THE SOBERING TRUTH

[signature]

John 8:32

"WHAT A POWERFUL STORY! I especially appreciate the author's honesty in describing the fear addiction forced him to live with. It's so hard to explain how incapacitating that fear becomes to someone who has never experienced it, but Steven Sellers really nailed it! His story shows that there is hope, there is a way out, that no matter how far we have fallen, we can still be lifted up.

The Sobering Truth should be required reading for patients in treatment centers everywhere as well as their families. I wish I could have read this earlier in my recovery. I hope my wife will read it too; I think it would really give her a clear picture of what it's like to be smothered in the grip of addiction.

It has become increasingly clearer to me that sobriety is not recovery, and without God, there will be no true recovery. I felt as if I was right there in the story with him; I was experiencing the fear, the confusion, and the guilt. I could also feel the salvation, a feeling I hope everyone who reads this book can experience!"

—BILL U.
Recovering Alcoholic

the SOBERING TRUTH

ONE MAN'S JOURNEY FROM FAILURE TO FAITH

Steven Sellers

AMBASSADOR INTERNATIONAL
GREENVILLE, SOUTH CAROLINA & BELFAST, NORTHERN IRELAND

www.ambassador-international.com

The Sobering Truth
One Man's Journey from Failure to Faith

Printed in the United States of America

ISBN: 9781935507611

Cover Design & Page Layout by David Siglin
Author photo by foto/jenn/inc

AMBASSADOR INTERNATIONAL
Emerald House
427 Wade Hampton Blvd.
Greenville, SC 29609, USA
www.ambassador-international.com

AMBASSADOR BOOKS
The Mount
2 Woodstock Link
Belfast, BT6 8DD, Northern Ireland, UK
www.ambassador-international.com

The colophon is a trademark of Ambassador

Wherever possible, actual names of people and places have been used with permission. However, some names have been changed to maintain privacy.

To Jim and Steve—

Men of God,
Brothers in Christ—
Thank you

"IF YOU WOULD LIKE TO go into the mind of an alcoholic and uncover the mysteries of addiction and recovery, you will find this book fascinating. I was surprised and amused by Steve's candor, imaginative use of language, and self-deprecating humor. He takes a serious subject and teaches us in a very entertaining way. Steve Sellers has written a book that you will not want to put down. I recommend this book to clients, therapists, pastors, medical doctors, and anyone who cares about an alcoholic and would like honest insight into his or her thinking. Do not miss this book—it is one you will want to buy several copies of to pass on to friends, family, and coworkers."

—DEBRA LACOCK, MSW, LISW
Psychotherapist

Acknowledgments

THANKS TO TIM LOWRY AT Ambassador International for his hard work and diligence in producing this work. Thanks also to his talented team, especially Alison, David, and Kacie; you all did an impressive job and I am appreciative of everything you've done. Thanks also to everyone who read and reviewed the manuscript and encouraged me to "take the next step." Special thanks to Jennifer Joyce for her photography and Dawn Burian for her website design. God has given you both incredible gifts; thank you for sharing them with us.

I am blessed by the prayers of people too numerous to mention but need to give special thanks for the support of Pat Rieck and Steve and Debbie Wells. Very simply, without them, this project would not have been possible.

To Katie and Laura, thank you for letting me be a dad again. I am proud of the women you've become and blessed beyond words to be a part of your lives. I love you both and am honored to be your father.

Most of all, thank you to Trisha for her love, support, insight, and wisdom. This story would have remained unfinished if not for the incredible sacrifices she made for me and for the work she's done to support me in this journey. A man could not ask for a more committed wife and partner.

Table of Contents

PART I

The Failure

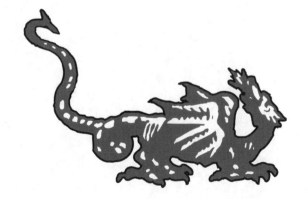

"Alcohol may be man's worst enemy but the Bible says to love your enemy."

—FRANK SINATRA

CHAPTER I

The Inquisition Begins

December 31, 1995
Mercy Medical Center
Cedar Rapids, Iowa

Name: Steven V. Sellers
Age: 41
Visit: 12/31/95
DOB: 11/21/54

HISTORY AND PHYSICAL
CONFIDENTIAL PATIENT—Special authorization is required
for release of information.

CHIEF COMPLAINT—"I need detox."

HISTORY OF THE PRESENT ILLNESS: Steve is a 41-year-old, married gentleman, who was brought in for voluntary detoxification last evening.

IT SEEMS LIKE A REASONABLE statement to a point. I was forty-one, married, and a gentleman when I needed to be one if it would advance my personal cause, but the term "voluntary" needs to be clarified a bit. When my wife, Mary, brought me in with her brother, Will, and our neighbor, Gary, my intention was to satisfy their desire to take me somewhere to get checked out and then go back home. I'm certain that my call to the police earlier in the evening to report a child abduction and my hallucinations that had been haunting me all day may have given them reason to think that there was something wrong with me, but I kept trying to tell them that all I really needed was some sleep. Mary ended up screaming at me that if I didn't go in "voluntarily" she would have me committed, and I remember thinking, *Why go through all that trouble this late at night?*

So I went in. Voluntarily? I think of people who volunteer as people who are eager to make a sacrifice in the line of duty. I was scared out of my mind at the thought of detox so there was no eagerness at all involved in the decision. My visions were of being strapped to a bed while spiders and snakes crawled all around me and sweat poured from my body while I waited for the cravings to cease or death to overwhelm me, whichever came first. I like to think that I was brought in for "agreeable" detoxification. I think anyone will agree to do anything when he comes to realize that he's going to do it one way or the other. I was going in no matter what. And "illness"? I didn't have any illness. I drank too much and hadn't figured out a way to stop yet. Doctors. To them, everything's an illness.

His alcohol consumption history dates back to about the first of the year . . .

Fortunately, nobody mentioned which year. I had been drinking heavily for about five years, *heavily* meaning that I was doing it every day and doing it, for the most part, secretly. I would drink mostly in the evenings, after Mary and our daughters, Katie and Laura, went to bed. But in the two years prior to my first admission to treatment, I had been drinking all day. My day would start with long pulls out of the vodka bottle I stashed behind the towels in the bathroom in the basement and end with the same long pulls usually out of the second bottle of the day. No glass, no ice, no company. Just me and Gilbey's, usually shut up in the bathroom, listening to the radio, doing a crossword, and waiting for the sweats to pass. At the end, I was drinking two fifths a day but would never own up to that. I never thought it was that much until I spoke at the treatment center to a group of patients one time and told them about it. You would have thought I'd told them I'd been drinking rhino urine. They couldn't believe it. Looking back, I guess it was quite a bit, but by then, it took that much to get me drunk.

. . . when there was considerable stress at home. His wife's mother was living with them a prolonged period of time with a severe health problem.

Gloria came down from her home in Woden, Iowa, because she was getting older and was still living in the same house she and her husband had lived in since before I had met Mary in 1975. Ed died the same year as my dad, 1992, and I don't think Gloria felt comfortable staying by herself through the winter. She got sick the first year and ended up staying in bed for prolonged periods of time. She had a little bell she would ring whenever she needed something, and eventually it made all of us crazy but Mary and the girls were able to adapt; I apparently didn't adapt as well. Looking back, I think that I had only mentioned this in my interview to justify my drinking. I was drinking pretty much all the time by then but I was able to use Gloria as one of my myriad of excuses. That's one of the many things I've learned in my recovery: an alcoholic will use anything to justify his next drink. "I've had a bad day; I need a drink." "I've had a good day; I need a drink." "Hey, it's day; I need a drink." Justification. Reason. That's all we look for. Gloria was my justification. Alcoholism was my problem.

Also, his daughter had pneumonia and his marriage was strained.

Laura ended up in the hospital and I remember curling up with her in a little bed and lying with her all night. The nurses thought I was such a good dad and they would keep bringing in movies for me to watch in the VCR because I couldn't get comfortable enough to sleep. What I remember most is reaching into the overnight bag I had brought with me and taking pulls out of the plastic vodka bottle I'd hidden in it. I drank all night and watched movies and held Laura so she wouldn't be afraid. I think I was the one who should have been afraid, but the only fears I ever had were the ones about not having enough vodka with me wherever I happened to be.

Was my marriage strained? No question. Mary suspected I was drinking too much because she kept finding empty vodka bottles behind the wet bar we had in our lower-level family room. I think she believed that the stress of Gloria's illness, Laura being in the hospital, and the job issues that were starting to come into play, many of which I never brought home with me, were all beginning to take a toll not only on me but on us. We just never talked about it. We never really talked about much of anything; that was my fault.

It got a lot worse this September when he was considering a job change back into education and his wife was not supportive of this, so he began drinking on a nightly basis . . .

It actually did get worse in September, but not because of any job change I was considering. I had taught high-school English for ten years in a small town in northwest Iowa before we moved to Cedar Rapids and I got into the insurance business. I actually taught for a year when we moved because my brother-in-law, Will, was the principal at a middle school in town and he got me an interview. I really didn't have any desire to get back into teaching but, again, I was looking for justification for my drinking.

I did have the conversation with Mary about wanting to get back into teaching but I wasn't sincere about it. I was starting to be a little scared about my inability to stop drinking and was worried about the confrontations I was having at work with my boss. Of course, I didn't tell Mary any of this; I told her I wasn't happy at work and wanted to do something else. What I really wanted to do was stop drinking for a couple of days just to see if I could do it. I couldn't, and it was starting to bother me. As far as the drinking on a nightly basis, I had been doing that for a number of years by then. Obviously, I wasn't up front with anyone about what was going on even as I was being interviewed in a treatment center. Ah, alcoholics and denial. We go together like vodka with a twist. Or an olive. Or a pearl onion.

. . . He would wait until everyone went to bed and then he would drink between a third and a fifth of a bottle of vodka a day.

True, I would wait until everyone went to bed, but I would also drink on my way home from work so I'd be drunk by the time I got there. At the time, I was driving an Olds 98 Touring Sedan, my first luxury car, with heated seats, steering wheel control buttons, the whole nine yards. I'd leave work and pour vodka into an Iowa

Hawkeye travel coffee cup the girls had given me for Christmas
one year, and I'd get on the interstate and head north about twenty
miles, turn around, and head back home. I'd sip vodka, listen to jazz,
and sweat like crazy but be as cool as could be when I'd walk in the
door. And like I said, by then I was drinking almost two fifths a day.
I wasn't denying that I was drinking; I was just fudging the facts a
bit. I think I did that with a lot of things in my life back then.

He has not had any alcohol for the past two weeks.

That's not exactly true either. I remember that my boss came to
our house the day after Christmas and I admitted to him that I had
a drinking problem. I remember that Mary and I sat with him at
our dining room table and I told him that, yes, he was right, I did
have a problem. However, I don't remember a thing about Christmas. I vaguely remember getting drunk downstairs after Mass on
Christmas Eve before we gathered with Mary's family. I remember
absolutely nothing about Christmas Day, so that "two week" thing
was off a bit. Once I told my boss about my "problem," the Board
of Directors made me sign a contract stating that I would get an
alcohol assessment done to determine if my problem required
treatment. I thought that if I stopped drinking for a few days and
cleaned out my system, any tests they might do at the assessment
wouldn't be able to detect any alcohol use. Never mind that my
liver enzymes were through the roof, something of which I had no
knowledge, or that my blood pressure was just about ready to blow
up my heart or that there were a million other things going wrong
with me and that I was as close to death as I have ever been in my
life. I thought I could up and quit and not have any problems at
all. There were a lot of things I thought I could do back then.

He and his wife have been separated for about a week.

Mary and the girls moved out after Christmas and went to live with her brother, Will, and his family. I don't remember if they moved Christmas Day or if it was the day after when I told my boss about my problem. Christmas was on a Monday that year, my boss came over on Tuesday, and I know that I was alone on Tuesday night and that I didn't drink. I remember that I had one long pull from a bottle on Wednesday night to calm myself a bit but didn't drink anything else the rest of the week. It was a mistake to think I could quit on my own after so many years of abuse. There wasn't one fiber of my body that was ready for the change.

He said he had a considerable episode of diarrhea last week and felt it was the flu. His appetite has been poor this week.

My body started revolting on Thursday. Even though I had a little to drink on Wednesday night, my body was screaming for more alcohol. I drank orange juice like it was going out of style because I was so dehydrated. I couldn't keep any food in me and eventually the juice ran through me as well. I was so sick that I would crawl from the couch to the bathroom and just sit there, too weak to move, until I would finally crawl back to the couch. I tried to make soup one day, Thursday or Friday, but I couldn't carry the soup bowl back to the couch because my hands were shaking so severely, spilling the soup all over the floor.

A coworker, Harry Whitehead, kept calling me because he was a recovering alcoholic. He told me that he would come over and take me to the hospital for my assessment. He kept telling me how serious the board was about me taking care of this "problem," but I told him that I had the flu and I was going to wait until after the first of the year to go in. I was spending so much time trying to convince Harry that I had the flu that it never dawned on me that all I was doing was trying to convince myself that was the problem. I have the feeling Harry knew that I didn't have the flu, but I was adamant about not going in until all the alcohol was out of my system. It was like smoking a cigarette and catching yourself on fire but not letting anyone put the fire out until you were done smoking the cigarette. I was dying and didn't know it, and even if I knew it I don't think I was going to let anyone do anything about it.

He has had no seizures.

I had no idea that seizures were even a possibility in the midst of my attempt to go without alcohol on my own—but then I had no idea at all what was happening to me. I was in full-blown, unmedicated withdrawal and things were getting worse by the minute. I had the d.t.'s, I was hallucinating, and I would most certainly have had seizures and in all probability have died if I hadn't gone in. It's remarkable to think that I was that close to death yet still tried to convince everyone—myself mostly—that all I really needed to do was go home and get some rest.

Last night he had some delusions and thought his daughter was kidnapped . . .

Saturday, December 30, 1995, was without question the most frightening day of my entire life. I remember that when I got up, I didn't feel as bad as I'd been feeling the past two days. I know that I was tired but I didn't have to crawl anywhere. I don't know if I ate anything in the morning or not, but my first conscious memory is sitting in my brown recliner, watching an NFL pre-game show, so it must have been late morning or early afternoon. There were two things that seemed out of the ordinary. We had two kittens at the time and I thought they had somehow crawled under my chair and were bumping against it because I kept feeling something hitting my legs from what I thought was under the chair. I even talked to the cats and told them to stop, but the bumping continued. I finally got out of the chair and looked under it but didn't see them anywhere. I went to the laundry room and opened the door and they were both sitting in there looking at me. They had been in there the entire time, but even when I sat back down in the chair and kept feeling the bumping on my legs, I was still convinced that they were somehow under the chair.

The other thing I noticed was that I kept hearing the sound of running water. I went through the entire house and checked all the faucets, but none of them was running. Still, I could not get the sound of the water out of my head. It wasn't a constant drip, drip. It was as if there was a faucet running somewhere. The sound wouldn't go away even when I turned up the television. It started wearing on me and I remember beginning to feel scared about something. There was a feeling beginning to weigh on me that there was something in the house that wasn't supposed to be there.

As the day progressed, I got very hot and started sweating a lot. I didn't think much about it, as I had convinced myself that I had the flu and this was no doubt one of the symptoms. I hadn't had the strength for a few days to take a shower, so I decided that I'd take one and that would clear my head and make me feel better. When I finished showering, I started shaving, standing in front of the large mirror over the sink in the lower-level bathroom, my bathroom where the vodka bottles were stashed behind the towels. While the thought of drinking no doubt entered my mind, I distinctly remember not drinking anything. I was still sweating and noticed that my hands were shaking and I kept thinking that I needed to be careful not to cut myself. While I was shaving, I started hearing footsteps upstairs and was immediately overcome with a sense of panic. My heart was pounding and my hands were almost shaking themselves off my arms. I knew that someone else was in the house and I was too afraid to go upstairs to see who it was. I was terrified. I called my neighbor, Ken, from across the street and asked him if he would come over. I met him at the front door. I was still shaking, and sweat was making the shave cream run down my face.

"You all right?" he asked.

"Yeah, I'm fine." *I always stand here in the middle of winter sweating like a pig, covered with shave cream and inviting my friends over to search my house for the source of the voices in my head.*

"You sure?"

"Sure, I'm sure. I just think there's someone in my house."

He looked at me, eyeing the sweat pouring from me and the cream starting to drip off my face. "You think someone's in your house?"

"Yeah, I heard someone walking around upstairs and I need you to go see who's up there."

He looked at me.

"Please."

He didn't say anything and went upstairs to the main floor. I waited for him in the doorway, too afraid to be alone but more afraid to follow. He didn't find anything.

He asked once more before he left if everything was okay, and I'm certain, no matter what I told him, he was convinced when he left that I was losing my mind. I had only just begun to do that.

CHAPTER 2

The Continuing Nightmare

AFTER KEN LEFT, I WENT back downstairs to try to finish shaving. I was terrified. It was then that I heard the voice for the first time. It was a female's voice, soft and alluring, almost hypnotic. It was coming from behind the closed door that led to the laundry room where the cats were. I could hear the voice very distinctly talking to the cats, comforting them, telling them that everything was going to be okay. It was a soothing voice, but I was frozen with fear. I couldn't even open the door to see what was going on. I just stood there and looked at the door in the reflection of the large mirror in front of me, absolutely horrified. She was playing with the cats, calling them by their names, and I was so scared that I began to cry softly and I remember being afraid that she would hear me. I knew I had to do something, so I wiped the shave cream off my face and went upstairs and grabbed a baseball bat that we had kept under our bed and then threw on some clothes. I went back downstairs, hoping it was all over, but the voice was still there, only now she was calling my name, telling me to open the door and come into the room.

In terror, I ran back upstairs and called my friend Laurie and told her that I needed to come over because I had to get out of the house. Laurie and I were close and she knew the struggles I was having with alcohol. The drive to her place was a blur but I remember being there and eating a salad and not telling her about what was going on in my house. It was the first food I'd been able to get down all week and I started to feel a little bit better. Even there, I heard the sound of running water and I kept asking her if it was raining because it sounded like rain was beating on the windows. It had started to snow but it was rain that I kept hearing.

I don't know how long I was there but I know it was dark when I got home. When I pulled into the garage, I was overcome with the same fear I had felt when I had left the house earlier. I was too terrified to go into the house. I shoveled what little snow there was off the driveway to avoid going inside. I saw Ken's son, Rich, come home and I went over to talk to him. When I looked back across the street, I began seeing people peeking at me out of the living room windows of the house next door to ours. I kept telling Rich that they were watching us, and I'm certain he thought there was something wrong with me because he went into his house and left me outside all alone. I looked back to my house and now saw people looking at me from the windows in my living room. I was horrified. I didn't know what to do and desperately wanted to ask Ken if he would let me in to stay with him and his family, but I figured by now they all thought I was crazy, so I gathered up what little courage I could muster, crossed the street, and went inside my house.

Once inside, I went upstairs right away and turned on all the lights and checked each room, baseball bat in hand. I looked in all the closets and under all the beds. I was shaking and the sweat was pouring from me. I don't know what I did next but I eventually called Phil, one of my oldest college friends who lives in Kentucky. He knew about my struggles with alcohol . . . most people did by then . . . and I talked to him for a while so I wouldn't have to think about what was happening to me. That's when I looked up and watched my youngest daughter, Laura, come from down the hallway and walk downstairs.

I was surprised to see her and I said something to her . . . I don't know what it was . . . and Phil was surprised too because I had told him that I was alone. I didn't remember how she got there but I knew she was there . . . downstairs . . . and I think it made me feel better for a minute knowing that I wasn't alone, even if it frightened me that she had gone downstairs.

I know Phil kept asking me if I was all right and I kept lying that I was. I hung up with Phil and called Mary at Will's house because I wanted to try to find out why my six-year-old daughter was with me. I didn't want to come out and ask Mary because I didn't want her to know what was happening to me.

At one point in our conversation, when we were talking about Laura, Mary said to me, "I'm going to give Laura a bath and put her to bed."

Simple. That should have convinced me that there was something desperately wrong with me, that Laura wasn't even there with me and that my mind had snapped and I was seeing and hearing things that weren't real. But when she said that to me, what I heard her say was, "Go give Laura a bath and put her to bed."

She confirmed what I thought I knew: Laura was with me, downstairs, and I needed to go get her ready for bed. I was confused about how she got there because I was certain she hadn't been there during the day, but however it happened, she was there and I needed to go back downstairs and get her.

The nightmare began when I went back downstairs and couldn't find her. I looked everywhere for her, except behind the closed doors of the laundry room, and I found myself choked with fear. I screamed for her, literally screamed her name, and was overwhelmed with the most utter sense of panic I had ever experienced in my life. The sweat poured from me as I realized that someone, no doubt the people who had been staring at me from my living room, had my little girl.

I still had my baseball bat with me and finally opened the door to the laundry room. Through the laundry room is our guest bedroom, the room in which I had been staying. I turned on all the lights and saw the two cats sitting on the floor staring at me. They never moved; they never made a sound but followed me with their eyes as I crept past them through the laundry room and into the bedroom, shaking with horrific fear. Tears were streaming down my face and I remember thinking that I was going to be sick. At the far end of the bedroom is a storage area under the steps. There are louvered doors that lead into the storage area, and as I began walking slowly toward the doors, I began to hear the woman's voice again. It was quiet and calm, almost reassuring. She called my name. I will never forget it as long as I live.

"Steve. Steve. Everything's okay. I have Laura and now I want you. Open the doors and everything will be fine. Just fine. . . . All you have to do is open the doors."

I had the bat in my left hand but I was shaking so hard I don't know how I held on to it. I was crying and the sweat was pouring out of me. I reached my right hand for the doors and she continued speaking to me in that hypnotic voice as I kept moving, inching toward the door.

"It's okay, Steve. Open the doors and everything will be fine. I have her. I want you. All you have to do is open the doors . . ."

I froze in my tracks. I tried to move but I couldn't, nor could I reach out any farther. Something was holding me back. I remember being angry because I had to open the doors and get my daughter out of there but I couldn't move.

"Steve, open the doors. Everything will be fine. Open the doors, Steve."

I snapped. Screaming, I broke the grip that was holding me back and ran upstairs. I called 9-1-1 and reported a child abduction. I gave the dispatcher a description of Laura and kept getting angry with her because she was asking too many questions. I screamed at her that I needed help and then hung up. I called Ken; his wife, Kelly, answered the phone. I told her that I had lost Laura and I needed them to come over and help me find her. I said nothing about the woman under the steps or the people looking at me through the windows. I didn't have to tell them anything about that. The panic in my voice and my odd behavior earlier in the day had already convinced them that something was going terribly wrong in my mind. I hung up the phone and ran to the front door to wait for them and for the police. I opened the door and stood in the doorway, bat in hand, so whoever it was that was downstairs could not get out.

There was a car parked across the street and I saw two people in the front seat. They were slouched down as if they didn't want to be seen but I saw them staring at me and I knew they had something to do with Laura being gone. I was convinced she was still in the house, still under the steps, but I was sobbing hysterically because I was afraid she was dead. I knew that I had to stay in the doorway so nobody would leave the house. I was gone. I had gone completely over the edge.

When Ken and Kelly came out of their house, I screamed at them to check the car because I knew that whoever was in the car had something to do with Laura. They didn't stop to look at the car and I was angry with them because of that. Of course, the reason they didn't stop was that it was their own car and there wasn't anyone in it. As they started running across the street and I heard the sound of the police siren in the distance, I felt a rush of cold air blow by me and I turned my head to see something misty and white blow down the steps and go around the corner toward the laundry room. I remember thinking that it had to have something to do with getting Laura out of the house and I at first wanted to follow it downstairs, but by then Ken and Kelly were there, and a minute or so later the police were as well. The police naturally attracted the attention of the rest of the neighborhood and everyone came running to the house to see what was wrong.

Gary, my neighbor from across the street, got there right away, and he and Ken grabbed hold of me and forced me upstairs and tried to calm me down because my heart was going a mile a minute. Looking back, it's a miracle that it didn't explode. I was crying and screaming at them to go downstairs and stop whoever was down there from leaving the house with Laura. Gary went down and looked and of course there was nothing there.

Things got a bit blurry after that, but I do remember that the police were questioning me and I was getting very angry with them because I thought they were accusing me of doing something with Laura. All I wanted was to have someone help me find her. I know that Mary's brother, Will, came over and the police talked to him outside while Ken and Gary stayed in the house with me trying to calm me down. The police told them to keep me away from the phone so they followed me wherever I went and wouldn't let me go downstairs. They kept telling me over and over that everything was going to be all right but I had an odd feeling that nothing was ever going to be all right again for a very long time.

When the police came back in the house, they told me that Laura was all right, that she was sleeping over at Will's house because Mary and the girls had been staying over there. Laura, of course, had never even been in the house with me.

In time, I had even come to believe that there had been no female in the laundry room with the cats, no one walking around upstairs, no one staring at me from the living room windows. I say that because eventually, when my spiritual walk became more sharply defined and the reality of what had happened to me became clearer, I came to understand what had really happened in the house that night. At the time, however, everything was explained away because of the fact that my body was rebelling against the absence of alcohol and my mind snapped. That night after Mary returned and I began to calm down, the reality hit me that maybe I really did have a problem with alcohol. I eventually admitted this fact to my neighbors, who were still obviously concerned over what they had witnessed. It remains to this day the most horrific experience of my life and one I pray no one else ever has to face.

... and had planned a detox this coming Tuesday, January 2, but was encouraged to come into the hospital and is admitted at this time.

December 15, 1995, had been my last day of work at Millhiser-Smith, the insurance agency I had worked at since December of 1989. I didn't actually lose my job at Millhiser until February 13, 1996, but never went back to the office after the fifteenth. I was sick and I was the only one in the world who wasn't accepting that fact yet.

The day after Mary and I met with my boss in our dining room, I was called into the office late in the day. I signed a contract with them agreeing to an alcohol assessment at Sedlacek Treatment Center in Cedar Rapids as soon as possible. If the assessment showed that treatment was necessary, I would have to complete the program before I could go back to work. Millhiser would file a disability claim and I would still get seventy-five percent of my pay. As I already said, I figured I could get through the assessment if I flushed my system of all the alcohol that I had consumed in the past six years, so I needed to buy some time. Given that I was as sick as I'd ever been in my life those few days after Christmas, I was convinced that I had the flu and managed to get my boss to agree to let me go in for the assessment after the first of January. I figured that would allow me enough time to convince everyone that I really was okay, that I could somehow find a way to become a smarter drinker. However, the "encouragement" I received on the night of the thirtieth changed all that. It changed a lot of things.

He has begun on Librium protocol.

Because alcohol is a nervous system depressant, the brain becomes irritable during withdrawal, leading to typical withdrawal syndrome. For this reason, the mainstay of treatment has been the use of various tranquilizers. The drugs chosen are those that remain in the body the longest, so pills are given less frequently. One of the most commonly used is chlorodiazepam, known as Librium. It is usually given in twenty-five to fifty milligram doses, four to six times daily. The medication reduces the symptoms of anxiety, shakiness, high blood pressure, and pulse elevation and protects against seizures. At the time of admission on the thirtieth, my blood pressure was 150/130 and my pulse was 138. I was a time bomb waiting to explode.

I was first examined by a physician sometime in the morning of December 31, 1995. My blood pressure had dropped to 130/104 and my pulse was at 100, so the drugs were beginning to do their job. I weighed only 182 pounds, down nearly forty pounds from what was then my normal weight. Body, soul, and spirit, I was sick, but more than anything, I needed a drink.

He is aware of his need for detoxification and voluntarily will be admitted.

I knew I was sick but was secretly denying my need for detox. When I first came in I insisted that I was tired and needed nothing more than to go home and get some rest. The doctor in the emergency room told Mary that if I didn't want to go in, he couldn't make me. The only way I could go in if I continued to deny a need was for her to commit me. He asked me if I wanted to talk to a nurse and I agreed to. My biggest fear was the process of detox. I had no idea what to expect, but it always sounded sinister so I fought it. The nurse came in and, after looking at my vitals, told me what they were telling her. If I didn't check in immediately and get medicated, I would more than likely have a seizure and I would die. I would be lucky to live through the night. Even if I did survive the night but continued to drink, I would be dead in three months. Period. If I ever wanted to live to see my daughters again, I knew I needed to get help. Still, it took Mary screaming at me and threatening me with committal before I finally agreed. I was admitted to Sedlacek Treatment Center in the early morning hours of December 31, 1995. Happy New Year.

Plan: He is agreeable to admission for detoxification. He seems to have a good support system.

Mary was, without a doubt, going to support me through this ordeal. However, I don't think either one of us would have ever imagined where this journey would lead and how quickly I would throw away the support she was so willing to give to me to save our marriage and my life.

This copy for: Medical Records.
Dr. John Roof. 12/31/95

CHAPTER 3

Just a Stopping Problem

Doctor's Progress Notes
Name: Sellers, Steven
Day 02
Date 01/01/96

Biopsychosocial Assessment
Identifying Data: This patient is a 41-year-old, white, married male from Cedar Rapids, Iowa, who voluntarily is admitted for his first admission to the Sedlacek Treatment Center. Chief complaint at the time of admission is alcohol withdrawal, which included hallucinations, severe shakes, and possible loss of employment.

I BEGAN WORKING AT MILLHISER–SMITH Insurance Agency in December of 1989, five days before the birth of our second daughter, Laura. I had just come off a six-month tenure as a life insurance salesman for Century Life Insurance Company and had hated every minute of it. Prior to that I had taught for eleven years and knew that I had to do something different.

I had put my name in with Management Recruiters, Inc. in Cedar Rapids and was working with a woman named Cathy Lammers, who soon put me in touch with Steve King, then the vice president of sales at Millhiser. I met Steve for my first interview in October of 1989 and we hit it off. My next meeting was with the board members, who also liked me. After that, I met the other agents. Everyone liked everyone, but the process was a long one because Millhiser believed that when they hired someone it was forever, and they wanted to be certain that I was a good fit. When I was initially offered the job, they wanted me to start on January 2, 1990, but I convinced them of my desire to start as soon as possible, so on December 11, 1989, I took the job.

At the time, Millhiser was one of the two largest independent insurance agencies in Cedar Rapids, and if you were in the insurance business, it was *the* place to be. The potential was unlimited and I was given every opportunity to be a success. Things went so well, in fact, that in March of 1993, three months after my dad died, Mary and I were awarded a trip to Hong Kong for ten days.

The pay was great, but the job was stressful. It was a salaried position, a situation rare in the insurance business, so the board was always keeping an eye on production. They wanted to make sure their sales force was justifying the salary. By the time I was hospitalized, I had been confronted more than once about my drinking, and when I went in I was under a contract with them to complete the program before I could return to work. If I didn't, they had the right to terminate me. I had just purchased stock in the company earlier in 1995, and the prospect of losing my job loomed darkly over me as I began rehab. It was probably the main reason I was in there, and that's never the right motivation to be in treatment.

Assessment: History of dependence: The patient states at the time of admission he is currently drinking one-third to one-fifth of a complete fifth of vodka on a daily basis. The patient has been drinking in this fashion for the past six to twelve months.

Like I said, this was way off. At the time I was admitted, I was drinking up to two complete fifths a day and had been doing so for at least three years. My tolerance was way up and I considered myself a functional alcoholic. I would drink before I went to work, again at home over the noon hour, on my way home from work, and then again, usually a lot before I went to bed at night. I wasn't sleeping well at all, the stress of my employment status, Mary's ever-growing suspicions about my alcohol use, and my body crying out for more alcohol in the middle of the night all combining to keep me awake virtually the entire night. It seemed the more I drank, the more I needed to drink. I felt that I wanted to stop, but I was becoming concerned at my inability to do so. To compensate for this fear, I drank more. Alcohol eased my anxiety and I had a lot of anxiety in my life. Ironically, most of it stemmed from the very thing I would pour into my body nearly twenty-four hours a day, but that fact couldn't make me stop.

He admits to loss of control with frequent blackouts and consistent intoxication.

The last three months of 1995 are pretty much wiped from my memory. There are pieces of things that I remember but larger chunks of things I don't. I have no recollection of Mary and me taking the girls to my mom's house for Thanksgiving. The entire weekend is a blank to me. I'm certain I drank a lot; otherwise I would remember the withdrawal from not having alcohol in my system. I don't remember any of it. The scary part is that I'm sure I drove over and back and I remember nothing of either trip. I've talked to people who panic when they realize a couple hours on a Saturday night disappear from their memory. I had huge chunks of days erased. Looking back, I recognize that the same grace that ultimately saved me ordered the events of my memory in a way that lets me fully appreciate my salvation and all that I was saved from.

My intoxication was constant. I had long since stopped drinking because I enjoyed it. I was drinking because I needed to have alcohol in my system. I was addicted. I couldn't stop drinking, couldn't stop feeding the beast. It was always me against the addict, and the addict would always win.

The patient states that recently his drinking has reached a point where he is now in alcohol withdrawal during the day; he is experiencing severe shakes and is unable to discontinue drinking despite repeated efforts.

Usually around ten every morning at work, my hands would start to shake. I would start to get irritable and notice that I felt flushed. I could feel that my heart was beating rapidly and could sense a pounding in my head. A lot of times, I'd go into the bathroom and throw some cold water on my face and spend some time on the john trying to calm down. I knew it was nothing more than the addict telling me, *"Okay, it's time to feed me again."* Your mind senses the desire but it's your body that gives you away.

I'd usually go back into my office and pretend I was on the phone with someone so no one would come in and want my signature on anything. My hands would shake so severely at times that I could barely hold on to a pen and my handwriting, bad to begin with, would turn into illegible hieroglyphics. Around eleven, I would check out of the office, telling my assistant I had an appointment and then was going to lunch. I'd go to the drug store across the street, buy a plastic fifth of Gilbey's that fit perfectly in my briefcase, and then head home. I'd go into my bathroom, and even though I was the only one at home I'd lock the door, turn on the radio, do a crossword, and drink right out of the bottle. I'd sit there for forty-five minutes or so, drinking and sweating, but I could feel the effects almost immediately. My heart would slow down, the pounding in my head would go away, my entire body would relax, and everything would be fine again. The process was no different from that of heroin addicts who would kill to stick a needle in their arms for the fix for which their body was screaming. I wasn't any different, but in my mind, as long as I knew there were people that were worse than me, I wasn't really that bad.

Recently, the patient was confronted at his place of employment with [sic] having alcohol on his breath. After this confrontation, the patient did quit drinking and now has gone into severe alcohol withdrawal.

I remember the first time I was confronted at work. The president of Millhiser, Bill Osborne, came to my door. He didn't come in; he just stuck his head in and asked if I would come down to his office for a minute. Bill was the kind of guy who liked to use the power of his office so that if you were being called in, he made sure you knew it was something important. If it wasn't any big deal, he'd come in and sit in your office, but going to his office meant serious business. Once I got there and he told me to close the door behind me, I knew it wasn't going to be a discussion about golf. He pointed to one of the chairs in front of his desk and I sat down. He looked at me and I made sure to return his gaze.

Breathe, relax, and be grateful it's before ten, I thought. *You'll be okay.*

I was drunk and knew I needed to be careful.

"Uh, Steve," he said with that awkward way he had about him when he knew he had to talk about something uncomfortable. He would spread his fingers and extend them straight up, his palms facing one another, and tap the fingertips on one hand against those on his other hand. I could tell he was nervous. "I'll get right to the point here. Do you have a drinking problem?"

There it was. The ball was clearly in my court. He surprised me a bit with the directness of the question, but really, how else do you ask something like that?

There was no question where I was going. Deny, deny, deny. *I don't have a drinking problem,* I thought. *It's really more of a stopping problem.* Maybe that's what I should have said, but I didn't think he'd understand that. "Of course not," I laughed. "Why do you ask?"

He frowned, even though he knew he was going to get that answer. He cleared his throat. I think he was more uncomfortable than I was. "I've received a report from someone who claimed to smell alcohol on your breath." He leaned in a bit. "Your numbers are down as well. We're just concerned about you. We want to make sure everything's okay."

I felt myself relax. He didn't have anything on me and wasn't going to push the issue more than making me defend my lousy production. I was going to dodge this bullet but still needed to be careful. I needed a diversion.

"Things are hard at home right now," I said, looking down. "Mary's mom is staying with us and she's been pretty sick. It's difficult right now but we're adapting. Everything's okay. It really is. There's nothing to be concerned about. My business is starting to pick up. I'm working on some really nice prospects right now." *Just don't ask me about them.*

He kept looking at me, tapping his stupid fingers together. Nothing. Silent finger tapping and that look you get when you know the other guy knows you're lying but can't do anything about it. He was hoping for the truth. *Well, get in line, Bill. There are a lot of people in front of you.* He faked a smile. "Just make sure you let us know if there's anything we can do to help. We want you to know that you can always come to us if you need anything."

That was it, but it was enough to make me realize that maybe it was time to make some changes in how and when I drank. I then embarked on a number of failed attempts to modify my drinking behaviors but nothing worked. I tried drinking on weekends but there was no way I could go five days without alcohol. I tried drinking every other day but that only lasted until just after dinner of my first off day. I had the shakes so bad earlier at work that I had to leave and spent the rest of the day driving around town listening to music to try to get my mind off of how much I needed a drink. After dinner I went downstairs and killed off about half a bottle in the bathroom. I tried drinking only at night but by noon I felt like I was going to die. I couldn't do it.

It wasn't until they laid the contract out in front of me and forced my hand in December that I knew I had to quit, even if only temporarily. I knew I was in trouble but didn't know what to do about it.

CHAPTER 4

The Acquaintance Who Wanted More

The patient began drinking alcohol at the age of 16; he states that he would have a beer with his father following athletic events while in high school. The patient reports minimal drinking while in high school, always with his father, and never to the point of intoxication.

ALCOHOL WAS MY MISTRESS. I met her for the first time a long time ago. Oh, I had known her since I was a child, watched her with my own father as she gave him pleasure. On occasions he would even let me touch her, let me taste her as I held her in my hands, and I found myself wishing I were old enough to have her for my own.

As the years passed, I got to know her better and found myself anxious to be wherever she was. She knew me well. She knew how to make me feel better when things in my life weren't as I wanted them to be, but she was also there to celebrate with me when times were good. She would be with me in a room full of people, innocently enough at first, but as more time passed, I found myself wanting to spend more time with her. Alone. When everyone else would go home, she and I would sit quietly and I would close my eyes while she took control of me and made everything good in my world. She gave me courage and took away my fears. I soon realized that I needed to be with her more and more and began meeting her alone, after work. We would spend time together in my car, soft jazz playing on the stereo, the din of the world unable to get through to me, and we would drive. Just the two of us.

She soon became the last thing I saw at night and the first thing I saw in the morning and I found myself accepting the fact that I couldn't live without her. Even when she started making me do things that I knew I shouldn't do, things that without her would have brought me shame, I couldn't let her go. I tried telling her goodbye. Oh, how I tried. I would leave her for a day, two days, but then I would catch a glimpse of her again and go running back to her and take her with a passion I had never known before. People became suspicious of us. *"You're spending too much time with her,"* they'd say. I knew I could leave her if I wanted to, but she soon took complete control over me. There wasn't a single minute that she wasn't a part of me. When we weren't able to be together, I could think of nothing but how much I needed her and how passionately I would embrace her when we finally met. And when she became a part of me, when her love would warmly meander through me, my heart would race and my temperature would rise as I gave myself completely to her, and everything would be right in my world again. I couldn't let her go. She wouldn't let go of me. She was my Juliet, my forbidden passion, and I would most certainly give my life for her.

I almost did.

I remember the first time I got drunk. I mean really drunk. I was sixteen and was uptown in Newton, Iowa, my hometown, on a hot July afternoon. Newton had a tradition called Ridiculous

Day, a day when all the merchants in town would move their merchandise out onto the sidewalks in front of their stores and try to sell things they hadn't been able to move at regular prices. However, because the prices were so, well, ridiculous, suddenly everything became a bargain. There was a parade, music on a stage in front of Mattingly's Music Store on the square, food vendors, and people everywhere. I remember that I was walking through the crowd of people with my best friend, Ronnie Olson, and we were scrounging change from everyone we saw. A quarter here, a couple of dimes there. Just walking up to people and asking for money. We had our own money; it was just that we were planning on getting drunk that night and had decided that we wanted other people to pay for it. Looking back, that was one of the first great lessons I learned about drinking. It's always a better drunk when you're drinking someone else's liquor or someone else is picking up the tab.

During the course of the day, we collected about sixteen dollars' worth of change and decided that much money should certainly buy us something good. We had already found someone who was willing to buy it for us but we didn't know what to get. Beer seemed out of the question. Too ordinary. We wanted something special, something . . . ridiculous. We sat on the curb and watched the bargain hunters fighting with each other over the orange plaid pants that the day before would have been buried on the last rack in the store, but today, everyone seemed to want them. We thought hard about what to get and finally decided on cherry brandy and crème de cacao. Chocolate-covered cherries had always been one of our favorites so we thought, *Why not? Let's do it.*

We went to one of the banks on the square and cashed in our change for bills and gave it to our connection. I remember the whole thing being very secretive, slipping the money to him while shaking his hand as if we were just making the biggest cocaine deal in the history of the world. He took off with our money and we drove to a park and waited for him to show up with the stuff. We ended up stashing the two bottles in the back seat of Ronnie's '68 Barracuda, the one with the backseat that folded down. He was going to pick me up at my house around seven that night. We had planned to go out to a cornfield out by the airport and get drunk.

At seven thirty we were heading back *into* town after deciding that we needed glasses, ice, and something to mix with the booze because our first sip had been a bit too much for us. We also decided that we wouldn't tell anyone about that. We wanted to remain as manly as possible, as my vision of hardcore drinking was long pulls straight out of the bottle. I used to watch *Gunsmoke* as a kid and always got a kick out of those guys that would buy a bottle of whiskey at the Long Branch for a nickel or whatever and then sit there and drink right out of the bottle. That's what we wanted to do. "No thanks, Kitty; we don't need no ice and Coke to go with that cherry chocolate stuff tonight. We'll do 'er straight out of the bottle."

Of course, not many cowboys drank in a cornfield with a blanket spread out to keep the bugs from crawling up their pant legs either.

We got back to the airport and parked the Barracuda beside one of the hangars, out of sight from the road, and made our way with blanket, bottles, ice, Coke, and glasses across the gravel road, over the barbed wire fence and about ten rows into the field. We matted down as many stalks as we could and spread the blanket out. It was hot—midsummer Iowa hot—with not a breath of air to move the bugs away. Not that we would have noticed the breeze if there was one given that we were surrounded by corn that was taller than we were. The stars were out and the moon was full, and we had no trouble seeing to pour the Coke and liquor into the glasses. I remember that it tasted so good, or at least that's what we were trying to convince ourselves.

We were sitting on the blanket, bumps from the clods of dirt making things uncomfortable at first, but the more we drank, the less we cared. Ronnie was drinking the crème de cacao and I was going after the cherry brandy and Coke. It tasted so sweet; I think I forgot what I was drinking. Like anything else, the excitement wore off pretty quickly, especially for Ronnie, what with the clods of dirt and the mosquitoes and the thick, sweaty air that wouldn't move. I don't know that he'd had a lot to drink but I know that I had really put a lot away. When he left, he took everything with him but the blanket and the bottle of cherry brandy and I sat there in the cornfield while he thrashed his way through the field. I heard him swear as he stumbled over the barbed wire fence and I laughed so hard at the sound that I thought I had actually wet my pants. Suddenly, everything seemed so funny.

I remember looking up at the stars and thinking that I was in the middle of a meteor shower. At first the stars looked like they were shooting across the sky but then I thought they weren't so much shooting as sort of floating, unable to stay in one place for any period of time. I kept taking long pulls from the bottle, sweat pouring down my face, and continued to watch the stars until I heard a car horn and someone calling out my name. I stood up and immediately fell back down, not on the blanket, but rather backwards into about five or six stalks of corn. It seemed like the funniest thing I'd ever done and I couldn't stop laughing. It took me forever to get my bearings and make my way to where Ronnie was on the gravel road, and I stumbled, as he had, headfirst over the barbed wire fence. I never once let go of the bottle.

I was drunk. I don't know if I realized it at the time, but I was really drunk. We both used to give each other a hard time and Ronnie was trying to make me think he was drunk, but I know he hadn't had that much to drink. He probably thought I was just messing around with him, making him think that I was looped, but I was drunk. There was no doubt about it. I was hot and dizzy and couldn't focus on anything. I couldn't talk but wouldn't shut up. We headed back to town and I was having a hard time remembering where we were. The sweat was pouring from me and I found that I didn't feel well. When we got back to town, we headed for the square where we knew everyone else would be, doing what every other small-town high-school kid was doing: making endless left turns around the court house.

We saw lots of people we knew and I remember that I was hanging out the window, yelling at everyone I saw. I don't know what I was saying but I'm certain it wasn't very profound. At some point, I knew I needed to lie down so I climbed in the back of the Barracuda with the seat down and just lay there, suddenly wishing that it was the afternoon again and we could give everyone their money back.

Ronnie kept on driving around the square, one left turn after another, and I found myself rolling from side to side in the back of the Barracuda, unable to make myself stop. I kept thinking I was still in the cornfield and wondered where the clods of dirt had gone. I thought if I could hang on to the blanket I wouldn't roll around so much, but I couldn't grab hold of it and thought that maybe I'd lost it. I closed my eyes but all I could see were the stars floating in the sky, only now they were spinning and I had a hard time seeing where they were going. I opened my eyes to make them stop, but the whole world was spinning and I kept rolling and rolling. There was loud music coming out of the speakers that always seemed to be right beside my head and Ronnie was honking the horn and yelling, then singing, then yelling some more. All I wanted him to do was shut up.

All of a sudden, I knew I was going to be sick. I didn't have time to think about it or try to wish it away; it hit me about as fast as the cherry brandy had. I tried to say something to Ronnie but he was oblivious to anything but the music and that stupid car horn, so I pulled myself up as best I could and stuck my head between the headrest of the passenger seat and the open window and threw up all over the outside of his car. I threw up a lot, and when I was done I hung my head out the window, dry heaves nearly throwing me out of the car. We ended up going to a car wash and Ronnie washed off the side of the car while I lay in the backseat, thankful that the stars weren't moving and that we weren't making any more left turns. I don't remember much about the rest of the night but I know that I made it home all right, and to my knowledge, my mother, who usually waited up for me to get home, didn't know anything about it.

That was my first drunk, but looking back, it was really a microcosm of my drinking later in my life. As I said, I learned that night that drinking on someone else's buck is usually the best way to go, especially if you have enough to get you really drunk. I also learned through the years that I tended to drink long after everyone else stopped, even if it meant drinking alone. Some, okay, *most* of my best drinking was when I did it alone. I lost control a lot when I drank. Not to the point where I was throwing up all over someone's car, but drinking to the point of not remembering what I did. If that's not losing control, I don't know what is. I also drank with the intent of getting drunk, even if no one else knew how drunk I was. I think the worst thing I learned was that I could drink every day. The next night I was back in Ronnie's Barracuda, sipping brandy and Coke as we rode around the square, this time making right turns and me trying to be a bit more restrained. Even then, I loved to drink. I don't know that it was even that much fun at the time, but I loved to do it anyway.

The patient states that he attended college and did no drinking while in college.

I met Mary at North Iowa Area Community College in Mason City, Iowa, where I had gone to play basketball and drinking was as normal as going to class. We lived in a co-ed dorm and everyone drank. Mary and I used to buy little bottles of Mateus wine, four or five at a time, and drink all of them and hang out with friends. There were always parties in town, and if we didn't go to a party, we would hang out at The Toadstool, the bar where I kissed her for the very first time. We drank while we drove to the places where we would drink next. When we went to my parents' house for the weekend, we would drink with my mom and dad, but Mary's parents didn't drink much so we stayed sober on those weekends. Mary and I usually drank beer and wine unless we were with my parents, and then, mainly because we were drinking my dad's booze, we had more elaborate drinks. We loved drinking Bloody Marys, especially in the mornings at Mom and Dad's. Beer and tomato juice, gimlets, whiskey and 7-Up, rum and coke, we pretty much drank anything Dad would make for us.

I broke my ankle my sophomore year and while the basketball team went somewhere in Minnesota for a game, Mary and I stayed in her room and got hammered drinking gin and tonics, not even listening to the game on the radio. We just drank. One night a bunch of us decided to go have a beer in every bar in Mason City. We counted thirty-nine bars in town but still felt we could get it done. We had six beers at the first bar and decided to try it again some other time. We had great fun at NIACC and when we graduated with our AA (yes, ironic, I know) degrees in May of 1975, we had decided that we were going to spend the rest of our lives together.

He attended a Baptist school and was on scholarship for athletics and did not consume alcohol.

I got a scholarship to play basketball at Stetson University in DeLand, Florida, and Mary went with me in August of 1975; we were married the next summer. I made great friends on the team, one of whom, Phil, the guy I called the night of my breakdown, still touches base with me once in a while. We all drank. When we had road games, we would leave the day before the game, flying out of Daytona Beach, about twenty miles from DeLand. Phil and I would usually drive to the airport together and split a six-pack on the way. When we got to wherever we were going, we'd have a light practice and then go out and enjoy the evening. Since we didn't have to get up until late the next day, we would all usually go find the college bars and sit around and get hammered with the locals. The next night we'd play, and after the game, since we didn't fly out until the following morning, we'd all go out and stay out all night. We got money from the coaches after the games, ten dollars if we lost and twenty if we won. Whatever the amount, we spent it on alcohol. I got drunk all over the country thanks to my time in college. Oh, I also got a degree in English. I almost forgot about that.

The patient states that he can remember the first time he was intoxicated which was in 1980, as a result of having other coaches at his house and he consumed beer to the point of intoxication. The patient states that he only drank beer at that time. Following coaching high school basket-

ball, he and several coaches would adjourn to his home
where they would watch game tapes and drink beer.

When I graduated from college in 1978, Mary and I moved back to Iowa and ended up living in Ruthven, a town of about 750 in the northwestern part of the state. I was the high school English teacher and boys' varsity basketball coach. We bought a large two-story house that had a wet bar in the basement. After games, my close friends would come to our place and we would sit at the bar and listen to music and rehash the game and get drunk. There was a bar in town where most people went, but our group wanted a little privacy and our basement gave us exactly what we were seeking. There were three brothers who farmed forever just outside of town, one my age, Frank, who was my assistant coach, one a year older, Pete, and one a year younger, Don. There was another guy, Craig, who was the hog buyer in town when I first met him, and the five of us would drink in our basement after every game. We drank beer, wine, shots of whiskey, whatever I happened to have in the bar. It didn't matter whether we won or lost the game; we were there and we never once watched a game tape.

I also bought a boat while I lived in Ruthven. There were seven lakes within seven miles of our front door and I had always wanted a boat. It was a bit of a bone of contention between Mary and me, but one Saturday, Pete, Frank, and I went to a marina in Spirit Lake and I came home with a runabout. It wasn't anything fancy, but we all had a lot of good times in it.

Mary and I would take Craig and his wife, Monica, out for boat rides in the evenings and I would do a lot of fishing in it during the summers, but some of the best times I had with it were when Craig and I would take it out on Thursday nights and just sit in the middle of Lost Island Lake, stereo playing, stars out, and each of us drinking wine out of huge jugs of Carlo Rossi. We had always told our wives that we were fishing but we never took our gear out of the truck. All we did was drink and then go ripping around the lake in the boat. We drank a lot in that boat. There's something about being around the water and drinking, especially late at night when you're the only ones on the lake and there are a million stars out. We would drink and laugh and there weren't any better times than that. Still, it's a miracle Craig didn't drown, because he couldn't swim and was always jumping out of the boat with his arms stuck through the straps of a boat cushion while I tore across the lake about thirty-five miles an hour. We had fun, except I always had a hard time dragging him back into the boat.

Alcohol took hold of us pretty good in Ruthven. One night, just before Christmas, I was home sick with a cold. There was a girls' basketball game and Mary went to it and then went downtown to the bar with our friends after the game. We were going to leave for my parents' the next day for Christmas. I was lying on the couch about eleven o'clock, sick as a dog, when I heard a commotion in the other room and looked up to see a couple of my friends come in with Mary between them, one arm around each, as drunk as I had ever seen her in my life. She had been drinking Peach Schnapps at the bar and had gotten sick all over everyone and couldn't even walk anymore. The poor woman was hammered. I got her upstairs and started getting her ready for bed when she threw up again, this time all over the bed and all over herself, and then she passed out. I ran some water in the tub and cleaned her up as best I could and then carried her into our spare room and made sure she was okay. I spent the rest of the night washing the sheets and trying to clean up the mattress without getting sick all over it myself. She spent the trip to my mom and dad's the next day with a paper bag between her legs in the car, and to this day, I don't think the poor woman has ever been able to eat a peach.

Other than maybe a very occasional glass of wine, I don't think she drinks at all anymore. Some of us learn our lessons well; others don't even open the stupid book.

The patient began drinking hard liquor in 1988 in the form of vodka, at which time he would drink only on a nightly basis. The patient stated that he moved to Cedar Rapids, Iowa to gain employment, and his family remained in Ruthven. The patient stated that he was living with his brother-in-law at the time and they would have a nightly martini. The patient states that his drinking at this time was not problematic, limited to one martini per occasion.

In 1988, I had resigned from my teaching position in Ruthven and Mary and I decided that we wanted to move to Cedar Rapids. She had a brother and a sister living in town and we were ready for a change. I ended up getting a one-year teaching job at a middle school in Marion where Will, Mary's brother, was the principal. We put our house up for sale in Ruthven and decided that Mary and our daughter Katie, who was five at the time, would stay there until the house sold. Mary had a good job at Eaton Corporation in Spencer and we didn't see any reason for her to leave until she had to. In the meantime, I was going to live with Mary's sister, Pam, and her husband, Allen. Allen owned a successful plumbing business and was an even more successful real estate investor. He'd had the vision years earlier of buying vacant farmland that eventually became valuable parts of Cedar Rapids. They lived in a beautiful home and they had a separate wing that they let me live in while we tried to sell our house.

I had met Allen when Mary and I were dating in college and we liked each other a lot. He was beginning his move into early retirement when I moved in with him but was still working most of the time. He and I would get home about the same time every night and we would sit at the bar that separated the kitchen from the "great room" and drink vodka on the rocks and watch Pam cook dinner. Allen would always have a bottle of Absolut in the freezer and also have chilled cocktail glasses in there as well. When he'd get home and I was settled at the bar, he'd pull out the Absolut ("mother's milk," he'd call it) and we'd have a couple of drinks in the chilled cocktail glasses. He'd throw some olives in or maybe a pearl onion, but never any ice, and we'd sit there and drink. It was the first time in my life that I had a structured drinking pattern where I would find myself looking forward to the first drink at the end of the day. After dinner, Allen and I would sit in the great room and watch sports on his satellite dish and play gin and drink more vodka. It was usually something like Smirnoff or Gilbey's or something like that but I know that we drank a lot; and I also began to realize that vodka didn't give me the hangover that I would get from beer or wine or anything else I would drink. I felt a little fuzzy in the morning but other than that, I would feel fine.

One night Allen and Pam had a dinner to go to at the country club so I brought home some Chinese food and sat at the bar and ate and started drinking the Absolut from the freezer. Before I knew it, I drank pretty much the whole thing and found myself driving to the liquor store to buy another bottle to replace it. I poured some of the vodka from the new bottle into the old so it didn't look like I'd had any then took the rest of the new bottle and hid it under my bed. That was the first time I did something so premeditated and secretive for my drinking, but it became a practice that I carried with me until the very last night I ever drank.

The patient relates his abuse of alcohol beginning in 1993 was a result of job stress. The patient states that he was very concerned and wanted to change jobs; however, he was limited in his finances and his wife did not support his change of employment. The patient states that he would begin drinking after his family went to bed at night. He would retire to his basement and drink vodka to the point of intoxication.

My drinking increased dramatically in 1993 after my dad died on December 16, 1992. My dad was my best friend, my biggest fan, and my unconditional supporter no matter what I did. My dad could have walked into a room with me standing there, gun smoking in my hand and a dead body with a bullet hole in it lying on the floor in front of me, and my dad would look at me and the gun and then at the body and say, "Son, I'm sure sorry I wasn't here to see it because it looks like that was some of the best shooting I would have ever seen. I'm sure proud of you, son."

I could do no wrong in the eyes of my father.

I'd had an unbelievable year at work in 1992. Every account I wanted to write, I wrote. I belonged to a Rotary Club that met for breakfast on Thursday mornings and I was writing just about everyone's business. I was a hero at work, but when Dad got sick, everything changed.

He had a heart attack in April of 1992 and, even though he survived, he was never the same. In November, he went back into the hospital in Ames to have a biopsy on a spot they had found on his lung. After the procedure, he suffered another heart attack; he never went home again. It was during this time that alcohol became my mistress, my strength, and my constant companion. She eased me out of the euphoria of my success at work into the stark realization that I had to make the drive to be with my dad and watch him die. She would then lift me again as I would have her ride with me on the way home late at night, sometimes even in the middle of the night, to face the next day at work. She eased my pain. She somehow managed to keep my life in balance when nothing else seemed to work. I was grateful for her and often took advantage of the escape she would offer. The hardest thing I had ever gone through in my life was when my dad died, and she grabbed me by the hand and pulled me through it and then wouldn't let me forget what she had done for me. I remember when Mary and I got to my mom's house the day Dad died, Mom met us at the door, crying, and said to me, "I need you to be strong for me." I excused myself, went downstairs to Dad's bar, sat on one of the stools, and cried for about ten minutes then threw down half a fifth of Gilbey's. I went back upstairs with all the strength alcohol could let me give everyone without ever having the opportunity to grieve myself.

Alcohol never let me forget what she did for me the day Dad died and I couldn't imagine spending another day without her. Oh, I would try to convince myself I didn't need her and vow to spend a few days here and there without her just to prove I could do it, but I couldn't. I'd see her with someone else, see the pleasure she was giving, remember what she would do for me and how she would make me feel, and run back to her. The stress I began to feel at work was simply the realization that alcohol was beginning to become the most important thing in my life. She got me through the worst experience of my life and I found myself needing her to get me through every single day.

CHAPTER 5

"I'm Not That Bad . . ."

MY PRODUCTION AT WORK PLUMMETED in 1993; not only was I not writing as much business, but I also didn't have my dad in my life anymore to support me. Alcohol had taken his place. She had dragged me through that time and made me realize that if she could get me through that, she could get me through anything. That was my trigger. That was the event in my life that turned me from a drinker into a drunk. It happens to all alcoholics. It just happens in a different way.

About nine years after I had been sober, I met Gina, who was drunk and had locked herself in her bathroom at home. She was married at the time, and even though I knew her husband, I had never met her. He had called me out of the blue one day and said his wife had a problem and asked if I would be willing to talk to her. I ended up talking her out of the bathroom and into treatment that same night.

She had lived in suburban Atlanta and worked as an engineer when her husband-to-be breezed into her life on a sales call at her company and swept her off her feet. He moved her, much to the dismay of her parents, to Cedar Rapids, where she got a job as an avionics communications engineer. However, she didn't know anyone, and her husband traveled a lot and left her at home with his two young children from his first marriage. Their babysitter was their own mother, who would show up and make herself at home playing mom to her own children. Gina was left to fend for herself and ended up seeking solace from a bottle. Her life soon got out of hand and she ended up in treatment, relapsed when she was released, and was committed by her husband, who promptly filed for divorce and then remarried his ex-wife less than three months later. Talk about a trigger. Ask any alcoholic what pushed him to become so dependent on alcohol and you'll hear about the trigger. It's the thing that makes us put the bottle in our mouth without even realizing we're doing it anymore. It's when we suddenly snap and unknowingly give up control of our lives to something that will slowly begin to take that very life away from us. It's when choosing to drink vanishes and is replaced by the need to feed what has suddenly become an addiction that we can't quit. It happened to me and it happened to Gina; it happens to every alcoholic. It's when we cease to exist alone and suddenly find ourselves fighting with the addict every day.

The patient relates that in November of 1994, his drinking then progressed to one-half of a fifth of vodka per occasion. This was a result of continued job stress and having his mother-in-law move into his home.

I think the only reason my drinking progressed was because my addiction was getting hold of me. The job stress would have been manageable if I had been sober. I think any job would be stressful if a person were drinking as much as I was and his employers were beginning to have suspicions about what was actually going on in his life. Poor Gloria, Mary's mother, was nothing more than my excuse to drink. All an alcoholic needs is an excuse, and she was a good one for me. But she wasn't why I was drinking more all the time, nor was the stress at work why I was drinking. I was drinking because I was an alcoholic but was obviously not anywhere near the point where I was ready to admit that to anyone, especially myself.

In early 1995, the patient discontinued drinking altogether for a period of eight days. He states that this was in anticipation of cataract surgery and at that time he experienced no withdrawal. The patient resumed drinking following this experience and immediately resumed abuse of vodka.

Alcoholics are funny people. We reach a point where we know something is wrong but we won't go to the doctor to figure out what to do about it. A lot of that has to do with the shame that's been attached to the disease. While most "normal" drinkers can stop and start as they please, we don't have that kind of luxury.

I'd had an eye problem for a long time and I knew it was something that wasn't going to get better on its own. My first concern was that it was somehow alcohol-related, but once I started researching a little about what was going on, I was convinced it was a cataract. I went to see an ophthalmologist for confirmation and scheduled an appointment for a pre-surgical physical. About the same time, I was planning a fishing trip to Louisiana with Allen and a bunch of my other in-laws. I had intended to not drink on the trip because I knew I needed to go to the doctor for my physical and wanted to not have any alcohol in my system when I went. So much for good intentions.

As was always the case when I was with Allen, we drank a lot on the trip. I stayed with him in his motor home, and in the mornings, after breakfast and the obligatory Bloody Marys, I would always conveniently forget something as we were loading the boats and I would dash back up to the motor home and take five or six long pulls out of one of the big one-liter jugs of vodka we had brought with us and then go fishing all day and drink beer out of the coolers in the boat.

When I got back home and ended up going in for my doctor's appointment, there was probably more alcohol in my system than anything else. Brian, my doctor, ended up calling me at work one day after I had seen him and asked if I would come in. I had a feeling I knew what he wanted to discuss with me, so it was no surprise when he came in the exam room and closed the door.

"Steve, do you have a drinking problem?"

I seemed to get asked this question a lot, and even though I knew it was coming, I was still caught off guard. "No," I smiled. "Why do you ask?"

He pulled out a chart and ran his fingers across some numbers. "Your liver enzymes are significantly high. That's an indicator of severe alcohol abuse."

I had no idea what he was talking about. What in the world were liver enzymes? Was he trying to trap me? I was getting good at tap dancing. "Well, I just got back from a fishing trip with a bunch of my family and we did drink a lot while we were gone." I was hoping he'd buy that.

He frowned at me. He wasn't buying anything. "Elevated liver enzymes are a sign of long-term abuse."

He didn't say anything else. He put the ball in my court and was waiting for a return. I wanted to pull off some miraculous, game-saving overhead smash or a lob over his head that even he couldn't get to, but I didn't have a shot.

"No," I said, shaking my head. "I'm fine, but thanks for your concern. Anything else?"

He just shook his head and smiled that smile that was saying, *You're a drunk and you're constipated with denial.* "No, that's it. I wanted to make sure everything was okay. Take care."

He knew. By now, I was pretty certain that everyone probably knew something was going on. I think I was the only one who didn't know.

I got so drunk the night before my surgery that they probably could have operated on me without any anesthesia. I was starting to believe that I was in some pretty serious trouble but, like all alcoholics, all addicts actually, we all look for someone worse to convince ourselves we're really not that bad. I always thought that as long as I could find someone worse than I was, then I must be okay. I remember sitting in a bar one night in Ruthven, drunk with my friend Craig. We were sitting at a table having a beer and the place was pretty empty except for one of the two bankers in town who was sitting at the bar. He was in a rumpled suit and was leaning back on the barstool fighting hard to stay there. After a few minutes he just fell off the stool, crumbling in a heap on the floor and out cold. While I *should* have been thinking, *Man, I hope he's okay. I wonder if we should go help him up and call someone to come and get him. . . ,* all I *was* thinking was, *At least I'm not as bad as he is.*

I think we all feel that way, that if we can find someone who seems to be having a harder time than we are, then we're not that bad. If I saw someone who got a DUI, or lost his job, or got a divorce, or died because of his alcohol abuse, then I always felt that I wasn't that bad.

I wonder how many people held me up as that guy in their lives.

CHAPTER 6

The Grip Tightens

He did attempt to discontinue drinking in the summer of 1995 as he took a trip to Atlanta with his wife. During this trip, this patient did experience severe alcohol withdrawal including cravings, severe tremors, and loss of appetite.

When Mary and I went to Hong Kong, we accumulated enough frequent flyer miles to go almost anywhere we wanted. I was pushing for a trip to Disney World because it was something I had always promised Katie we would do, but Mary decided that we were going to go to Atlanta to, of all things, an Amway convention. My friend Phil and his wife Ellen were into Amway and Phil had been after us for a long time to get involved. I guess Mary decided that the time away together would be good for us and that maybe being around Phil might help me out. Phil had long since quit drinking and I think Mary was beginning to reach the point where she knew I needed some help.

We left Cedar Rapids early on a Friday morning and I got drunk before we left for the airport. I had thought about taking a bottle with me in my suitcase but didn't want to run the risk of being found out. Besides, I thought that if things got bad, I'd be able to get a drink somewhere down there during dinner or something. Shows you what I knew about Amway people.

I slept from Cedar Rapids to St. Louis and woke up just before we landed needing something to drink. I began to get the feeling that it was going to be a long weekend. I don't remember much about getting to Atlanta. I think Phil and Ellen and their son, John, met us at the airport, but I really don't remember. I know that the convention was at the Georgia Dome and there were about 40,000 people there.

By Friday night, I was having a hard time functioning. It got to be pretty late; I was tired and hadn't had anything to drink since early in the morning. We were sitting in the upper deck and every time I stood up, it seemed as if I were going to fall over. My legs were heavy and I was beginning to feel tremors in my hands. My whole body ached and was screaming for a drink. After the Friday night session, we all shared a motel room and I remember being so hot lying in bed but I couldn't stop shaking. Mary knew something was going on but I don't think she'd ever been around me before when something like this was happening so she didn't have any idea what it was all about.

I know the next night, she grabbed my hand and pulled me out of my seat and led me to one of the corridors surrounding the Dome. She confronted me about needing a drink and I admitted to her that, yes, I'd *like* to have a drink but certainly didn't *need* one and that I would be okay.

I don't recall much after that except that the next morning before we went to the church assembly, Phil took me aside and told me that he thought he smelled alcohol on me and wondered how and when I'd had a drink. I told him I hadn't had anything but thought that maybe the alcohol that was in me was seeping through my pores or something. I didn't know what to say to him except deny that I'd had anything to drink. That was the first and only denial that was actually true. I know we went to the church service and I ended up going to the altar call and that Mary was crying and everyone there that knew Phil was crying because they were all so happy that I was giving myself to the Lord. I brought home a small copy of the New Testament and honestly think everyone believed I was going to be okay.

On the way home, we flew through Minneapolis and my sister, Laurisa, met us at the airport. Mary had me hold my hands out to show Laurisa how much I was shaking, but I passed it off as being afraid of the next leg. The weather had turned lousy and I dreaded flying anyway. I think, in my mind at least, that they both bought it because in the plane, before takeoff, Mary kept praying over me to have the Lord give me strength for the flight to Cedar Rapids. But I know that when we got home that Sunday night, one of the first things I did was go downstairs to my bathroom and take a long drink. Everything was fine as soon as the alcohol hit my system. It was so good to be home with her again. I had missed her more than I would have ever imagined.

Upon returning from Atlanta in August of 1995, the patient continued his use of alcohol to the point of intoxication on a nightly basis.

I was drunk all day every day by then, and people started to become suspicious. Even though my tolerance was high, I found myself slurring my words on occasion and sometimes stumbling a bit when I walked. If those things weren't giving me away, all anyone had to do was look at me to see how much the alcohol was affecting me physically. My skin was gray and dry from dehydration. I had dry, scaly splotches everywhere and was constantly putting lotion on my face. There were dark circles under my eyes because I wasn't getting enough sleep. By then I had lost about thirty pounds because I wasn't eating very much and what I was eating wasn't staying in me very long.

I drank before work and was now leaving during the mid-morning to have a couple of pulls so I wouldn't start going through withdrawals at work. I was still drinking over the noon hour, again in the afternoon, on my way home from work, and after dinner. All of this before finally relaxing at night when the kids went to bed, when I would go downstairs to watch television and really get hammered. There were a lot of nights when I would wake up in my chair with the vodka bottle resting on my chest, and I remember thinking how lucky I was that Mary hadn't come down and found me like that.

Alcohol was in complete control of my life. I quit working out. I quit working period. My assistant, Sandi, covered for me at work and I'm certain she did things for me that I'll never know to protect me. My life was about drinking and nothing else. All I ever found myself thinking about was when I was going to get my next drink. My next fix. I was always planning on when I was going to feed the beast—the addict—again. All I could do was go along with whatever he told me because he was now in charge of my life.

I was drinking out of the plastic "traveler" bottles because they fit so well in my briefcase and they were easier to get rid of. Usually when I would empty a bottle, I would put it above the drop ceiling in the spare bedroom downstairs. I would go back where the furnace was and reach up over the wooden framing and lay the bottles up there. They were light enough that they wouldn't come through the ceiling tiles and I would usually put two empties a day up there. About once every other week, when I was home alone during the day, I'd grab a big, black garbage bag and take all the empties out from the ceiling. I'd usually have anywhere between twenty-five and thirty bottles and sometimes it would take two bags to get rid of them all. I'd take the bags out and put them in my trunk and then later that night, after it got dark, I'd find a dumpster somewhere in town and get rid of them. I think I knew where every unlocked dumpster was in Cedar Rapids.

I also found myself starting to go to different places to buy my vodka. There was a drug store right across the street from my office. I used to go there every day, but I started getting paranoid about the clerks noticing that I was coming in so often so I started driving all over town just to buy my vodka. I'd go to drug stores, grocery stores, liquor stores—everywhere that would sell it, I'd go there. I was getting paranoid about everything. I had good reason to be.

The patient has experienced consequences as a result of his alcohol use. His spouse has separated from him recently—one separation for one-week duration when the patient left home, the patient then returning home for the Christmas holidays.

On Monday, December 11, Sandi was in my office and we were joking around about Mary throwing me out of the house. I don't know why we were even talking about it, but we were and Sandi told me that if it ever happened to let her know and I could stay with her and her husband, Bud.

That night, when I got home, Mary and Katie met me at the door. They were both crying and Mary was holding a one-liter empty that I had hidden under a chair in the family room one night and had forgotten about. Neither one of them said anything. They just stood there and cried. The only thing I remember saying is that I thought I should probably leave and the next thing I remember is being at Sandi's house, and it was late, and she and I were sitting on the couch in her living room talking about what was going on. I don't remember calling her about me coming over and I don't remember going over there. I don't even remember packing clothes at home but I must have done that. I don't remember. I don't know what we talked about but I do remember sleeping in the lower level of their house and drinking all night, wondering what was happening to me and why I couldn't stop doing what I was doing.

The next day is a complete blank. I'm certain I went to work because I know Sandi came in and closed my door and told me that Bud was uncomfortable having me at the house and I needed to find someplace else to stay. I know that I called a friend of mine, a guy I had known since we had moved to Cedar Rapids and who, along with his wife, hung out with Mary and me quite a bit. I asked him if I could stay with them and he told me that he didn't want to get involved. Those are the last words that man has ever spoken to me even though I've tried to get in touch with him three times since I've recovered. Some people are funny about alcoholics.

The next thing I remember is sitting in Mary's brother's car in a parking lot between our house and his. Will was lecturing me about staying with them for the night but that there was absolutely no way they would tolerate alcohol in the house. I sat up all night in their basement draining a fifth of Gilbey's and not staying there the next night. I have no idea what happened but it must not have been very good.

The next night is when the first of many strange occurrences happened in my life. I actually had never admitted this to anyone before until recently because it was too bizarre and was one of those things that take years to understand. I have a very good friend, Jim Iverson, who had become almost like a father figure to me after my dad died. He's in the insurance business and I met him right after I started at Millhiser. He's a deeply religious and spiritual man and I know he struggled as he watched me fall. On Wednesday he told me, and I don't know where or how, but he told me that he had a friend who owned a cheap motel on the southwest side of town and that I could stay there for the night if I wanted. I went there, and it must have been after work but I don't know for sure, and got a room. I know it was dark when I went into the room but I don't know what time it was.

My car had a phone in it but it was permanently attached and not portable at all. I mention that only because the room had no phone. I don't even know if it had a television or not; I simply don't remember. The one thing I do remember is that the room smelled like gas. It was like someone had tried to turn on a gas burner and the flame didn't catch but the gas stayed on. That's how it smelled. I remember that I went out to my car and called someone, though I don't remember who it was or what I said, but I ended up going back into the room and the smell was still there. I think I might have opened a window but because it was so cold out, I didn't keep it open for long.

I lay in bed and kept telling myself that I really should leave, that I shouldn't stay in that room because of the gas. I kept seeing the picture of Mary and Katie standing in the door on Monday crying and holding that empty bottle and I started to become overwhelmed by an incredible feeling of absolute failure. I felt that I was letting everyone down at home, at work, everywhere. For the first time, the reality of what was happening to me began to settle over me and I sobbed uncontrollably in bed and prayed for some sort of deliverance. I didn't want to be like this anymore and I suddenly found myself overcome with the most peaceful feeling I'd had in a long time. It was as if someone or something somewhere was telling me to let go. Just let go and it would all be all right, and I remember thinking, *Why not? Why not just let go? I don't want to do this anymore and I don't want anyone to be hurt by this anymore. Why not just let go?*

I know I was conscious of what would happen to me if I went to sleep. The gas smell was overwhelming and I knew if I went to sleep that I'd never wake up, but I also knew that I didn't really care anymore if that happened. I wanted the pain to stop; I wanted to stop hurting everyone else and felt that there wasn't any other way to do it, and while I was thinking that, thinking about how nice it would be to fall asleep and how everything would be done, I closed my eyes.

I slowly became aware of waking up. I was comfortable; I was lying on my stomach and I was warm and everything around me was soft. I tried to think of where I was and was searching my memory, trying to place where I had been last. I thought of the smell of gas and became aware of the fact that the scent around me was fresh. I thought of falling asleep and remembered how much I wanted to stop everyone's pain and I remembered that I quit caring and I couldn't figure out where I was. I opened my eyes and saw the sun streaming through a window that wasn't there the night before. I slowly raised my head and looked around and realized that I had no idea where I was. The bedroom I was in was large and bright and neat. The clock on the table beside the bed showed 11:14 and I figured it must be the next day but still had no idea as to where I was. I was dressed but I didn't have my shoes on. I tried to remember if I was dressed the night before when I lay down in bed but that memory was gone.

As I lay there, I became aware of footsteps coming my way. It sounded like they were coming up some stairs and that there wasn't any carpet on the stairs. They sounded like men's shoes. I thought I should be afraid but the fear never came. A man walked into the room. He never looked at me so I couldn't see his face and the only thing he said to me was, "Are you all right?"

I knew I wasn't but, as always, said, "Yes, I think so."

He turned and walked out of the room and down the wooden stairs. I heard a door shut and then there was nothing. I didn't hear a car start; I didn't hear anything. All I knew was that there wasn't the smell of gas and that I wanted to get out of that house.

My shoes were on the floor beside the bed and I put them on, and as I did I looked around the room but saw nothing that would give me any idea as to where I was. There were no photos of any people, no names anywhere, nothing. After I got my shoes on, I saw my coat draped over a chair on the other side of the bed. I put it on; my keys were in one of the pockets, but not the pocket I would normally put them in. I walked down the wooden stairs and could see through the window by the door that my car was parked in the driveway. I went outside, closing the door behind me. I just wanted to get out of there as fast as possible. When I got in the car, my duffel bag was in the front seat but I couldn't remember if I had taken it into the motel with me the night before. When I pulled out of the drive and headed down the street, it took me a few minutes to figure out where I was. Even though I knew the street, I had no idea who lived in that house. To this day, I don't know how I got there.

When I left the house, I have no idea where I went. I know that I spent the next two nights at a friend's house but I have no recollection of how I ended up staying with him and his wife. Their house was festive and I think they even had a holiday party on Friday night that I was part of but don't remember. I know I went home on Saturday but I don't remember anything about it. The next memory I have is a vague one of me getting drunk after Mass on Christmas Eve, but that's it until the day after Christmas when Mary and I met with my boss. Gone. Everything's gone. It's probably best that way.

The patient continues to suffer withdrawal from alcohol at the time of this writing. He continues to have tremors, although they are diminished in severity. The patient does have an acceptance of chemical dependency and he is willing if not yet able to call himself an alcoholic; however, he has very little understanding of the disease.

I think I had come to terms with the fact that I was sick but was having a hard time grasping the idea that I had a disease. Cancer was a disease. I figured that even if I didn't stop drinking, I'd eventually figure out a way to modify my drinking behavior, get everyone off my back about it, and begin to feel better. I may have wanted everyone to believe that I was willing to call myself an alcoholic, but I wouldn't actually do it. An alcoholic was someone who couldn't stop and who had lost his job and his family and didn't have anywhere to live. I wasn't that bad. As I said, I think we all hold up others who are "worse off" than we are as our own symbols of alcoholics, and as long as we aren't where they are, we think we're still reasonably okay. I looked at myself as someone who was drinking too much and needed to find a way to drink less.

The patient is experiencing some resistance to treatment, as he does feel superior to most other patients in the treatment setting.

People in treatment, much like people in any social setting, tend to break off into their own little cliques. In high school it was the jocks, the nerds, and the hoods. In business, it was the high-dollar commercial producers, the customer service reps, the personal lines people, the stockholders, and the board members. In treatment, one would think the natural tendency would be to group up by choice of drug, but that's not how it was when I was in.

Most of the time, you would hang out with people who came in the same time you did or who had been in for only a little while before you got there.

My first time in, my closest friend was Chris, a nineteen-year-old kid from a small town outside Cedar Rapids. He had come in a couple of nights after I had and was having a pretty tough time trying to come off a meth episode. When he was taken upstairs to detox on the psyche ward, he was strapped to the bed to protect himself and was still in pretty bad shape when he came down to the fourth floor. He ended up being my roommate and, despite the age difference, we became pretty close.

I was the oldest of the batch of inpatients when I was first admitted, and that, plus the attitude I developed about my view of the insignificance of my problem, tended to set me apart from everyone else. Early on I found myself telling everyone how great everything was for me. I painted this picture of confidence; I wasn't going to let this thing get me down. I set out to try to convince everyone who would listen to me, and oftentimes even those who wouldn't, that everything was great, just great. People found hope in me; they liked my attitude and wanted to have the same kind of confidence I had. The inpatients got robin-egg blue and white striped cotton bathrobes when we were admitted and I would wear mine everyday over my jeans and sweatshirt as if it were a symbol of royalty. I found I had a group of followers who wanted to be just like me. They apparently wanted to be as phony as I, as confident in my desire to change my drinking behavior, as willing to lie to the counselors who, I was certain, were buying into the act as well. I was the king; everyone else was my court. The addict became my assassin, secretly plotting my overthrow.

CHAPTER 7

Romance Matters of an Intellectual Genius

The patient has significant relapse potential in that he has unresolved marital conflict, and he seems to be minimizing the effects of his alcohol abuse on his family's life.

My marriage had never been one based on positive communication. I grew up in an environment in which my parents rarely discussed anything reasonably and rationally. My dad was never one to have a discussion with my mother who, to say the least, was more than a bit overbearing. She would rag on him unmercifully about something, anything really, and he would sit there and boil until he would be ready to erupt. My dad *never* hit my mom and rarely would even have any verbal confrontations with her, but I do remember the screaming and cursing when he would. Mostly, though, I remember Dad stomping out of the room and either heading outside to blow off steam or, more often than not, heading downstairs to get away from her.

I remember following him downstairs once after he had flipped off my mom behind her back, his face beet red and the veins on his forehead looking like thick blue worms trying to wiggle their way out of his skull. I was afraid for him, not *of* him, and just wanted some reassurance that he was going to be okay. I sneaked down the steps and saw him in the corner behind the bar standing there chugging down a bottle of Seagram's like it was water. That's how my dad dealt with confrontation. Maybe that's how my dad dealt with a lot of things, and maybe that's why I had convinced myself that it was okay to deal with things the same way in my marriage and in my life.

I was a terrible husband mostly because I never let Mary in on what was going on in my life. Given that definition, I was lousy in general because I never opened up to anyone about anything and, looking back, that trait got me into most of the trouble that dogged me throughout my adult life. I didn't want to talk to anyone about my fears, my imperfections, my anxieties, my doubts, my abilities, anything. I found that if Mary called me on something, I would allow whatever feelings I had to stay somewhere deep inside me and, at the first opportunity I had, I would find myself sneaking down the steps to the corner behind my own bar and chugging down a bottle of vodka. I think I always found it easier to allow for the chance to escape reality than to face it, even if it would still be there when the effects of the liquor would wear off. That's how my dad did it; that's how I was choosing to do it.

No wonder I had significant relapse potential. If all I was ever doing was drinking to avoid any conflict in my life, to avoid uncomfortable situations or circumstances, and given that I was in treatment to figure out a way to be a smarter drinker, I think it's safe to say the odds were definitely not in my favor. It would be interesting to see how I would respond if and when the time came to test myself.

Psychological Condition/Mental Status Exam: The patient had an adequate attention span during the interview and appeared to have appropriate recent and long term recall. His language was logical and goal oriented. The patient was a good historian; he was able to supply information specific with dates and times.

I've always had an intellectual superiority around people, even if only in my own mind. It seems that no matter where I was or whom I was with, I would try to convince myself that I was somehow "above" them intellectually even if I knew the other person was smarter than I. I think a lot of that came from being an English major at a private southern Baptist university. People used to be freaked out by that when they would find out.

"So, what do you do for a living?" they'd ask.

"Oh," I'd say nonchalantly, "I'm the head of the English department at a local school. I majored in English and literature in college and I'm positively enamored by the study of our language."

I'd say it with polished confidence and not sound the least bit pompous even if I was the *only* English teacher in the school. I'd say it like it was no big deal, say it like everyone in the world should know how Jim Casey symbolized Christ in *The Grapes of Wrath*, why Lady Macbeth walked in her sleep, how to never split an infinitive, or why a preposition is a word you should never end a sentence with. People would rarely talk to me after they knew that, and even if it meant absolutely nothing in the grand scheme of things, I used it to my advantage whenever I could.

The point is, I realized that I was a much more confident person when I could use my intellectual experiences when dealing with people. This was especially true when I was dealing with people whom I perceived as being more intelligent in their particular field, say, substance abuse counselors for example. "Logical language, goal-oriented speech, a good historian." Language has always been my way of trying to dodge the reality of any situation. I gave my counselors what I thought they wanted me to say and what they needed to hear from me. That's how I planned to get through the program. I had been able to lie my way through most of my life up to that point and I saw no reason to change the way I worked now. I was fairly certain these people had never seen anyone like me before; I had them right where I wanted them.

Social, Family, and Spiritual: The patient is the younger of two children born to his parents. He states his mother is age 66, currently living in Jefferson, Iowa. He describes having a positive relationship with his mother.

After Dad died, it got harder and harder to spend time with my mom. Mom has always felt like anything bad happening to someone else was the worst thing that's ever happened to her. I'm pretty sure she could have used some serious therapy at some point in her life, but I discovered that it was easier for me to drink when I was around her than try to convince her that she needed help.

She had been completely dependent upon Dad. He did everything for her. He drove her everywhere they went; I have very few recollections of my mom ever driving the car until after Dad died. Once, when we were on a family trip to Michigan to see my uncle, Dad decided to take a nap and told my mom to stay on the road we were on, which happened to be I-80. She made one wrong turn, or maybe she didn't make a turn when she was supposed to, but either way, she ended up on the wrong road. If Dad hadn't awakened when he did, we would have probably ended up somewhere in New Jersey. She didn't drive again after that.

After Dad died, Mom became dependent and clingy and needy, mostly needing me to be strong, like I was on the day Dad died. I think that's when I first started hauling vodka with me on trips when Mary and I would take the girls over to see her. I'd usually take a couple of bottles in my suitcase and then hide them under the bed in her guest room and sneak in when I could to take a couple of pulls to distance myself emotionally from her and her selfishness. I don't know that she ever asked me how I felt about Dad being gone; she just needed to make sure that I knew how hard it was on her. I'm pretty sure Dad drank a lot; I'm certain, in fact, that he was an alcoholic, but I'm pretty certain he had to drink a lot just to put up with her. I know I did.

The patient has one sister, age 46, who currently resides in Minnesota. He describes this as a close relationship; however, he does not see her very often.

Laurisa got her name from my two grandmothers, Laura and Isabelle. I never knew my parents were so creative, but I'm glad their experimenting ended with her; otherwise I would have ended up as either Welph or Raldon. As far as names go, she got the better end of the deal. Other than that, I seem to have gotten the better end of the stick growing up.

We had absolutely nothing in common. Laurisa was deep, intellectual, and artistic. She actually stood up in front of a fairly large crowd in the Newton Public Library and sang "People" for a recital one time. She was smart. I remember being in junior high and having the teachers say things to me like, "Well, if you're Laurisa's brother, we're going to be expecting big things from you." I never felt as smart as she was but always felt that people were expecting me to be. I often felt that the pedestal my parents put me on, especially my dad, should have been reserved for her.

My dad had huge, red, three-ring binders that he'd bring home from work, and he'd keep scrapbooks of me and all my athletic

accomplishments from the time I started playing Pee Wee Basketball at the Y when I was in third grade. I played football, basketball,
baseball, ran track, and had pretty good success at just about everything. My sister's biggest athletic accomplishment was walking
all the way to B.C. Berg Junior High School, all six blocks in an
ice storm, only having to turn around and walk all the way home
when she found out school had been canceled—and not falling
down once. At least, not until she got back to our driveway and
was in the process of telling my mom how excited she was that
she hadn't fallen down.

When my sister moved out of the house and started college, I
was starting ninth grade and my parents let me move into their
bedroom, and they moved into Laurisa's. It was a pretty big deal,
and I'm sure Laurisa was pretty upset about it; she was pretty much
left out in the cold. Once I turned sixteen, Dad decided to buy a
second car so I could have something to drive around. It ended
up being a 1965 Mustang Fastback, red with a white racing stripe,
something that's worth about $24,000 today if only we hadn't
traded it in on a new 1975 Pinto station wagon when I left to go
to school in Florida.

The point is, I ended up with a lot more perks as an "only child"
than she ever got as the older child, and I think this had something to do with the distance that always seemed to be between
the two of us. Even as kids, we'd fight a lot. We always had to do
the dishes after dinner, and she would always sing this old Andy
Williams song, "Moon River," to me, only instead of singing the
real words, she'd sing, "Steve Sellers, wider than a mile . . ." and
I remember that it made me so angry at her. It was the stupidest
thing in the world but it really used to make me mad. I'd go into
her room and read her diary when she wasn't around just because
I knew I wasn't supposed to do it.

We probably weren't any different than every other brother and sister with five years between them, but the differences seemed more pronounced as we got older. We tried to connect a bit once I got to college, while she was living with Mark before they got married. But at the time, I realized I was enjoying being around her more because I really liked Mark a lot. I'd never had a brother and he was a neat brother to have, so it seemed like Laurisa and I were getting closer. Really, it was just me getting closer to him.

Some years later after she and Mark had moved to Minneapolis, we saw less of them, and it was always more of a production to go since we now had two girls; when we went, it had to be for the whole weekend. It wasn't that we didn't enjoy going but more that Mary and I had always felt intellectually and professionally inferior to them. They didn't ever do anything to make us feel that way, but we were obviously pretty insecure about our intellect and professions so the feelings were magnified when we were around them.

Laurisa ended up divorcing Mark and marrying her current husband, Arnie, who, like Mark, is a really good guy. I don't think Arnie liked me much early on, as he was smart enough to see through my nonsense, and the times we'd spend up there were difficult because there was always this cloud of uncertainty about my drinking hanging around everywhere. I don't think it was uncertainty about the fact that I was drinking; I think it was more the fact that no one seemed to know exactly what to do about it.

I guess if Laurisa and I had been closer, I would have been more comfortable talking to her about what I knew was becoming a pretty severe problem. I think I had gotten to the point where I would have liked to reach out to her, but because of that stupid song she used to torture me with, I never felt like I could get close to her. That always irritated me to no end but she really did have a nice voice.

He states his father did drink alcohol and [he] did observe his father intoxicated; however, he did not feel his father had a problem with chemical dependency.

Dad *did* have a problem with alcohol. I think anyone who had to spend any amount of time with my mother would have to have developed a chemical dependency of some kind just to get by. There was never a time when my parents socialized when alcohol wasn't involved. My uncle had built a nice bar in our basement for my dad and it was always stocked with every kind of booze imaginable. He had beer signs hanging behind his bar. You know, like the caricature of the fat, stumbling drunk with a red nose and his hat sitting cockeyed on his head and he's saying, "I don't have a drinking problem. I drink. I get drunk. I fall down. No problem." Or the one that says, "He who drinks, gets drunk. He who gets drunk, falls asleep. He who falls asleep, doesn't sin. He who doesn't sin, goes to heaven. So let's all get drunk and go to heaven."

He had great bar glasses and all the tools you needed to mix any drink imaginable. His nickname was Slim and he had a sign that said "Slim: Bartender on duty" that hung on the wall. He even used to tend bar at the Elks on weekends and some evenings, so he obviously knew his way around a drink menu.

I think Dad and I were a lot alike in that we drank in order to stuff problems somewhere down inside where we wouldn't have to deal with them and most certainly wouldn't have to talk about them. In 1980, Dad lost the only job he'd ever had when the small manufacturing plant where he'd worked as a cost accountant for twenty-eight years closed; he lost everything he'd ever worked for. Mary and I were living in Ruthven at the time and I don't think I realized for a long time how hard that was on him.

When he had his first heart attack in April of 1992, the doctors figured out that he'd had a heart attack about ten or twelve years earlier, about the time he'd lost his job, and he'd never told anyone about it. Talk about keeping things inside. I know from experience when something that traumatic happens and you're an alcoholic, you start drinking like there's no tomorrow, and for my dad, when he lost his job, he probably felt that he had run out of tomorrows.

In the spring of 1986, Mom and Dad came up to Ruthven for the weekend. I loved it when they would come up because Dad and I would hang out together and play cribbage or gin, watch any kind of sports on TV, and drink all weekend long. We'd have Bloody Marys in the morning, beer during the day, something with vodka before dinner, Gimlets or screwdrivers, and then usually drink wine with dinner and also into the evening with a snifter of brandy or a cordial of Drambuie before bed. We did that all the time and loved every minute of it. We'd play games with Mary and Katie and Mom, and then after Katie went to bed, we'd all stay up late and play cards and Dad and I would never stop drinking.

This particular weekend, we decided we were going to take the boat out, so Dad and I drove my truck out to the lake and pulled the boat while Mary, Mom, and Katie followed us out in the car. We had packed a cooler full of beer, vodka, mix of some kind, and some snacks and were going to make a day out of it. I put the boat in at the ramp and then tooled over to the docks and everybody hopped in. It was a nice, sunny day but once we got out on the lake, the wind had picked up and the water was rough. It got worse the farther away from the boat ramp we got and we finally decided that it was too rough to be out there, so I headed for land and followed the shoreline around to the boat ramp on the far side of the lake. We let Mary, Mom, and Katie out and told them we'd take the boat back across the lake and then I'd drive over and pick them up. When Dad and I got back to the other side of the lake, I tied up the boat at the dock and then got in the car and headed over to pick up Mary, Mom, and Katie while Dad stayed in the boat, listening to the radio and sipping a beer.

When I picked them up, we headed back for the dock, and when we turned the corner and saw the boat, there sat Dad with the jog of vodka, guzzling that thing like it was water and he had just crawled out of Death Valley. By the time we got to him, he was so drunk he couldn't even stand up. I had to carry him to the car and Mary drove him home while I got the boat out of the lake and onto the trailer. I remember thinking as I was driving home that I had seen my dad drunk quite a few times but never to the point where he couldn't walk. He was absolutely smashed and it wasn't the funny kind of smashed, the Foster Brooks kind of smashed where everyone is laughing at how bad he is. Mom was beside herself and Mary, I'm sure, didn't know what to think. By the time I got home, they were already there and everyone was sitting in our family room, not really knowing what to do. Mary took Mom outside to go for a walk to try to calm her down and I sat inside with my dad asking him what was wrong.

He broke down. He told me how he felt like a failure for losing his job, that he had let everyone down and felt worthless to everyone. This was six years after he had lost his job, and I have the feeling it wasn't the first time he'd guzzled booze to squash the feelings of inadequacy that had overwhelmed him. He had never been able to talk about his feelings; it was one of the many things I inherited from him, and I discovered later that we also shared the same way of dealing with those inadequacies. My dad was an alcoholic. So is his son.

The patient is currently married to a 40-year-old woman and they reside in Cedar Rapids.

I met Mary in the spring of 1974 when we were freshmen at North Iowa Area Community College in Mason City, Iowa. In high school, I'd had this terrible crush on Janie Collins but she was never interested in me. She was a junior when I was a senior so the only class we had together was chorus and I would sit in my seat in the top row and just stare at her. She was a terrific singer and I loved to watch her mouth move when she sang; I would pretend when I'd watch her mouth move that she was talking to me and telling me how crazy she was about me. The first thing I noticed about Mary was that she looked like Janie Collins and the second thing I noticed was that she wasn't interested in me either.

I used to plan my trips to the cafeteria at NIACC to make sure I'd see Mary. She'd be sitting with all of her friends and they all knew that I had a thing for her, but I was such an idiot around her that she must have thought I was crazy. I wasn't like that around any other girls I'd hung out with so I'm not sure why I was that way with her. This was back in the seventies and clogs were in. I remember walking on the sidewalk going to class one day when I saw her coming and desperately wanted to be cool, which I figured would be easy seeing as how I was wearing clogs and all. When she got close, I made eye contact with her, which was a really good thing, but since I was looking at her, I wasn't looking where I was going anymore and stepped off the edge of the sidewalk. I don't know if you've ever even worn clogs, let alone step off the edge of a sidewalk with them, but I ended up losing my balance and staggering around like someone who had just done one of those dizzy bat contests at a baseball game. You know, where people bend over and put their forehead on a baseball bat and spin around in circles for two minutes and then stand up and try to walk in a straight line. It would have probably been easier if I had fallen down but I thought that would be far too un-cool so I kept staggering around while Mary kept on walking past with her friends wondering what in the world was wrong with me.

I don't know how I did it, but I eventually won her over, and when I went to Florida in August of 1975, she went with me, all of our stuff loaded in that brand new Pinto station wagon, and a year later we were married. She blessed me with two beautiful daughters in the nineteen years we were married, and for a long time, they were the only things in my life that I had ever created that I was proud of. I've always believed that Mary deserved better than me or at least a better me than I was during the last few years of our marriage. My alcoholism was harder on her than I'll ever know and by the time I went in the first time, I don't think she had any idea what she was in for.

The patient has two children from this union, a 12-year-old daughter and a 6-year-old daughter. The patient's youngest daughter suffers from Down's [sic] Syndrome.

The nice thing about Laura being six when all of this happened is that she probably won't remember much of what actually did happen. As far as "suffering," Katie was the one that was hit harder by this. Laura's affliction can hardly be called suffering. She is the most forgiving, loving, and loveable girl anyone could ever hope to be around, and because of her age she will be spared from most if not all of the memories of that time of her life. I try hard to think back to being six and I don't remember much of that time in my life. Of course, I didn't have anything traumatic happen to me like my dad flipping out and being locked up in the psyche ward of the local hospital. Katie got the brunt of all of this. I remember twelve; I know she'll never forget it either. The night I ended up in the hospital, Katie was at her cousin Ellie's house and I know that it was an excruciatingly painful night for both of them. Katie has learned forgiveness and today I'm blessed to have wonderful relationships with both of my girls. Ellie has never spoken to me again.

The patient is a college graduate, graduating from Stetson University in Florida where he was on scholarship for basketball. The patient is satisfied with his educational level.

When I signed my letter of intent to go to school in DeLand, my dad jumped up and clicked his heels. He was forty-nine at the time and a pretty heavy smoker and not much of an athlete. I don't smoke at all and try to stay in pretty good shape, and I don't think I could even do that, so he must have been pretty excited. I would probably have had a tough time going to school if it weren't for basketball. Dad would have done anything to have been able to have me go, so I know he was pretty happy to have someone else pick up the tab.

Mary and I had a blast in Florida. Dad used to tell everyone that DeLand is about twenty miles from "de water," Daytona Beach to be exact, so we spent a lot of time hanging around the beach. We'd load up the Pinto on Saturday mornings and head over to the beach and spend most of the day lying in the sun, playing in the water, throwing Frisbees, all sorts of stuff. Oh, we drank a lot too. We were on a Busch beer kick while we lived in Florida and had it all the time. It was everywhere.

I don't remember why I decided to major in English. I think it had something to do with the fact that when I went to NIACC I wanted to be an accounting major and do what my dad was doing. The first day of our accounting class we had an exam that was supposed to review everything we'd learned in our high school accounting classes. Given that I'd never taken an accounting class in high school, I didn't do so well on the test. My faculty advisor called me in a couple of days later and suggested I go in a different direction, so I hadn't declared a major when I went to Stetson. It is a private Baptist university, and just about everyone there was either a religion major or music major. Laurisa had pretty much soured me on music, what with "Moon River" and all, so I picked English. I struggled with it during my first semester, ending up with three D's and an F at midterm and getting hit with academic probation, but by the time I graduated, I was on the Dean's List, so something must have clicked somewhere along the line.

By the time I graduated, Mary and I had decided that even though we had the opportunity to stay in Florida, we wanted to go back home. It seemed that whenever someone in our families had a vacation, they would always come to see us and the only vacations we ever took were going back home. Plus, Mary's dad had a heart attack while we lived down there and we wanted to be closer to her family. I missed my family too. Especially my dad.

The patient has been employed in the past as an English teacher at a high school in Iowa.

When we made the decision to move back to Iowa, Dad started looking for jobs in the Des Moines *Register* for me. He would find the high school basketball coach/English teacher combinations and circle them with a red ink pen and send the ads to me every week. It shouldn't be a big surprise that there weren't a lot of those jobs out there.

The first person I heard back from was a guy by the name of Bill Johnson, the superintendent of Ruthven Community Schools. We had never heard of the place. When we looked it up on the map, we saw that it was only about fourteen miles from Spencer,

Iowa, and the only thing we knew about Spencer was that it was always the coldest place in the state every winter. I applied, got a call from Bill a week or so later, interviewed on the phone, and took the job sight unseen. We figured we'd stay a year or two and then move on. We were there ten years.

I always told people I was the head of the English department, but I was the *only* English teacher in the school. I taught ninth grade through twelfth grade, and every student in high school had to take English, so I had, to say the least, a fairly diverse classroom full of characters. My freshmen worked a lot on grammar and composition and read *The Adventures of Huckleberry Finn*. It was the first novel a lot of them had ever read. They also studied *Romeo and Juliet* and they had a blast with that. I'd learned in college that no one should ever have to read Shakespeare, so my kids listened to it, scene by scene, and then we talked about what was going on. After we got through the whole play, they would watch it, and by then they loved it. Ah, the arts. It was probably the first time anyone in Ruthven, Iowa, had ever been exposed to something like that.

The sophomores did more creative writing and read Steinbeck's *Of Mice and Men* and studied a lot more American literature. My juniors wrote more, studied English literature, read *Lord of the Flies*, and studied *Macbeth*. The seniors wrote research papers and short stories, studied *The Grapes of Wrath,* and broke down *2001: A Space Odyssey*. I think I learned more about writing and literature and the English language during that ten-year period than most people would learn, or *care* to learn, in a lifetime.

Coaching basketball was great fun, especially the after-the-game parties I had in my basement. I knew my kids because I taught them all, so I knew who I could depend on and who would be most apt to let me down. Given that there were only 750 people in Ruthven, there wasn't a whole lot for my kids to do on weekends and, needless to say, I had more than a few problems with kids drinking. I found, especially later on, that I was being as hypocritical as could be when I would lecture them about drinking when, the weekend before, I was lying on top of a rented station wagon with my friend Craig, flying down a county road at ninety miles an hour with another friend far too drunk to be behind the wheel swerving to see if we would let go of the luggage rack. Ah, alcohol. I *know* that the people in Ruthven had been exposed to *that* before.

The patient describes a significant amount of social support including his family, his spouse's family, various friends at work, and friends through his church. He believes that his social support will be a support for him in his continuing sobriety.

I don't actually know how much support I had when I first went into the hospital. My mom was freaked out by everything and has never been one to show much support in desperate times, so I wasn't really counting on a lot of support from her. Laurisa and I weren't really close yet and she lived in Minneapolis, so I didn't see her at all. Mary's family was praying for me and probably offering more than I knew. People at work, my boss especially, were supportive, but other than a card I got from a woman I was working with at the time, a card I still carry to this day, I don't think I heard from anyone other than the request for an occasional update on my condition from my boss. I really didn't have that many friends through the church. I think I told them that because they were looking for a spiritual base of some kind and I really didn't have one. I belonged to a board of some kind at church but I ran for that mostly because I thought it would look good. I didn't even win in the election, but our priest, Father John, wanted me on, so he created an extra position so I could be on the board.

I have a feeling that most people were just freaked out by the fact that someone they knew had flipped out and ended up in the hospital, locked in the psyche ward. Nobody really knew how to handle something like that. It's like dropping money in the Salvation Army kettle during Christmas. People do that with no trouble at all because it's so impersonal. But these same people will go out of their way to avoid a homeless person begging for money because it's personal and nobody wants to deal with it directly. What happened to me hadn't ever happened to anyone else that my friends, coworkers, or family had ever known. We were all in the dark about what to do and what to expect.

Oh, and that idea about "continuing sobriety"—my "support staff" really didn't have to worry a whole lot about that being a very big deal. The only "continuing" I was planning on was drinking.

The patient states that he has been very vocal with his neighbors, his minister, as well as several of his family members regarding his alcohol problem.

I guess if you define being "vocal" as in "I don't have a drinking problem," then that's a pretty accurate statement. The only time I admitted a drinking problem to my neighbors was the night I went into the hospital and I didn't have much of a choice in the matter. I think it was safe to say that everyone knew that I had a problem that night so confession seemed like the best way to get everyone out of my house. As far as my minister goes, I did go to Father John's one night in late November and told him I was drinking too much. He said I should stop.

There was obviously a lot of concern among my family members, but Mary was the only one who ever called me on it though I continued to deny my addiction around her. My mom did call me once after we had been to her house for a weekend and most of a full fifth of vodka had mysteriously disappeared from the liquor cabinet that she kept in the garage. She asked me if I was having any problems. I told her no. That was that.

He describes being faithful to his spouse within his marriage and believes that his wife has also been faithful to him.

I was involved with another woman when I uttered those very words at my interview. I had gotten to know Laurie when we had first moved to Cedar Rapids. She had asked her husband to move out in 1992 because their marriage was dead and she needed passion in her life. I needed someone who would leave me alone about my drinking and love me unconditionally. We both fit each other's needs.

The very first night I was with her, I drank about half a fifth of Gilbey's to calm myself then stopped and bought a couple bottles of wine. We drank wine every time we were together, and before we'd get together, I'd have that half a fifth of vodka. I was never with her when I was sober. I'm not trying to justify what happened; it's simply a fact. I was scared then and thought I needed someone to support me and love me without telling me that I needed to change what I was doing. I was wracked with guilt about what was going on, but my fear weighed more heavily upon me and she made me less afraid. I could be what I thought was myself with her—even though the scary part was that the "myself" I was with her was always—and I mean *always*—drunk. She eventually came to know how sick I was but never once told me that I needed to get help or that I should stop drinking or that she was concerned about it in any way.

I think . . . no, I'm certain . . . that's why I believed I loved her. She never judged me, never condemned me or made me feel like I had any problem at all. She just wanted to be with me. Even when I kept trying to tell her how bad my drinking was and how she should leave and find someone who could give her more than I was able to give her, she never once wavered. She, without even knowing what it meant, was the ultimate enabler. She was also soon caught up with me in a nightmare that neither one of us ever anticipated even if we should have seen it coming a mile away.

CHAPTER 8

The All-Knowing Voice and the Blonde

ONE DAY AT WORK, I got a call from someone I didn't know, a man who seemed to know more about what was going on in my life than I was able to remember or ever be willing to admit. He knew about what was going on between me and Laurie and he was threatening to tell Mary.

Laurie and I hadn't been careful and most of that was my fault. Every day, I would leave work about eleven and go home, lock myself in the downstairs bathroom, and get drunk while doing a crossword and listening to the radio. About 11:45 I would head to Laurie's office and park in the back lot, as far away from the building as I could get, and wait for her to come out. We would go somewhere and have lunch or go sit in a park somewhere and talk or just drive around. We weren't being very careful so it really shouldn't have been a surprise that someone knew that there was something going on, but this got out of hand in a hurry.

By then, I was paranoid about everything that was going on in my life. The addiction was doing that to me even if I didn't know it at the time. I was hiding everything from everyone and I got scared in a hurry when he started calling me. At first he would call me at work and say things like, "Hey, how's your girlfriend? You guys have fun at Papa Juan's at lunch yesterday? Your wife know what's going on?"

"Who is this?" I'd ask, as brave and tough as a frightened, paranoid alcoholic could sound.

"I'm your new best friend," he'd laugh and then hang up.

This went on for two, maybe three weeks. He'd call me every day, never at the same time, and sometimes two or three times a day. I never told anyone about it, not even Laurie at first, but it started to get worse one day when I was in my car and my cell phone rang. It was him.

"Hey Stevie," he'd taunt, "headed out to see your girlfriend? You better hurry; you're leaving the office a little later than usual. You drinking on the way home to save some time?"

I panicked and looked at the cars around me. He was watching me. He knew more than the fact that I was just seeing someone. He knew I was drinking. I felt the knot tighten in my stomach. "Who are you?" I asked. I was trying not to sound scared but I was too scared to try not to be scared.

"Enjoy your lunch. Be careful."

And then, he'd be gone.

He was following me, or at least he got me believing he was following me. It got to the point where every time my phone would ring at work or in my car, I would panic. There were days at work when I would go into the bathroom nearly sick because of how afraid I was becoming. He knew everything I was doing, everywhere I was going. I started to fear for my family, but the only threats he would throw out at me were those of exposing everything that I was so desperately trying to hide from everyone.

I tried to think of who it was but had no idea where to start. So much of my life was wiped away in an alcoholic haze; who knew what I had said or done to the wrong person and not even known it? I thought for a minute that Laurie knew something about what was going on, but what happened next made me certain that she was far too valuable to him in her role as my mistress.

A woman, maybe in her late twenties or early thirties, blonde and attractive, started appearing at the same places I was. I noticed her at first in church one Sunday only because she was new and she was attractive. I didn't think anything about it, but one day, maybe two or three weeks later, still in the midst of my daily phone calls from my new best friend, I realized when Laurie and I were having lunch at Xavier's that the blonde woman was there and it hit me, as the haze lifted long enough for me to see through it, that I'd seen her more than just at church and more than sitting at the crowded bar at Xavier's. I remembered seeing her at the drug store when I'd bought vodka, at the Hy-Vee on Wilson Boulevard when I'd bought vodka, at Target and Walgreens and Papa Juan's and just about every other place I'd been; she was there too. I found out her name was Angela; he told me one afternoon when he called.

"So, you like Angela?" he asked, that voice a cross between a cowboy and a science professor, relaxed yet ice-cold, tearing bits of me apart while he spoke. "She's been keeping tabs on you and your girlfriend for me. Knows exactly what you've been up to. Cute, isn't she? Cold, but cute. You've got something she wants and it ain't what you think it is. I want it too and it ain't gonna be much longer before we get it. Bye-bye, Stevie boy."

I was really getting scared now. He kept calling me on the phone and she kept showing up everywhere I went. She would look at me when I would see her but she knew, as he did, that I was too scared to do anything. I was gripped in a fear I had never known. They knew what they were doing to me; they knew why they were doing it. I didn't know anything except that I was never so afraid of anything in my life. I know that all I had to do was to tell someone, Mary especially. All I had to do was the one thing that I hadn't ever been able to do, simply tell someone the truth. My problem, well, one of my problems, was that I hadn't ever really learned to do that and my fear was that no one would believe me if I told the truth anyway.

Eventually it got too big for me, and one afternoon Laurie and I were in her car in a park on the outskirts of town and I told her. It was then that I told her about my drinking problem, about the phone calls, about Angela, about how paralyzed I had become, and about how I thought she should pack it in and walk away from me. I was on the edge of something; I had no idea what it was but I didn't think anyone should be there with me.

She wouldn't leave. She was into this whole thing too far with me and had somehow convinced herself that maybe she would be able to be the one who could pull me back. Enablers will believe that anything they do will help. She needed to leave me; she needed to walk away for her sake and my own but she sat there in the car and cried and held on to me and told me that everything was going to be all right. She had told me so many things in the drunken fogs in which I had found myself with her. She had told me how wronged I had been by everyone and how I deserved so much more than what others were giving me. They were things that I had made myself believe because they were things I thought I needed to hear. Maybe I thought I would believe her when she told me everything was going to be okay, but for the first time since I had started seeing her, I could not shake the feeling that she was wrong. I started to believe that this was not going to end well.

One day he called me at work and the first thing he said was that he wanted to play a tape for me. When I asked him what he was talking about, he said, "You and your girlfriend on the phone.

You talk to her all the time. You need to be more careful about what you say. I got pictures too. I think your poor wife might be the only one that doesn't have a clue about what's going on. I'm thinking it may be about time for that to change."

I used to call Laurie at night, after I'd had enough Gilbey's to make sure I had the confidence to use my home phone to call my girlfriend while my wife and daughters slept upstairs. We would talk about everything and nothing and plan lunch for the next day and after a while, we'd hang up. That day, when he called, he told me he had taped the calls. I had no idea how he could have done it, or if he had even done it, but I believed him and told him, nearly screamed at him, not to play it. I thought I was going to throw up.

I immediately left the office and called Laurie on my car phone to tell her what had happened, but when I got her, she was in tears. I could hear the same fear in her voice that I knew I had in mine. He had already called her; she had heard the same threats. I think part of me wanted to believe that Laurie had something to do with all of this because none of it made any sense, but I knew in my heart that try as she might to enable me to death, she would never do anything like this to hurt me. She believed she was in love with me; she was trapped now. He had us both.

The calls continued and Angela was everywhere. I would even see her at social functions I'd be at with Mary. She would always mingle with whoever was around her but it never looked like she had come with anyone. I was terrified every time I saw her and even though there seemed to be a voice somewhere telling me to say something to Mary, the fear would completely take away my ability to think rationally about anything. I found myself constantly looking over my shoulder wherever I went, always looking for a man on the phone or a blonde with a smirk on her face. Paranoia had overwhelmed me; I lived my life choked in fear.

One day it all started to come to a head. He called me at work but his tone this time lacked the good-old-boy quality; he was all business this time. I know that it was early December; my breakdown was looming. He had become a big part of the insanity.

"Hey, Stevie boy, it's time to deal and we're not messin' around with you. Let's make a trade; the tapes and the pictures and everything else we've got for, let's say, twenty-five hundred."

I didn't say a word. I was waiting for my heart to explode. Sweat was pouring from me as I sat at my desk and prayed that no one would come in. I got up and closed my door and then sat back down and tried not to be sick. I couldn't believe this was happening.

"You want . . . you mean you want me to give you . . . twenty-five hundred . . . dollars? You want twenty-five hundred dollars?"

He laughed at me. "We want more and we may get more, but let's just see how well you play with us, okay, Stevie boy?"

I didn't know what to do or say. The addict was screaming for a drink, and I was terrified about what was going on. I know that what I should have done, all I needed to do, was call his bluff, tell him to go ahead and do what he needed to do, and then go home and tell Mary. There probably weren't any tapes or pictures, but the paranoia had convinced me that he might be right. Still, it would have been the smartest thing to do, but when a person's decision-making process is controlled by alcohol and fear, he doesn't tend to make the wisest decisions.

"I can't get that much money."

He knew he had me. "C'mon, Stevie boy, don't mess with me. You make enough money."

"Look, it's not that; I . . . I don't know how to do it without, you know . . ." I couldn't even say her name. ". . . I don't want her to know what's going on."

"How much?" he asked. "Two grand? Surely you can get two grand."

I wiped my brow and lowered my voice even further.

"Eighteen hundred," I whispered into the phone. "I can get . . . eighteen hundred." I couldn't believe it. I was bargaining like I was trying to get a deal on a used car.

He didn't say anything for a minute and I was hoping he had somehow decided he couldn't do this to me anymore.

"Eighteen hundred it is, Stevie boy, but listen to me. If there's any problem with this going down, this isn't going to end for you."

He told me what he wanted me to do and I wrote everything down but was having a hard time holding the pen. He wanted me to take the money after work on Friday to an empty lot not too far from my house. It was an area between a new residential division going up and part of an industrial park on the northeast side of town. He told me there was a big oak tree in the middle of the field and there would be a paper bag at the base of the tree. I was supposed to put the money in the bag and then get in my car and go home. If everything went the way it was supposed to, if no one saw me or followed me and he was able to get the money, then he would leave everything he'd told me he had in a big manila envelope under the pine tree on the side of our garage. Mary and I were going to an Iowa basketball game that night, and I knew that it was going to be the longest night of my life.

I barely remember getting the cash. I have a recollection of Laurie being involved somehow because I was afraid to go to my own bank, but I don't remember the details. I was so scared; my alcohol intake was through the roof and fear was controlling everything I did. All I remember is that late Friday afternoon, a little before five o'clock, I had parked my car on a side street and found myself trudging through a field. I was dressed in a suit and a long winter coat and had an envelope full of eighteen one hundred dollar bills in my hand. I could not believe this was happening to me.

As I slogged through the field toward the empty tree that loomed ahead in the early evening darkness, I remember how with every step I took, the shame weighed itself down on me heavier and heavier. I had never been so ashamed of myself as I was at that moment. I was paying, literally, and in more ways than one, for the consequences of my actions, and yet I knew in my heart that by paying this man, I had no intention of stopping the very things that had brought me to this point. It wasn't about Laurie; it was about the destruction of my soul. It was about the disintegration of the man that I may have at one time believed I could have become until I let the addict take complete control over every aspect of my life. Yet I knew as I made my way to the tree that nothing was going to change, and with that thought, the shame nearly pulled me over.

I knew that somewhere he was watching me, and in my paranoia, I suddenly found myself waiting for a shot to ring out and a bullet to tear through me. I don't think I would have been surprised if it had happened, and the sad part is I remember feeling a sick sort of disappointment when it didn't. It would have been the easy way out for me and somehow it was how I saw this nightmare ending, but it didn't happen. I finally got to the tree and found the paper bag. I knelt in the frosty grass and opened the bag to put the money in but there was something inside. It was an envelope. "To Stevie Boy . . . ," and when I opened it up, I saw that it was a sympathy card. "We are so sorry for your loss." It was signed, "Angela and Your New Best Friend."

I stuffed the money in the bag and turned and ran back to my car and drove home, taking the long way so I could drink some sanity back into my life so when I got there Mary wouldn't know I had been crying.

When we got back from the basketball game that night, and after Mary had gone into the bathroom to get ready for bed, I sneaked outside to the pine tree beside the garage to get the envelope that would end the nightmare in which I had found myself.

There was nothing there.

Mary ended up finding out about Laurie and me, but that was because of my own stupidity . . . go figure. And shortly after I had finally stopped drinking, Mary found out everything anyway. I don't know what she heard or how she heard it, but I know that the next time I saw her she was as hurt and as angry as I had ever seen another person in my life. Whoever he was, he was real and he got some sort of perverted satisfaction from doing as much damage to me as I had already done to myself. The funny thing is, well, it's actually more of a sad thing, but the thing is my entire life was falling apart around me while all of this was happening and I would simply continue to deny that anything was going on. No, I don't have a drinking problem. No, I've never been unfaithful to my wife. No, I'm not having trouble at work. No. No! *No!!* Just shut up and leave me alone!

I was a sick man.

CHAPTER 9

Dysfunctional Communication at Its Best

The patient is a churched Catholic.

I WAS RAISED IN A Presbyterian church in Newton but went to a Catholic church with my girlfriend in high school. Mary was raised in a strict Catholic family and we were married in a Catholic church. Still, on Sunday mornings, Mary would go to Mass and I would stay home and watch television and have a Bloody Mary. When we moved to Cedar Rapids, I started going more because Mary's family would all go together and it was nice being with them.

Katie was baptized in the Catholic Church but it wasn't until Laura was born that I decided to convert. I'm not sure to this day if I did it because I wanted to or because I felt that people were expecting me to but, either way, I did it. I don't think it had a profound impact on my life. I know it didn't change me at all spiritually but, back then, I didn't have much of a grasp on the spiritual aspect of life. To me, Mass was an hour a week of listening to some scripture, singing a couple of songs, standing, kneeling, and, oh yes, getting to drink a little wine during communion. Toward the end of my struggles with alcohol, I was usually pretty well lit up when we'd go to Mass, but you have to remember that I was pretty well lit up wherever we went. I'm not sure if it is significant in any way, but I've never been back to a Catholic church since I quit drinking. We'll blame it on the wine.

In addition, the patient is on several church councils and feels very connected with his spiritual beliefs.

Like I said, I was on one board or council or something. We met once a month and I always felt uncomfortable at the meetings. I would always sweat and drink water like there was no tomorrow. I had no idea what anyone was talking about and never really had any significant contributions to any of the conversations we would have. When something was open for discussion I would always study our agenda like I was a third grader who didn't know the answer to a math question and would stare at the book so the teacher wouldn't call on him. My spiritual beliefs were nonexistent. I only knew that AA preached to the belief in and dependence upon a Higher Power and I wanted to make sure that everyone knew that I had my act together.

Perceived Strengths and Weaknesses: The patient believes that his ability to communicate with others, and his compassion and care for others are his primary strengths of character.

I think the thing to remember here is that I had the ability to communicate with others but never really used it. I felt that I had a terrific command of the language and could speak very superfluously but it was always more of a "willingness" issue with me. I'm not sure how compassionate or caring a man can be when he places alcohol on such a high pedestal and is willing to climb over anything, especially his family, when he needs a drink, which for me was all the time. Saying that I was compassionate and caring reeks of the selfishness that alcoholics exhibit, perhaps consciously, perhaps not, but it is pure selfishness nonetheless. We think only of ourselves in everything we do and are focused only on how and when we're going to get our next drink. That, sadly, was my only care and concern.

He believes his primary weakness is his strong drive to win.

I've often wondered where in the world *that* came from. One would think a strong drive to win would be a strength, and I've tried to figure out what I was trying to prove here. The only thing I've been able to come up with is that I was trying somehow to elicit sympathy of some sort from my counselor.

"Oh, yes," I'm certain I sobbed. "If only I weren't so darn competitive; (sniffling a bit for effect) then I wouldn't have felt like such a failure when things didn't work out. (Wiping my eyes now.) I . . . I just couldn't handle the agony of defeat and nothing seemed to help so I would drink to ease the pain. (Bury my head in my hands. Don't forget to shake the shoulders a little.) Oh, *darn* my competitiveness. Why couldn't I just be happy being a loser?"

Wait a minute. I think I was a loser.

In addition, the patient does not express his emotions freely; he believes he has difficulty communicating with his spouse regarding his feelings.

This must certainly be genetic. The environment in which I grew up certainly fostered this kind of dysfunctional communication. I don't ever remember my dad putting up a fight with my mom or talking about anything significant in front of me and my sister. All I remember is the rage and the anger and the finger he'd flip at her when she wasn't looking. I wasn't like that with Mary; I just never let her in on what was going on inside me. I didn't let anyone in. Even when I was seeing Laurie, I never let her know until she couldn't help but notice herself how sick I was. Everything in my life was always just great.

"How are you feeling?"

"Great."

"Is there anything wrong?"

"No, everything's great."

"Is everything going okay at work?"

"Everything's great."

"Do you think you have a drinking problem?"

"Me? No! Of course not. Everything's great!"

"You have a lump the size of Rhode Island sticking out of the side of your head and it's leaking some green syrupy ooze that smells like a septic tank that's ruptured. Do you think you should go get it checked out?"

"Oh no. I'm sure everything's fine. I feel great!"

The main reason I got kicked out of treatment the first time in wasn't because I relapsed. It was because I never told Mary about it and that was the only thing they asked of me when they sent me home. Here I was, with my job on the line, and all I had to do was go home and say, "Mary, I relapsed. I'm sorry it happened, but this addiction is pretty tough on me. I wanted to tell you about it so you can help me come to an understanding as to how I can work to overcome this. I want you to be a part of my recovery and I really need your help."

It sounds so easy to say that now, but back then, even with all I had to lose, I couldn't do it. When Mary came to our couple's session on Tuesday, Brenda, my counselor, asked her what she thought about my relapse. It was the first Mary had heard about it. I got kicked out because instead of talking to Mary about it over the weekend, I stuck my head further in the sand and drank as much as I could, hoping it would all go away and everything would be better. It doesn't work, does it Dad?

Integrated Summary:
Clinical Impression: Primarily, the patient appears to have a high tolerance to alcohol; he has a need for markedly increased amounts of the substance in order to reach intoxication.

Near the end, I wasn't even drinking to get drunk. I was drinking because the addict was in need of the fix. I'd drink before I went to bed and then sleep for a couple hours before waking up and not being able to go back to sleep. This happened every single night and it wasn't until later that I realized that all I had to do was go back downstairs and have a couple of long pulls of vodka and my system would be satisfied and I'd be able to go back to sleep. I think by then my system seemed more normal when I had my two fifths in me than when I was craving a drink. If I got caught in a situation where there wasn't anything around to drink, I'd get irritable, my hands would start shaking, and I'd sweat like I was in a sauna wrapped up in a down comforter. I don't think I ever believed I got drunk. I would blow way over the limit if anyone called me on it, but most of the time it seemed that I would simply pass from the state I was normally in, my functional alcoholic state, to the state of oblivion where I didn't remember anything that happened. But it rarely seemed that I was drunk. All I was, was dying.

Identified Problems:
1) The patient is experiencing physical difficulty with withdrawal at this time. He continues to have minor tremors and feels agitated within. In addition, the patient continues to struggle with his weight as he is far below his normal weight as a result of not eating properly.

Of course I was agitated. I wanted a drink! And as far as not eating goes, my ex-brother-in-law always said, "Why screw up a twenty dollar drunk with a two dollar cheeseburger?"

I always thought that was pretty sound advice.

2) The patient will need to address his chemical dependency in treatment; that is he will need to come to an understanding of the disease and become actively involved in support groups such as Alcoholics Anonymous.

I remember the first time I went to an AA meeting. I didn't actually *go* to the meeting but told Mary I went. What communication problem? It was sometime in the fall of 1995, and we both knew I was dancing on the edge of some serious trouble with alcohol. Mary was after me to do something—anything—to try to get some sort of help, but neither of us knew at the time what options were available other than AA. Mostly to appease her, I agreed to go to a meeting.

There was a meeting scheduled on the other side of town and I got in my car and headed over there, but I knew in my mind that I wasn't going to go. That's kind of the way treatment became for me; I was in there for her and in there for my job but not in there at all for me. I wasn't going to that meeting; Mary knew I needed help more than I knew it and I wasn't going to go just to find out that she was right.

I knew that when you went to your first AA meeting you got a white poker chip as a sign of surrender. Armed with that knowledge, I drove to a drug store, bought a package of poker chips and a fifth of Gilbey's, and drove around for about an hour and drank nearly the whole bottle and listened to music, wondering where all of this was going to take me. I think I was starting to get scared because of the very reason I'd bought the stupid poker chips. I knew I couldn't surrender. I think I was starting to feel that I was losing the fight, maybe even losing the whole war, but I wasn't ready to surrender. The funny thing is, I was ready to make everyone believe that I was ready to quit even though I knew I wasn't. That's why, after an hour or so of driving around and drinking, I went to a rest area on the interstate, opened the box of poker chips, and took out a white chip. I threw the rest of them away and then drove home.

I remember the look on Mary's face when I walked in and showed her the white chip. She was so proud of me because I had finally surrendered. I remember being angry with myself because I realized I should have bought another bottle of vodka. I was afraid I wasn't going to have enough to get me through the night.

3) The patient will need to address his marital problems as a result of his alcohol [abuse].

Mary and I were having problems but I'm certain I didn't realize the severity of things, given my constant intoxication, my fear and paranoia about my drinking and my relationship with Laurie, the threat of losing my job, and all the other junk that was driving me farther and farther into the oblivion alcohol gave me. I've tried to come to some sort of realization through the years of how hard all of this was on not only Mary but on Katie and Laura as well, and there is no way that I can do it. I especially couldn't do it then because, as is the case with all alcoholics, my primary concern was me. How was *I* going to get through this? How was *I* going to make everyone believe *I* was sincere about everything? How was *I* going to be able to be more responsibly secretive about *my* drinking? How was *I* going to continue to live *my* life the way *I* had been living it and making everyone else believe that everything was changing when, in fact, nothing at all was changing?

Alcoholics are a selfish lot. Anyone who would push aside a beautiful and loving wife and the two most adorable daughters in the world to escape willingly into the hell he had created in his own life and then want to keep going back is something I'll never understand. But I plotted to continue to do it anyway. The sad thing is that I actually believed I could pull it off.

The patient will need to face fellow employees and address his work situation once he returns to work.

No real problem with that. I had been deceiving everyone at work for so long that this was never a concern to me. It had never entered my mind that everyone there was onto me already. I think that's the funny thing about denial. We're the only ones who buy into the garbage we're flinging out there for everyone else to catch. It never entered my mind that I wouldn't go back to Millhiser at all. They were obviously more serious about this than I was.

The patient needs to learn to identify emotions and to learn to express them effectively.

I was doing okay with the identification part; it was the expressing part that was throwing me off. I knew I was angry, paranoid, and afraid, but the only thing I was focusing on was making sure

I said and did exactly what everyone wanted to hear and see from me. I was the most condescending and pathetically sorry person in the world at that time. I was craving sympathy and creating the illusion, in my mind at least, that I was truly sorry for all that had happened and I was going to whip this thing. Yes, that's it. I'm going to turn my life around! I'm positive! I'm upbeat! I know I can do this! Why, I feel just great! Hey, I guess I was able to express emotions. The problem was they weren't really mine.

The patient needs to improve his physical fitness.

There are a lot of ironies when a person is consumed by alcohol, or actually any substance that's no good for you and has taken over your life. One of the biggest ironies in my own life was how hard I was working out in the months prior to my breakdown. I lifted weights three times a week in our family room, usually at night after the kids had gone to bed. Every other morning, I'd get up and go downstairs and get on my cross-country ski machine and go at it for a half hour or so and really feel like I was making a positive change in my life. The irony was in the fact that every night after I'd work out I'd sit in my recliner and watch television and suck down about half a fifth of Gilbey's. In the mornings, after my ski trip to nowhere, I'd go into the bathroom and lock the door and sit there drinking, getting ready for the day. It was like running on a treadmill with a Marlboro hanging out of my mouth. I don't know what I was thinking but have come to realize that it's part of the self-deception we go through when we drink. It's like we're saying to ourselves, *How can I possibly have a drinking problem? I mean, look at me. I work out all the time and I'm in great shape.*

It's all part of the denial. It's all part of the game we're playing with anyone who will join in until it's become nothing more than

Solitaire. We're the only ones holding any cards and we can't get anything to line up right anymore. I mean, come on, who was I fooling anyway? By the time I went into the hospital I had lost almost forty pounds and my skin was the color of an old nickel. Great ad for a cross-country ski machine, don't you think?

The patient needs to participate in a self-esteem program as his identity is primarily through achievements.

Without question, my identity was through achievements at that time of my life. Looking back on everything I was telling people during my initial interview, my life had been very much "me" oriented and I was judging myself primarily on what I had accomplished in my life rather than on the kind of man I was. If I had had the courage to strip away all of what I thought that I was, based on my accomplishments, and take a hard look at the very core of my soul, I wouldn't have liked much of what was there. I didn't look, though, because I'm certain, deep inside, I knew there was some pretty evil stuff lurking down there swimming around in all the poison I'd been pouring into my body for so long.

Sitting there during my initial interview, I didn't acknowledge any self-esteem issues; doing that would have indicated a lack of confidence, and a lack of confidence would have shouted out to people that I've got a problem. I hyped my accomplishments to show everyone how strong I was, how driven I was to succeed, how successful I was in everything I had done. I was an athlete, a scholar, a rising star on the local business horizon. Take that all away and I was scared to death about what was happening to me, and eventually I was horrified about the wreckage I was leaving in my wake. At that moment, however, because I was still so far removed from acceptance of my disease, I was comfortable with my self-esteem. More importantly, I needed to make sure everyone else knew that too. I knew I needed to stay one step ahead of these people. They were pretty smart, but I knew they hadn't met someone like me yet. How right I ended up being.

Initial Treatment Plan:
1) Goals: Orient this patient to treatment. Encourage the patient to make a commitment to a full term treatment experience.

There was a lot of encouragement going on at this time. They wanted to encourage me to do what they knew needed to be done to help me get well. I, on the other hand, was trying to encourage them that I already knew what needed to be done even if I had no idea what it was. I only knew that I couldn't let them know that my real encouragement during treatment was to become more aware of my limitations when I drank so I could still continue to do it and not have a repeat of what had happened on the thirtieth. I don't believe I would have survived another night like that but was also still convinced that I couldn't survive at all without alcohol.

2) Encourage this patient to begin communication with his wife, in particular, encourage the patient to begin addressing long-standing marital issues within group and individual settings.

More encouragement. When I went in the first time, I thought it was going to be all about my drinking. I thought that's what treatment was all about, getting someone to acknowledge that he *may* have a drinking problem and begin to learn how to address that situation. I had no idea they were going to be dragging the rest of my life out in front of everyone as well. This was not at all what I had anticipated. I had far too many secrets buried in far too many empty Gilbey's bottles to be laying all that out in front of people I didn't know. I wasn't even talking to Mary about any of the things that were going on in my life and now everyone wanted me to talk about it in front of other people. This actually might be more uncomfortable than I had first imagined. By this time, I really needed a drink to be able to think through all this nonsense. I mean, come on, I was only in here because everyone else thought I needed to get some help. I really wasn't that bad. Not yet, anyway.

3) Discharge planning: The patient will be in the hospital for approximately one week of therapy. Following that, he will be transferred to an intensive outpatient program.

One week in the hospital. I had no idea when they dragged me in on the night of the thirtieth that I would end up hospitalized for a whole week. I remember when they told me how long I would be there, I was angry. Angry with Mary, my neighbors, everyone involved with Sedlacek, my boss, *God*, everyone that had even the slightest bit to do with this happening to me. It never once dawned on me during this fit of anger that smoldered inside me for that one week and beyond that I was there because of what I had done. And I was millions of miles away from the spiritual realization that I was there because God knew that's exactly where I needed to be.

No, I was just angry. Oh, I was going to allow myself to become "oriented to treatment," but I was going to do it my way. I wasn't going to let them know anything about me other than what I knew they wanted to believe they were learning. They couldn't do this to me!

CHAPTER 10

The Wasted Week

Discharge Date: January 5, 1996. Inpatient Treatment Program. Treatment Progress: This patient was accepted at the Sedlacek Treatment Center and a Comprehensive Treatment Plan was developed based on needs and goals identified. As Steve improved physically, he began to attend groups and classes.

THIS WAS NOT THE VACATION I thought it was going to be. We were up every morning at seven and went to the small dining area for breakfast. The food was brought up from the cafeteria but was much better than I thought it was going to be. The reason was simple: most of us in the hospital for treatment (there were nine of us at the time) had long since stopped having anything of any nutritional value make its way through our systems. Even though I didn't know anyone except for my roommate, Chris, you could tell that people hadn't eaten good food for a very long time. We got pretty much whatever we wanted to eat. There was a menu card we would fill out after we ate, giving us plenty of options, and they allowed us to eat as much as we wanted.

After breakfast, we went back to our rooms and got cleaned up and made our beds, unless it was a day when they did laundry.

There were two single beds in each room and a bathroom with a stool, sink, and shower. It was just like a normal hospital room except the beds were regular beds. There were no IVs or heart monitors hooked up to anyone and if it weren't for the fact that I knew I was in a hospital, it really reminded me more of a dorm room in college. Without the keggers, of course.

We had classes all day interspersed with individual counseling sessions and, later in the day, sessions with our partners. Everything was done on the clock and there was little time off. The reason for this, naturally, was to instill a sense of discipline into people who, if they were anything like me, had been disciplining themselves to drink, and nothing else. I had always gone to work when I was supposed to and left at a reasonable time, but even those actions were dictated by my drinking. They were more like reactions. I knew if I was standing in front of the mirror in the morning with shave cream on my face, a razor in one hand and a fifth of Gilbey's in the other, it must be time to go to work. If I was sitting in my car and the jazz was on the radio and my Hawkeye mug was full of Gilbey's, it must be time to head home. Drinking was my only discipline. Sedlacek worked hard at creating a better structure in our lives. That was hard for me; doing it without alcohol was even harder.

Our first group session was usually a film about addictions or about people who had overcome terrible obstacles in their lives. I remember one movie we watched was about a woman who didn't have any arms and they showed how she was able to do everything with her feet. She would comb her hair, brush her teeth, cook, drive a car, everything except clip her fingernails. Now *that* would have been motivational. It was pretty hard for me to get too excited about seeing someone overcome that kind of obstacle. I was impressed with what she was able to do but it really wasn't anything I could relate to.

We also watched films about the dangers of smoking because a lot of people would start smoking in treatment and we were getting an education about the dangers of cross addictions, replacing one addiction with another. I didn't start smoking until my second time in, so I spent the time watching the non-smoking movies biting my fingernails just to irritate the woman with no arms.

After the movie, we'd have a group session with just the inpatients. We'd talk about whatever anyone wanted to talk about. Most of the time we'd just sit there until the counselor would ask us something to try to stimulate a discussion about something.

"So, Steve, what did you think about that woman with no arms? Wasn't it remarkable how she was able to overcome such a difficult obstacle and create such a wonderful life for herself?"

I'd sit there and want to ask how she was able to go to the bathroom and pick her nose and all those other things that I know someone else had to be doing for her but that's not what anyone wanted to hear.

"My goodness," I'd say, shaking my head because I've always felt that good body language is important when you're trying to make someone believe that what you're about to say is deep and heart-felt. "I hope that someday I can overcome the obstacle that alcohol has become in my life and learn to live in a positive and fruitful manner, just like she did."

The rest of the people in the group would look at the floor and nod their heads as if that's exactly what they would have said if they had been called on, but what they were really wondering was how *did* that woman take care of things in the bathroom? We would sit for fifty minutes like that every morning and the time would crawl. Nobody would volunteer anything because nobody was ready to admit the need to be there and it was as if by saying something . . . anything . . . you were going to expose a part of yourself that you weren't ready to have anyone see yet. Maybe you weren't ready to see it yourself.

During the movies and the group, counselors would wander in and whisk people away for individual sessions. It was hard to say which was more difficult: sitting with a group of people you didn't know that well and saying nothing while watching the second hand on the wall clock move so slowly it seemed like it was moving backwards, or going into a one-on-one with a counselor you didn't know that well and be expected to admit to everything. I always hated it most when I was the one being whisked.

My first counselor was Dave Robertson, a rail of a man who wasn't interested in anything but yes or no answers to the yes or no questions he would ask. No nonsense, no excuses, no justification, just yes or no.

"Steve, do you think your drinking is out of control?"

"Well, Dave, my mother-in-law was here for—"

"Yes or no, Steve."

"But she—"

"Yes or no."

"My boss—"

"Steve, is your drinking out of control?"

I could do this job, I'd think. *I mean, really, what do they expect me to say? If I say "no" they know I'm lying. I'm in a treatment facility for Pete's sake. If I say "yes," which is what they want me to say, they'll think I'm making progress but then I'm admitting a problem. What do I do? I know. Distraction always works.* "How did that woman with no arms go to the bathroom, Dave?"

I wasn't ready to admit anything that first week in. I wasn't used to what treatment was yet and didn't know the expectations other than not having any alcohol. All I was doing was trying to get through the week without going crazy not thinking about drinking. I had been drinking for years, day after day, and now not only was I not able to drink, but they wanted to know why I drank, how strong my marriage was, what it was like growing up. Where were all these questions coming from? We were alcoholics, meth addicts, morphine abusers, pot smokers, crack heads. Weren't they just supposed to give us some pills and make everything go away? Certainly there had to be an easier way.

After lunch, we got a break for about forty-five minutes or so. I usually hung out in my room with Chris and learned about how many ways there are to ingest meth. I didn't even know what meth was but by the time I was done talking to him about it, I knew I was glad I had never done it before. I suppose some addictions can be worse than others but that doesn't lessen the severity of a person's own. Chris and I, along with everyone else in that place, each struggled with our own addiction, but I'm certain none of us would have ever changed places with anyone else there, no matter how bad things got for each of us.

Around two or so, we'd go to the gym for a while. Even though there were weight machines and basketball hoops, we had to do aerobics. Sometimes we even had to do them with steps. It was embarrassing to dance around like that; even though I had been riding my ski machine to nowhere, I was in horrible shape and was having a difficult time keeping up with everyone else. The only saving grace was that the instructor was pretty attractive but that actually made it worse for me given that I was sweating and stumbling around, especially when she brought out the steps. Alcohol had taken a pretty severe toll on me in a lot of ways, and every afternoon in the gym reminded me of how much it was controlling me even if I was nowhere near being able to admit that to Dave. I always thought I danced better when I was drunk. Stumbling around the gym floor, I became pretty convinced that was the case.

At three, the intensive outpatients, the IOPs, came in and we all met for our self-esteem class. These were the people that had either already been discharged as inpatients or who hadn't been bad enough to be hospitalized but still needed to be in treatment. Most of these people were working and able to leave work early to get to the hospital. I was jealous of them because they got a taste of the outdoors and I wanted to hang around them to be able to smell the fresh air they would bring in with them. I felt trapped on the fourth floor and these people represented freedom to me even though they had to come in every day from 3:00 to 8:30. They still got to go home at night; home didn't seem to exist for us during that week.

The self-esteem class was one of those things that I didn't fully appreciate until long after I had gotten out of the program. We all knew our self-esteem had taken a pretty severe beating, but, again, no one wanted to appear to be too beat up because then, heaven forbid, we were admitting that the addiction had gotten the best of us. Now wasn't the time for me to own up to something like that. I was too busy trying to figure out how serious I was about this "not drinking" thing that was hounding me every single moment.

By the third or fourth day in treatment, I knew I was missing alcohol. I had pretty much stopped shaking but I had this deep hunger that wouldn't leave me alone and I knew the addict was calling me. My biggest fear at the time was the hallucinations that had wracked me on the thirtieth, but I had been assured that things like that wouldn't happen to me again unless, naturally, I started drinking again. I'm certain they were right in telling me that, but at the time, I thought maybe they were just scaring me into staying sober. It was a delicate balance, trying to decide if I wanted to fight to stay sober, or drink and run the risk of hearing those horrifying voices again. It should have been an easy choice; I was beginning to learn how difficult it really was.

The counselors pounded us with improving our self-esteem. The class itself was cyclical; when we completed the book, we started it over again and kept going through it time after time. I bet I went through that yellow book five or six times while I was in treatment, which shows how hard treatment centers like Sedlacek work to improve the one thing that gets beat up the worst. Physically we healed with the diet and exercise they were pushing our way, but it was the feelings of failure, the realizations that we had caused some pretty serious damage to the people we loved most that ate at us. Even knowing that, I would sit there and think about my next drink. And the voices.

After self-esteem, we would have a break and then we'd have group therapy, again an opportunity for discussion about anything, which usually meant it was pretty quiet in the room. The IOPs would be more willing to talk about things than the inpatients. They were a little more comfortable in their sobriety and the nine of us kind of looked at them with some degree of respect because they seemed so much more well-adjusted than we felt.

I know now that they, for the most part, were just as out of whack as we were, but because their insurance had run out, they weren't able to stay in the hospital and had been turned loose to try staying sober for a good part of the day on their own. Some were working; some had lost their jobs and were dealing with that as well as dealing with staying straight. Some, in time, disappeared from the program, either dismissed by the counselors or chased off by the call of the fix that was too strong to ignore. More people didn't make it than did. Success in that place was hard to rate; was not drinking the only way to rate success? How about drinking and not dying? How many people were going to simply rate their success on how long they lived while continuing to pour the poison in their bodies or stick the needles in their thighs? Was it really an all or nothing? For me, at that time and in that place, the answer was no. As much as I thought I could quit if I really wanted to, I was beginning to have this gnawing feeling deep inside that if I could get out and keep drinking and not die, then my life would be okay and treatment would be a success for me. I was seeing how much the IOPs were struggling; I didn't want to go through life like that for very long.

It was also during this time that a lot of us had counseling sessions with our spouses, significant others, parents, whoever it was that was there to support us. Mary would come during this time and we would go visit Dave, and these were the most uncomfortable times of that first week in treatment. While I felt comfortable in a one-on-one with Dave because he didn't know me that well yet, it was harder to lie to him when Mary was there. She pretty much made me accountable for the answers I'd give him to the questions he'd ask. I tried to be as honest as I could but there was a gigantic barrier between me and the truth. The Great Wall of Denial was too high to get over most of the time. I should know—I built it.

I found myself beginning to tell them what I thought they wanted to hear, which was really never the truth and not what I needed to be saying to actually come to grips with what was happening to me. That first week of treatment was becoming nothing more to me than the realization that I didn't want to be there and didn't really have the need to be there. Most of that stemmed from the fact that this was becoming about more than my drinking. It was about my behaviors, my infidelity, my past, things I had always hoped would stay buried away in a place where no one could ever find them. People were getting too close; I had to figure out a way to keep them from getting even closer. As always, I turned to the things I knew best: denial and lying. I figured early on that I needed to sound contrite, really sorry about all that had happened, while still denying that I was anything more than a man who had a bit of a drinking problem.

"Yes," I'd say, looking down at the floor as if too ashamed to look at Mary or Dave directly. "I realize how much alcohol has impacted my life, our lives (quick glance and sad smile to Mary), and I know now that I need to make some changes in my life."

Wonderful! Truthful yet such garbage that I could almost smell the words on my breath. Alcohol *had* impacted my life. I was in a treatment center and could lose my job. I had blacked out about three months of my life. I nearly died only a few days earlier and was now being forced to find inspiration in the life of a woman who could change a light bulb with her feet. So obviously I needed to make some changes in my life.

Here's where we no doubt had our differences. The changes I was referring to involved none of those issues that were buried away, the ones Dave kept wanting me to dig into and uncover and lay out for everyone to see and say, "Aha! There they are! Those despicable issues that have turned me into the sot that I am. Now that they're out there, why, there's no way that I'll ever have need of another drink again. Look at them! Sniveling little issues. I'm better than you, I am. I don't need this poison to crush you with my new-found truthfulness and honesty."

No, for me it was more like, "I need to drink less and on a more acceptable (to me at least) schedule."

My changes sounded so much easier. Come to think of it, I think that may be the reason I had those sniveling little issues in the first place. It was simply easier to drink and ignore them and let them fester like an infected boil that's tucked away neatly in a fold in your skin someplace where you can't see it so you simply choose to ignore it. It never gets any better until one day it explodes, and now you've got a bit of a mess on your hands. Oh, just deal with it later. It's much easier that way. That's the way I was; that's the way all alcoholics are. Too bad I didn't know that then.

After group, we had dinner. The IOPs headed downstairs to the cafeteria or out to grab a bite if they had time. We had no such luxury. Again, it was to the small dining area on the fourth floor to our own tables and our own food. There never seemed to be much conversation during dinner at night. A lot of that came from the fact that we were starting to feel a bit more exposed as the week went on. We were learning more about ourselves and hoping others weren't seeing everything.

I don't think any of us needed to worry about that though. I know that I was pretty much focused on how I felt I was getting through the early process of being sober and not letting Dave and Mary in on too much of what was really going on. I found that I really didn't care about anyone else's problems up there. I liked Chris but that was probably because we were roommates; I couldn't relate to his struggles nor could he to mine. I found I was pretty much isolating myself from everyone and trying to concentrate on getting through the week and getting out of there. It was not a pleasant place to be, especially for someone who wasn't exactly embracing the ideas that were being pitched.

After dinner, we would all gather in the small auditorium and have an hour-and-a-half talk about whatever the counselor that night had chosen to talk about. Some of the patients had their partners in with them but that was usually because they had an individual session scheduled. The meetings themselves were pretty unremarkable but I do remember one night when Bill Martin, then the director of Sedlacek, was talking about how he ended up in jail. He was talking about how the entire time he was being hauled into jail he kept screaming, "You can't do this to me! You can't do this to me!"

He talked about how he was being dragged down the hallway of the jail and kept screaming, "You can't do this to me!"

They opened his cell door and threw him in and he said he went to the bars and grabbed them and shook them and kept screaming down the hall, "You can't do this to me!"

He said he stopped and looked around and realized that apparently they *could* do this to him. Everyone laughed either nervously or politely depending on whether or not you were the one actually in treatment. The polite laughter came from the people who got to go home after the meeting. The nervous laughter came from the patients who wondered if Bill was talking about them. I think the point he was trying to make was something about denial, how we can continue to deny all we want that we need help, but eventually we wake up one day in treatment and realize that, hey, maybe I do need help. I suppose it was a pretty good analogy for those in the room who actually needed help. For those of us still denying, he needed a different story.

The last thing we did during the day was play volleyball. We went to the gym and divided up into teams and played some of the worst volleyball imaginable. If you took a volleyball net to some remote village in Africa and set it up and didn't even explain the rules to anyone and then handed the ball to the natives without even motioning what they were supposed to do, they would have played volleyball better than the people in that gym played. I'm sure at some point in life when everyone was at a family picnic and had about ten or twelve beers in them or had hidden behind a tree somewhere and got loaded on pot or crack or meth or coke and then gone and played volleyball, everyone would have played fairly well. Like I said, I know I always danced pretty well when I was drunk. I'm sure it was the same with everyone else when it came to volleyball. But put us all in a gym, everyone struggling with being straight for the first time in a long time, and coordination becomes an issue. One would think the opposite would be true, given that there was no alcohol or meth or anything getting in the way, but this was probably the first time in a long time that anyone had done anything like this clean and sober. It wasn't a pretty sight. Volleyballs were flying everywhere. The people who were the worst were the ones who were convinced that they were pretty good. Kind of like the worst drivers on the road are the drunks who are convinced, even though they've had twelve beers, that, "Hey, I'm fine. I actually drive better when I've been drinking. It really helps me focus."

I can't believe people used to say that. I would have said it too but it was true for me. I really did drive better when I was drunk. No, really, I did.

Once we were done, at exactly eight thirty, the IOPs left the building and went home and the rest of us headed upstairs to the fourth floor. Our day was officially done, but a lot of times we'd sit out in the lounge and watch television and try to get caught up on what was going on outside the confines of the prison in which we had found ourselves. I know that we were there because we needed help; the problem is I know that now—at the time, I had no idea.

On 1/05/96, this individual was discharged from the inpatient program per a staff decision. He was determined to be medically stable and appropriate for the intensive outpatient program at this facility. All of the issues addressed in the biopsychosocial assessment remain unresolved and will be addressed in the intensive outpatient program at this facility.

My insurance wouldn't allow me to stay any longer as an inpatient. Besides, I needed a haircut. Other than that, I think things went well.

CHAPTER 11

Unabashed Failure

Intensive Outpatient Program—Encourage this individual to attend AA regularly, and continue to maintain a chemically free lifestyle. This individual was not placed on Antabuse due to his elevated liver enzymes. It is further recommended that an exit interview be set up for this individual before he returns to work. The individual's relapse potential is high.

I WAS A RELAPSE WAITING to happen. I can't blame anyone; my entire focus throughout the time in the hospital was to modify the way I drank. When I was discharged, I hadn't had a drink for eight days. There had been improvement physically during that time; the food helped, as did getting more sleep, but emotionally, I was a wreck. The worst part was that during the day, I was going to be alone and I didn't know how well I was going to handle that. AA would have been a good idea for me, but given that I was only "encouraged" to attend, I had none of it. I knew that the first thing you had to do at a meeting was stand up, tell everyone your first name, and then tell them that you're an alcoholic. Everyone says, "Hi, Steve," and then you tell them what's bugging you. I saw a lot of problems with that whole process.

First of all, I didn't want anyone to know who I was and certainly didn't want to tell anyone that I was an alcoholic. If I couldn't admit it to myself, why in the world would I want to admit it to a bunch of people I didn't know? There was also no desire to hear a bunch of strangers complain about how bad their lives were. I'm sure they were bad; I didn't need to hear about it. To me, they were all a bunch of losers and I was too far above them in so many ways that I didn't need to be exposed to all that garbage. I'd been exposed to enough things I wasn't buying into during my time in the hospital that I didn't need to hear anything else. Plus, I wasn't about to accept a white chip. I couldn't surrender, not while the addict was plotting his next move.

Another thing I had working against me was the decision *not* to put me on Antabuse. It's a pink-colored drug, liquid in form, that's given to people in treatment to keep them from drinking. It's called the "Anti-Alcoholic" because if you're taking it and you ingest alcohol, a lot of strange things start happening to you. You mostly get flushed; your face gets beet red and you start to sweat. It's like an allergic reaction and it's a dead giveaway that you've been drinking. It's not given to *keep* you from drinking. It's not a magic potion that takes away your desire or anything like that. It's a deterrent that's supposed to make you think of the consequences if you *do* drink. You can't drink and get away with it if you're on Antabuse. Because of all the damage I'd done to my liver, I couldn't take it.

The biggest thing that I had trouble with was the fact that I couldn't go back to work. Pretty much everyone else in the program was working, assuming of course they hadn't lost their jobs yet. The boys at Millhiser were going to follow the contract they had with me to the letter. Bill Osborne and Steve King had come to check on me one day while I was in the hospital to see how I was doing but they weren't going to budge on the issue. I could go back to work once I completed the program, so I was looking at another six weeks or so before they would even consider bringing me back. It was going to be a long haul.

Initially upon entering the intensive outpatient program this patient did identify himself as alcoholic; however, he has a very minimal understanding of the disease concept of chemical dependency.

I began working off and on with a new counselor, a young woman named Brenda, and she was trying her best to help me but I had absolutely no understanding of the disease. Like most of us in there, we all thought we drank too much, smoked too much, injected too much but really hadn't come to terms with the concept of quitting. We hadn't come to realize how important alcohol, meth, coke, crack, or pot was to us. Even though I drank all the time, I didn't realize how important it was to me until I tried to ease back into life without it. Being at home without the comfort of Gilbey's was more difficult than I had imagined. The very discipline I complained about in the hospital, I craved at home and found myself at a loss as to what to do.

I busied myself as best I could around the house. Mary was at work and the girls were both in school so it was just me and the cats. We never got along real well; I was kind of freaked out by them and the way they would stare at me like they knew something about me that I didn't know and they didn't like. In the mornings, I would try to work out, lifting weights and working the ski machine. It was odd doing it and not having the alcohol carrot dangling in front of me. I found myself struggling and realized how much I had been beaten down physically by my drinking. I had gained back some of the weight I had lost but was in terrible physical condition. I'm sure I had been for a long time but had been too drunk to realize it.

I watched a lot of television and started getting hooked on soaps. I think part of that was the fact that watching all the drama going on in everyone's lives made me feel that I wasn't so crazy after all. Those people were freaks. I think that must be why a lot of people watch soaps so they can justify all the drama that's going on with them. People drink a lot in soaps too. I suppose if your life is as messed up as theirs, you need the alcohol to maintain the balance. I know that's why I drank. It wasn't because I was an alcoholic; I'm sure those people on the soaps weren't either. Except that guy on *The Bold and the Beautiful*, Dirk or Kirk or something like that. Now, there was a guy that had some issues. Maybe that's why I liked him so much.

As a family, we tried to carry on as best as we could, but it was hard given that I was gone from 3:00 to 8:30 every day. I didn't see much of Katie and Laura and I missed them a lot. On weekends, we tried to start putting things together but I know there was always this undercurrent of uncertainty with Katie and Mary. They knew what was going on and they were both tiptoeing around to make sure nothing upset me. Laura was too young to realize what was happening but I think anyone who walked into our house, even if they had no idea what had happened, would have guessed that there was something way out of the ordinary going on. It would be like walking into a house where the husband was an axe murderer and everyone else was being careful not to give him an axe to grind, so to speak. The discomfort hung everywhere and no one talked much about it. Mary and I would make a point of sitting on the couch as often as we could, especially when I got home from the hospital at night, and we'd try to talk but I never felt that we were making much headway. I was still in denial about a lot of things and the conversations were always stiff and unnatural. That was how everything was in my life at the time, stiff and unnatural.

I kept waiting for everything to get easier, but nothing did. I kept waiting for a revelation of some kind, but nothing came. I kept going to the hospital at three every day waiting for someone or something to impact me and help me see that everything was going to be all right, but it didn't happen. I existed in a fog that wouldn't lift. I felt almost detached from my body as if I was trying to manipulate my own movements like a puppeteer. I didn't feel in control of anything that was going on, which is odd given that I had already given up control of everything else in my life to the alcohol that had gotten me in this mess in the first place. Alcohol *did* control me and I didn't know how to manage when it wasn't doing that anymore.

Things weren't much different at the hospital either. I was getting pretty tired of the same people being around complaining about the same things. Chris had been released, and he ended up going to a facility in Independence for his outpatient work. It was closer to home and they were going to let him start going back to school. It was hard to see him go but I was happy for him. I was happy for anyone who didn't have to be in that place.

Counseling sessions didn't change much either. Along with my time with Brenda, I was still working with Dave, but we weren't making much headway. He kept digging around in places I didn't want to go. I downplayed the significance of my relationship with Laurie and kept passing everything off as being alcohol-related even if I never once admitted that I was an alcoholic. I think if I would have made that admission and they would have believed it, things would have been a lot different. I suppose I could have lied about it; I was lying about everything else and knew I was good at it. I just couldn't bring myself to do it, even to lie about it. I could not get those words to pass my lips.

I slogged along and never felt that I was making any progress. I thought a lot about drinking, especially after dinner. I ate in the cafeteria with everyone else and then just hung out until it was time to go back upstairs. There wasn't a whole lot of time to go anywhere but I did find myself thinking about Gilbey's. I wasn't really counting the days but I knew anyway how many it had been since I had had my last drink. Ten became fifteen, fifteen became twenty, but the urge never eased. I'd tell everyone that things were going great, but I was struggling.

On Friday, January 26, 1996, after I was discharged from the inpatient program, we were sent home early because of a snow-storm. I had not had a drink for nearly thirty days. By then, I was in the Intensive Outpatient Program, meeting from three in the afternoon until eight thirty in the evenings. Most people at this stage of the program were allowed to go back to work, but Mill-hiser was adamant that I not come back until after I completed the entire program. Looking back, there were a lot of problems with that decision, but since neither they nor I had ever had any experience with this kind of thing, everyone must have figured that it was the best thing to do. I'm sure the staff at Sedlacek had their hands tied by the demands of the president, Bill Osborne, and the board at Millhiser.

That Friday night we were all pretty happy about getting out early. I drove home with the snow blowing all around and felt a sense of freedom that I hadn't felt in a long time. Recovery is all about discipline, and being able to leave the structured environment of Sedlacek, especially when it was so unexpected, was nice. The drive was peaceful and quiet, the snow making everything clean and pure. I was one month into a sober world that hadn't seen me for years upon years, and I distinctly remember thinking that there was something symbolic about the purity that surrounded me on the drive home.

There was quite a bit of snow on the ground by the time I got to the house, and as I turned into the driveway, I got stuck. I tried rocking the car a couple of times in an attempt to free myself but soon realized that I wasn't going anywhere. I thought I'd feel anger at being stuck but remember sitting in the car, watching it snow and trying desperately not to think about the last time I had shoveled the drive and the faces that had haunted me from inside the house.

I went inside, talked to Mary and our girls for a minute, then went downstairs to change clothes to go out and try to get my car dug out from the end of the drive. I had a pair of coveralls that I had bought a few years earlier in Minneapolis. They looked like something a farmer would wear and I always thought I looked pretty silly when I wore them, but they were warm and that was all that mattered. I kept them hung up on a hook in the furnace room, the same furnace room I used to go in to toss my empty Gilbey's bottles over the wooden frame onto the ceiling tiles. I took the coveralls off the hook; they felt heavy and when I laid them down onto the floor to get ready to pull them up, I heard a *thud*. There was a zippered pocket on the front and when I picked the coveralls up off the floor and opened the zipper, there was a full, unopened fifth of Gilbey's. I half expected to hear *"It's okay, Steve. Open the bottle and everything will be okay."*

I realized I was shaking.

I took the fifth and sat down on the edge of the bed, knowing that I now had a very big decision to make. I had yet to reach the point in my journey where I understood the simple concept of life being nothing more than a matter of choice. A person either goes forward or backward, up or down, left or right. As I sat there, I thought back to the days before I went into treatment. I thought about the lies, the denial, the agony, and the frustration, and I began to faintly realize that the thing, the beast that caused it all, was sitting in my hands. I realized that for the first time, I had the opportunity to take control of it instead of having it control me.

I thought of the past thirty days and the fact that I hadn't had a single drop of alcohol in my system for the first time in I don't know how long. I thought of Mary and Katie crying at the door. I thought of Bill Osborne and the confrontations and the contract, and I thought of the night in the motel and the smell of gas luring me to sleep.

Sweat was popping out on my brow as I heard the voice and saw the faces and listened to the sound of the rain in my head. I knew I needed to open the bottle and take it into the bathroom and pour it down the drain and then take the empty bottle up to Mary and show her how strong I was, and I thought of how proud she would be. I thought of all of those things as I stood up and walked into the bathroom and slowly snapped open the plastic lid.

I looked up at the reflection in the large mirror that stood over the sink and saw the man who had stood in that same spot a month ago, face covered in sweat and shave cream as he heard the footsteps that nearly stopped his heart. I twisted the lid off the bottle and thought of the hundreds of times I'd done that and never once thought about taking that first step I knew I needed to take and pour it down the drain and walk away.

I held the bottle up and looked past the label and stared at the liquid poison I'd been pouring into my body for so many years causing damage that I probably wouldn't be aware of until it was too late. I peered through the liquid and looked at the distorted face in the mirror . . . the face of the addict . . . and knew that my whole life was distorted now and that I wasn't going to be strong enough to make it all right again. Not yet. Not now. Especially not here, not in my safe house.

I closed the door and pushed the lock and then, eyes closed so as not to have to see what I was doing, I put the bottle to my lips and took her back again. Oh, how I had missed her. She raced through my body, touching every nerve, easing every fear, and I didn't let her go until I knew I'd had enough, and then, sweat pouring from my body, I sat on the toilet and cried like I had never cried in my life. I couldn't do it. I knew what she was going to cost me but I knew I could not let her go. Somewhere in my mind, I heard the laughter of the addict. He knew it too.

The relapse happened because alcoholics relapse. That's not how I saw it at the time but that's why it happened. When the addict took over that night, downstairs where he always seemed to lurk, the barrier crumbled. I had been sober for thirty days when he unscrewed the cap off the Gilbey's bottle and I again allowed him to take complete control of everything that was happening in my dysfunctional life. There was no stopping with one drink, one bottle. I was right back where I'd been before I went into the hospital. Right back to inviting the voices and the sound of the rain and the faces staring at me from the windows back into my life. Right back into the horror and the time that's wiped away from my memory—and I didn't even care. I had everything to lose and I kept right on drinking, hiding the bottles where I'd always hidden them, hiding my fears in the same place too, where no one would ever find them. Hey, Dave. You want yes or no? The answer is yes. The answer is always yes.

During the patient's involvement on an intensive outpatient basis, it was suspected he had drank [sic] on 01/31/96. This patient was confronted on 02/02/96. A Breathalyzer was done at that time and this patient was registering 0.108. He denied drinking at that time and was sent home.

On Wednesday the thirty-first, I was drunk when I went to the IOP. I had been drinking steadily since the twenty-sixth, that Friday night when the addict in the mirror uncapped the bottle. I drank all weekend, and on that Monday there was no way I was going to stop just so I could go to treatment. I had always believed myself to be pretty functional when I drank so I saw no real problem with drinking in the car on my way to the hospital. I planned it so the sweats would pass and I'd have enough time to stop in the bathroom downstairs to throw some cold water on my face and then grab a cup of coffee in the cafeteria before getting on the elevator. I'd stick a couple of peppermints in my mouth and when the doors opened, I was good to go. I'd done it a thousand times; I could do it now.

I had made friends with a guy named Mike in the IOP. He was an alcoholic but hadn't been an inpatient. We were about the same age and he was a good guy, so we started hanging out together and I think he was the guy who turned me in.

I remember that after volleyball on that Wednesday night, he and I were walking down the hall together and we ended up riding the elevator down to the parking lot. I hadn't eaten dinner that night because I didn't want to ruin what was left of my buzz but hadn't had anything to drink since before three. I know that by 8:30 I was sober, but when I later got hauled in to the nurses' station to blow, they told me that someone had smelled alcohol on my breath on Wednesday night. They never told me who it was but I know it had to be Mike. Since I couldn't prove anything, I couldn't call him on it and he never told me he'd done it, but I knew he had to be the one.

I drank again on Thursday and Friday before I got to the hospital and it was Friday when they nailed me. We had finished our self-esteem class and I was heading down the hall to take the elevator downstairs to call someone; I don't even remember who. Sarah, the counselor who had taught class, followed me out into the hallway. I was drunk and suddenly didn't think I was the only one who knew that.

"Steve, I need to see you in the nurses' station."

It didn't sound good when she said it; I kept walking, reaching into my pocket and popping another peppermint into my mouth.

"I need to go make a call," I told her over my shoulder.

"Steve. You need to come to the nurses' station. *Now.*"

I can take her, I thought. *I can turn around and knock her down and then run, get in my car, and never come back to this place. They'd never find me.*

I stopped, knowing I couldn't do any of that, and turned around to see her standing there, hands on her hips almost like she was ready for me to come after her. I thought that maybe someone had done that to her before and realized how desperate people can be in this place. Something in the pit of my stomach was telling me that they had me. I walked to where she was standing. "What's going on?" I asked as nonchalantly as possible as the fear rolled through my stomach.

"I need you to blow."

I forced a laugh, trying hard not to make it seem as full of fear as it sounded to me. "Blow? Why?"

She didn't say anything as we walked into the station. The duty nurse already had the Breathalyzer out when we got there and she was standing there holding it with a little smirk on her face.

"Why am I doing this?" I asked again, the fear more apparent in my voice.

Sarah was staring at me with a strange look on her face. It wasn't like the snotty little smirk the duty nurse was wearing. It was more a look of sadness. Not sadness that she had just nailed someone who'd been drinking. This was more like she was sad that she was seeing the frightful reality creep over the face of someone who suddenly knew that everything wasn't so great after all.

I'd never blown before and played my ignorance for all it was worth. I think I was buying time to let the peppermint hide any remnants of alcohol on my breath. I didn't even know how the thing worked; I didn't realize they already had me. Even when I finally blew and I was drunk enough to get a DUI if I'd been driving, I denied everything. For the first time in my life, I was staring consequences in the face and didn't like what I was seeing. I was angry at the addict for doing this to me, but mostly I was scared. And when I got scared, afraid that someone was getting too close to anything going on in my life, I did what I did best—deny, deny, deny.

"Yeah . . . okay, I drank," I finally blurted out. "But it was Wednesday night; it wasn't today. I don't know how this happened."

"Steve, you're intoxicated," said Sarah as she folded her hands behind her. "You have to leave now. You have to go home."

I looked at her and I think she saw the fear. It was all starting to drape itself over me. Work. The contract I'd signed. I could lose my job and all I could do was stand there and continue to deny. It was the only thing I knew how to do anymore. "I'm not drunk. It must still be in my system from Wednesday night." What was I thinking? Maybe if I kept telling her that at least I might start believing it.

She said it again. She never flinched, never blinked. She stood there with sadness in her eyes and her hands folded behind her back. "You're intoxicated and you have to leave the center. You have to go home."

I looked at the duty nurse; the smirk was gone. She was shaking her head and writing something down in my file.

I lost it. "I can't go home!" I screamed as I looked back at Sarah. "I could lose my job! You can't send me home! You have to let me stay! Please!"

I was sweating and my pulse was racing. I needed to move. I needed to sit. I needed another drink.

"Steve, you need to calm down. Let's go sit in the group room a minute and we can talk about this." She nodded toward the double doors that led to the room where the aftercare patients would meet. She moved toward me but didn't touch me; she never unfolded her hands from behind her back. I turned and moved out of the nurses' station and pushed open the doors and immediately sat down in one of the chairs. Sarah followed me in and pulled a chair up to face me. I put my head in my hands and started to cry. Show time was over. I was scared out of my mind.

"Don't you understand?" I sobbed. "I could lose my job if you send me home. I can't go home."

"Look at me," she said softly. "I need you to look at me."

I didn't want to look at her. I didn't want her to see the fear and didn't want her to see that the addict was getting the best of me. She didn't say anything again until I finally looked at her. I was expecting sympathy . . . a change of heart. She knew I was afraid and maybe this was what they were all waiting for. She'd see the tears and she'd know how terrified I was about losing my job and she would say, *"Ah, there's the breakthrough. Good for you, old sot. You've finally come to grips with what could happen to you if you don't change your ways. Sorry to have put such a fright in you but I think we'll be all right now, don't you? Come now, give us a hug."*

That's not at all what I heard. I guess I wasn't surprised.

"You're going to go home now. You can come back on Tuesday. I want you to tell Mary what happened and talk to her about this and then you both can talk to your counselor about this when you come back. It's imperative that you share this with Mary. Do you understand me?"

I looked at her and all I could see was Bill Martin shaking the bars on his jail cell and yelling, "You can't do this to me!"

CHAPTER 12

The Match Meets the Wood

This patient did not attend programming on Monday, 02/05/96, but did return on 02/06/96. He was confronted regarding the suspicions of his having relapsed Wednesday and over the weekend, including Monday. He denied this and reported that he had only drank [sic] on Friday. It was stressed to this individual it was going to be very important for him to get honest in regard to his relapse. This patient never deviated from his insistence that he had only drank [sic] on Friday. He had not shared his relapse with his wife and was encouraged to do this in a family session on Tuesday. He was also then encouraged to talk with the group about his recent relapse. The patient's discharge planning was not resolved.

I WAS PULLED OUT OF group on Tuesday after saying nothing about my relapse. Sarah was in charge of the group and asked me if there was anything significant I wanted to talk about to the group. I looked at her and hated her for what she had done and said nothing. As if on cue, Brenda came into the room and called my name. Everyone in the room knew something serious was going down but no one said anything. My eyes were fixed on the floor as I walked out of the room and followed Brenda into her office to where Mary was waiting.

I think I still believed that somehow this was all going to work out. Even when I walked into that room and saw Mary sitting in the corner with red eyes and about ten tissues crumpled in her lap, I still thought everything was going to be okay. I'd always figured out a way to get out of all the messes I found myself in during my life. Always been able to lie my way through everything. Why should this be any different? Of course everyone would believe me. The only problem was that I had no idea what to say anymore.

Yes, I denied drinking even though I drank all weekend hoping the whole mess would simply disappear. Mary and I went to an Iowa basketball game on Saturday night with her sister and brother-in-law . . . old mother's milk himself . . . and I drank the whole day before we left. I even passed out in the car on the way home and told everyone it was because I was tired from working so hard at treatment. I drank all day Monday, leaving the house at 2:30 and not getting home until 9:00, remembering vaguely the gnawing fear that was growing inside me. It was an unfamiliar fear that maybe this time, no matter what I was trying to make myself believe, this time things weren't going to work out so well. I even drank Tuesday before I went in, figuring that I always did my best thinking, like my best driving, when I was drunk.

But when I walked into that room and I saw Mary and knew she knew, it hit me that maybe the hard surface I felt behind me was that great wall of denial I had built and my back was firmly up against it.

Brenda asked me one question: "Steve, did you discuss your relapse with Mary?"

As I looked first at Brenda and then at Mary, the anger and disappointment I expected to see pushed out of sight by the sadness

in her eyes, I gave my one and only honest answer I had given in
the whole time I had been in that place. "No."

There were no explanations, no qualifications, no excuses. There
was only "No."

I was told to leave but I remember thinking that at least Dave
would have finally been proud of me.

*His employer was contacted after this patient's discharge
from the program and was informed that this patient had
relapsed with alcohol and had unsuccessfully completed
treatment.*

When I left Tuesday night, I don't remember where I went
but I know that I left alone and that I didn't drink. I was as depressed as I've ever been because I knew that if it hadn't been
done already, someone at Sedlacek was going to contact Bill
Osborne at Millhiser and tell him what had happened. I thought
of how I was going to first try to convince somebody, anybody,
at Sedlacek to give me another chance and second try to convince everyone at Millhiser that I should have a tenth chance or
twelve chance or however many chances I was up to now with
them. I was slowly beginning to come to uncomfortable grips
with the fact that, as Bill Martin had said of the night he got
locked away where he deserved to be, they *could* do this to me.
It wasn't a very good feeling.

*Throughout his involvement in the outpatient program, his
employer was involved. His employer stayed very concerned
about this person returning to his previous position as he had
been very secretive, had difficulty in communicating, and
was very superficial in his approach to addressing feelings.*

I do think everyone at Millhiser was pulling for me, but they didn't have a choice once I left the program. They had drawn a line in the sand and I crossed it. I was fortunate that they gave me the chances they did, but I think I always believed that they liked me enough and had enough faith in what I was capable of doing that they would give me another chance.

I think that's part of the warped thinking with anyone who uses. All we're looking for is one more chance. Then another. And another. The next day, I spent a lot of time on the phone with Dave Robertson, pleading my case, and all he would tell me was that Brenda was addressing the matter with the people at Millhiser and that they would let me know when a final decision was made. I was out of the program. That much was clear and that fact alone was okay with me. At least I knew I wouldn't have to put up with any more of the stuff they were trying to spoon-feed me there. My concern at this point in time was the status of my job.

Like a good wife and wonderful kids, a dream job is something we tend to take for granted, thinking that no matter what, it will always be there. As much as I tried to convince myself that was the case, I was beginning to feel things really starting to slip away. I talked to Steve King . . . Bill Osborne was letting his underlings handle this mess . . . but he was vague about what was happening behind the closed doors at Millhiser, telling me only that they needed time to talk about all that had transpired and that they would be in contact with me early the next week. Next week? How in the world was I going to get by until next week? Oh, wait I minute. I knew someone who had gotten me through worse times than this. There's always hope when there's vodka. I needed a lot of hope. I drank a lot of vodka.

The rest of the week and the weekend are lost in an alcoholic haze and it's probably better that way. My next tangible memory is getting a call from Steve on Monday the twelfth telling me that they wanted to meet with me the following day after everyone else had gone home. I tried to rationalize why an after-hours meeting was a good thing but remember having a hard time coming up with anything positive at all. I went into the office on Tuesday, a little after five, and was directed by Steve to the large and suddenly ominous conference room in the back of the building. I went in alone and sat for a few minutes thinking back to all the sales meetings that I had sat through in that same room. Back then I was too lit up to care about anything other than drinking enough ice water to stop the sweats and hoping I wouldn't be asked anything that would require too much thought. But now, I was calm as I sat there, the alcohol making everything right in my world, as always, even though it was all about to come crashing down around me.

Steve and Bill came in, Steve closing the door and sitting next to me, Bill sitting at the head of the table where he usually perched during our sales meetings. Bill leaned back a bit in his chair, his fingertips tapping together as usual, but this time he wasn't nervous at all. This meeting had been rehearsed and that didn't seem like such a good thing to me.

Steve swiveled his chair slightly to look at me and waited a moment before he said anything because I could tell that what he was going to say wasn't going to be easy for him. That didn't seem like such a good thing either.

"Uh, Steve. I think it's time that we parted company."

That was it. I was being fired. I remember as a kid when my dad told my mom at the dinner table that our ice cream man, the old codger that drove a little three-wheeled icebox on wheels around town playing "Pop Goes the Weasel" on a loop and selling ice cream bars to the neighborhood kids, was getting fired. I had a vision of the poor old guy tied up to a stake surrounded by a big pile of wood that was being lit by the parents of all the kids that got an ice cream sandwich when they had ordered a fudge bar, and I remember thinking at the time that being fired sounded like a pretty painful thing. Sitting there in the conference room at Millhiser, I felt like Steve had just piled up the wood and Bill was holding the match. I turned slightly and looked at him.

"Is this final?" What was I expecting him to say? *"Of course, not, old man! We're just making sure your sales skills are still sharp! You know . . . can you still negotiate? Still can't take no for an answer?"*

But, in true Dave Robertson form, all I got from Bill was, "Yes."

There went the match. The wood was burning now.

I looked back to Steve. "Can I resign?" I surprised myself at that. It seemed to be the right thing to ask at the time. Maybe I was thinking about potential employers.

"So, Steve, why did you leave your last position?"

"I resigned."

That had a better ring than, *"Oh, I had a mental breakdown during an un-medicated attempt to quit a two-fifth-a-day vodka habit and then relapsed in treatment even though I knew I'd get fired from the best-paying job I'll ever have, leaving my wife and children destitute because I was always too drunk to ever establish any kind of contingency plan to avoid this kind of thing."*

They both agreed that I could "quit" on my own and I thought at the time it was the right thing to do. They agreed to give me positive references in exchange for avoiding any black eye the whole episode would give them. They told me they would pay me through the next week and even throw in the mechanized desk chair they had bought for me to boot.

I was too numb to say anything but "thanks," and I remember leaving and getting in my car and wondering just where in the world I was going to go and what I was going to do. Drinking even more sounded nice but I know I didn't do that because by the time I got home and told Mary about what had happened, I was remarkably calm. Maybe it was the thought of that mechanized desk chair that I had just inherited.

All I know is that on February 13, 1996, I felt that I couldn't lose any more than I had lost that day. And that night, to better come to grips with it all, I sat downstairs in the bathroom and drank a fifth of vodka that I had lugged home in my briefcase. Looking back, it was a little like a man pouring gasoline on the fire that was burning down his home and everything he owned. I found myself hoping the chair was worth it.

This patient's mental and emotional health remain unresolved.

I was talking to someone recently while we were watching an old movie about a Broadway production and how everyone was worried because the director had already had one "nervous break-down" and they were all afraid he would have another. We talked about how that term isn't used much anymore, and it hit me then that that's exactly what I had in December of 1995. I had been locked up in a psyche ward; I was drugged so I wouldn't hurt my-self; I had seen and heard and felt things that weren't there. I never once acknowledged that I had a problem. I flaunted my superiority over the others in treatment and had a terrible time of identifying or resolving any feelings I was trying to hide. I was encouraged in group, family, and individual sessions to discuss how I felt about anything and I couldn't . . . or wouldn't . . . do it. Treatment wasn't simply about dealing with my drinking but about all the things in my life that may have led up to my world turning completely inside out. I had failed miserably in every aspect of the program but I never once thought that there was really anything wrong with me that I couldn't fix. I think Brenda was pretty accurate in this assessment. My mind was a pretty unresolved place.

The patient's marital situation remained unresolved.

I had a lot of sessions with Mary during the time I was in treatment but I had a terrible time being honest and communicative with her. I was called on this a lot during our time with Dave first, and then Brenda, and came to realize that I had in fact sabotaged our relationship, but I had a difficult time rectifying the situation. I think a lot of the difficulty came from the fact that I hadn't been very honest with her about much of anything during most of our marriage. My first priority was me; later it was the addiction.

That night, after I left the hospital, Brenda met with Mary to discuss why I was being discharged. She accepted the decision but still didn't quite know how she was going to deal with our marriage. When I walked into the house on February thirteenth I couldn't believe that she was still willing to support me. If she had followed me to the bathroom that night, I'm pretty certain she would have changed her mind. And to think, all I probably needed to do that night was sit down on the couch with her and talk about everything that had happened and try to figure out as a couple how to make things better; but the addict would have none of that. As always, I ended up doing what he wanted me to do.

This patient's peer relationships remained unresolved.

In treatment, I was always very caught up in maintaining the image that I was in complete control and having everything in my life taken care of by others. This was true to an extent at work where Sandi would cover for me more times than I'll ever know, partly to protect me but mostly, I'm sure, to protect the clients who had unfortunately put their trust in me. At home, Mary played the role of dutiful wife and mother because I was making enough money to justify allowing her to do that. Long before either Sandi or Mary had ever heard of the word *enabler*, they were playing the role perfectly. This image—this dysfunctional belief that I was in complete control of my life—was a fact I did not let pass by the less fortunate souls with me in treatment. I was better than they were. I didn't have a problem and if they hung around me long enough, they wouldn't either.

His self-esteem remained unresolved.

I pretended to understand the concepts that were preached in our class, but purely on an intellectual level. Applying them was another story because, at the time, I didn't think I had a self-esteem issue. I thought I esteemed myself rather highly, thank you.

This patient's spirituality remained unresolved.

I was not a spiritual man. I was a good Catholic who, for one hour a week, was the most religious man in the world. I would stand and sit and kneel with the best of them. I would nod my head as Father John would read scripture and preach his sermon, knowing that, for that one hour, I was being saved from all the misery I lived during the week. I ate the bread and drank the wine and nodded politely to all the other good Catholics who, for that same hour every week, were erasing all their own misery from their own lives and who, for the other 167 hours each week, felt free to mess things up all over again. There was no spirituality in my life. There was only that one hour a week. And the wine.

Growing up, I was never a big fan of prayer. I knew about prayer and was prayed over every Sunday by Reverend William Johnson of the United Presbyterian Church in Newton, Iowa. He would stand up behind his oaken pulpit and raise his robed arms and look up to the heavens and pray over all of us. I don't remember what he'd say and I don't know that I felt as if I had been particularly blessed in any way when I left the church, but I remember that he did it. To me it was nothing more than the sign that church was finally over.

My family didn't pray regularly other than saying a prayer before we ate: "God is great, God is good, and we thank Him for this food. Amen."

I don't think I ever thought about the prayer but rather would spend my time looking at the food Mom had made or making faces at my sister. Our prayer was simply a prelude to food. The focus wasn't on how great God was to me; it was all about the food. It wasn't even about giving thanks. All it was to me was something we had to say before we could eat just like Reverend Johnson's prayer was something we had to hear before we could go home.

Bedtime was different. My prayers at night were said with either my dad or my mom, whoever happened to be tucking me in that night. It was the standard, the timeless classic that millions of kids have prayed every night: "Now I lay me down to sleep, I pray the Lord my soul to keep. If I should die before I wake, I pray the Lord my soul to take."

Simple enough until you break it down, as I did every night, and focus on the one part that, as far as I was concerned, was the focal point in the whole thing. *If I should die. . . .* That prayer to me was about nothing but death and every night, right after Mom or Dad would leave the room, I'd pray again and ask God not to let me die. It wasn't about salvation or mercy. It was about death, and I was terrified every night that it was going to be my last night on earth. As with the prayer we said before we ate, my focus was obviously pretty narrow and directed at the wrong thing.

When I was about nine years old, my uncle Dale, Mom's older brother, was diagnosed with leukemia. Even though I had no idea what that was, I knew that it was bad and that he might die from it. I remember sitting out on our patio one morning eating breakfast when our phone rang. Mom went in to answer it and all of a sudden we heard her start to cry. Not quiet, sniffling sobs but rather mournful wails that you knew were proclaiming that something very bad had happened. My uncle, whose cancer had been in remission, was sick again and was near death. I remember sitting on the couch with my mom and crying as well, not so much because of the news about my uncle, but rather because I felt so bad for my mom.

I started praying in earnest that night, after of course praying that I not die, that God would save Uncle Dale because I didn't want my mom to go through the pain she was suffering. I prayed every night and I prayed hard, pleading with God to spare him and thereby spare my mom from the grief she was feeling. Days went by, weeks perhaps, and I kept praying, and Uncle Dale didn't die. I found myself marveling at the power not only of prayer but at my own power as well, for it was my words alone that were keeping him alive. There was simply no other explanation.

In time, as with many things in our lives, complacency set in and, figuring my work was done, I stopped praying. My uncle died a short time later and the most vivid reminder of his death was not the grief of my mother who had lost a brother or my aunt who had lost a husband or my cousins who had lost their father. It was my anger at God for letting him die, which was soon followed by the realization that I had killed him when I stopped praying for him. I carried that guilt around with me for a very long time and didn't pray again for years. I even quit listening to Reverend John-son on Sundays, focusing instead on the United States flag beside his pulpit and trying to recite the Pledge of Allegiance backwards so I wouldn't have to hear him pray.

Prayer resurfaced in my life when I was playing basketball in high school and we would recite the Lord's Prayer as a team before games. I don't know if we were praying that we would win, but I think all of us believed that if we prayed hard enough, we'd have a better chance. Of course, if the other team was praying as well, all it really boiled down to was what school's colors God was choosing to wear that night and who He was going to allow to feel better at the end of the game. I prayed before tests; I prayed for Cathy Huggins to wise up and dump Keenan Griffin and come back to me. I found that I was praying again but was really only praying for things that I thought I wanted but knew weren't going to change my life if I didn't get them.

The point is, I didn't get the concept of prayer. I was still a little intimidated by it because of what happened with my uncle Dale. I didn't understand anything about God's will and don't think I ever believed that much in prayer because to me, one had never been answered yet. I was smart enough to realize that we won basketball games because our team was better, I passed tests because I had studied, and Cathy finally came back to me because . . . well, I don't think I ever figured that one out.

I finally reached a point during my drinking when I knew I might be in trouble. I wasn't ready to admit that to anyone else yet because it would be too real, but I was beginning to accept it because I was starting to be uncomfortable that other people knew what was go-ing on. I started praying hard. I would lie in bed every night and pray that Mary wouldn't find any more empties that I had hidden—and forgotten about—in the basement. I prayed that Bill Osborne wouldn't confront me again with his concerns about my drinking. I would pray that I had enough vodka in the house to get me through a weekend without having to think of an excuse to leave the house to buy more. I prayed that no one would look under the bed in the guest room where we would stay at my mom's or my sister's and see the liquor bottles I'd stashed to get through the time away.

I still didn't get it. Prayer and God's will. You cannot have one without having the other. As I continued to slip further toward the long sleep, when I would doze fitfully only a couple hours a night because the alcohol had coursed its way through my system and I would wake up, my body screaming for more, reality began to settle uncomfortably around me. I couldn't stop. All the times I thought I could stop whenever I wanted to, the reality that cried out to me in the night was that I couldn't. I needed help.

I don't remember the first time I prayed the kind of prayer that God had desired so long to hear. I don't remember the words, but I remember feeling overwhelmed by what was happening to me and I desperately wanted to stop drinking, and I know that I asked Him to help. While I don't remember what I said, I know that I was angry that it seemed that He wasn't hearing me. Every morning I'd wake up and expect to be "cured" and have no desire to drink anymore. Yet, every morning I'd stand downstairs and shave and drink out of my plastic Gilbey's bottle and be angry that He hadn't answered me. I even remember thinking that He must still have been mad at me because I had let my uncle down. I didn't get it. I knew He didn't want me to drink; why wasn't He answering me?

Due to the difficulty this patient had in meeting treatment concepts, he was discharged from this program for non-compliance on 2/16/96.

For the rest of that week, after I had lost my job and after Steve had delivered my chair and my last paycheck, the staff at Sedlacek put my file aside and met a few times on whether or not they should let me come back. I'd like to think that there were fierce arguments and fist fights among the counselors and that people didn't speak to each other for months after the decision was made. Of course, it was already a foregone conclusion that I was done. I wanted to believe that I was as special as I'd been trying to make everyone else believe I was the whole time I was in there. All I was, though, was another one of the thousands of people who pass through the doors of hundreds of treatment centers all around the country. People who can't or won't accept the simple fact that they're sick and that they can get better. People who think they can rein in a problem that is bigger than any of them had ever imagined it could be but one that if looked squarely in the eye could be overcome. If only we would show the same resolve to put aside the alcohol as we show when we plot our next drink, putting the addict in his place would be a relatively simple task. It's the convoluted idea we have that our lives are made better because of the peace that comes with the poison. That's what keeps us from accepting that a *truly* peaceful life is one free from the shackles of shame that the addiction uses to lock us up.

They weren't going to give me another chance. At some point in time, we all have to own up to the consequences of our actions and our behaviors. If my time hadn't come yet, it was about to hit me in a way that would change my life forever.

DISCHARGE RECOMMENDATIONS: Due to this patient being at high risk for relapse and not being appropriate due to lack of motivation, at the time of his discharge there are no recommendations.

PART II

The Forgiveness

"You, Lord, are forgiving and good, abounding in love to all who call to you."

PSALM 86:5 (NIV)

CHAPTER 13

An Imprisoned Freedom

I WAS LIKE A SAILOR on leave. After months at sea, without wine or women, he more than makes up for lost time when he hits the shore. I was no different. In an odd and more than sad sort of way, I felt free for the first time in a long time. Free from the suspicions at work, free from the rigors of the discipline of treatment, free from feeling that there was anything significant to worry about, well, except for the fact that I had been fired and had absolutely no idea what I was going to do. While I wanted to enjoy the freedom, I'm certain it was those realities that made me pour more alcohol into my system that weekend than I had poured into myself in a long time.

I have no recollection of that first weekend after I left treatment except for the visions I have of being in the bathroom in the basement pulling a bottle of Gilbey's out from behind the pile of towels in the closet and drinking nonstop. I can only imagine what was going on in my house at the time but all I remember is that whatever it was, I didn't believe I could handle it without the addict being with me, controlling my every move, just as he always had.

The first tangible memory I have is one of Tuesday the twentieth. I was sitting at the dining room table and Mary was with me. Katie and Laura were both in school but I don't remember why Mary wasn't at work. The vision that is forever burned into my memory is of her sitting on my lap and holding me and crying, telling me over and over that everything was going to be okay. It was hard for me to fathom at the time that she was still there with me given all that I'd put her through, but she was and she continued to believe that we were going to be all right. She had no idea that I was still drinking, let alone how much. I think she believed that the enormity of all that had happened must have certainly hit me by then, but the irony was that the enormity was the thing that kept me pouring vodka into my system. I was completely unable to handle anything that went wrong in my life without the courage I believed I got from alcohol. Like the day when Dad died and she took me by the hand and gave me the strength I needed to get by, I continued to let her do it to me over and over. Even on good days, she made me feel better. A bad day without her would have been unbearable.

I told Mary that I was going to go to Minneapolis. My sister lived there with her husband, Arnie, but they had made it clear that they wouldn't let me stay with them. They were smart enough to see through my nonsense even if they had never caught me stuck in any of it. Instead, I told her I felt the need to go see Laurisa's ex-husband, Mark, and his wife, Meta. Mark was the first brother I ever had and a man who had stayed a good friend even after his divorce from Laurisa. He had struggled in his life as well, alcohol and depression dragging him down a path far too familiar to me, and I felt the need to be around someone who understood everything I was going through. That's what most people would have guessed at the time and I would have probably agreed with them. But there was something at work that was much greater than I would have ever imagined even if it took a long time for me to figure it out.

Maybe Mary knew; maybe that's why she didn't put up much of a fight when I told her I was leaving the next day to go see Mark. Maybe she thought it would be good for me as well. I don't know. The only thing I know is that after that day, Tuesday, February 20, 1996, I never held that woman in my arms again. It's funny how we remember little things like that and can't remember an entire Thanksgiving holiday. I think it's one of the million ways God works in us when we have no idea He even thinks enough about us to care, but He always wants us to remember the things that mean the most to us, even if we don't know it at the time.

I left home around three on the afternoon of the twenty-first. Mark knew I was coming and, because I had been to his house before, I had a pretty good idea of where I was going. It was a funny trip. I always, *always*, drank in the car when I was alone. I drank *before* I'd leave on a trip when I was driving other people, so it was only natural that I'd drink *in* the car when I was alone. But when I left Cedar Rapids that day, I took nothing with me. I had thought about stopping at the Osco down the street and picking up something for the road and something extra for my suitcase so I wouldn't get caught short, but I didn't do it. It was odd; one of my biggest fears when I went anywhere was running out of vodka, so I always took extra with me to stash under the bed. But on that day, I took nothing.

It was a nice day and I had always enjoyed the solitude of my car; plus the trip was a nice diversion from everything else that was going on in my life. I thought about work and what I was going to do but found myself not worrying about it as much as I should have. I thought about Mary and our girls and how hard I had just made their lives but I found I wasn't dwelling as much on that as I should have. I thought about how I had failed at treatment and wanted to feel bad, but all I kept thinking was that I was free to drink as much as I wanted now and all I had to do was be careful so no one knew. I believed that I had been good at that for a lot of years; my experiences in treatment had made me more aware of my need to get even better at it.

I must have had fifteen or twenty opportunities to stop on the way and buy my bottles, but I never did. I drove past a Tom Thumb convenience store and thought I should go in but wondered if they even sold vodka and then, by the time I decided that maybe I should stop, I was already past the store. That kept happening over and over and I was starting to wonder why I wasn't stopping anywhere. The addict was starting to wonder as well and I could tell he wasn't very happy about it. By the time I got to Minneapolis, it was dark, and I suddenly found myself slipping into a bit of a panic. I was on 494 heading west to Highway 69 . . . at least that's where I thought I wanted to go . . . but as I was driving, the addict took hold of the wheel. I could tell he'd had enough.

I ended up driving toward my sister's house because I knew there was a mall with a grocery store near her place, a Byerly's that my dad and I had gone to when we were in Minneapolis for my sister's fortieth birthday party about six years earlier. We had run out of wine so I knew they had a large liquor selection. I had no idea where Mark's was from there, but getting to his house was the last thing on my mind. Panic had taken hold of me and I needed a drink. It was a little after eight thirty.

I parked and walked into the store and turned to the right to go down the short hallway leading to the liquor section. You could get into the liquor section by either going down the hallway to the door or by walking through the store. That was too far. I couldn't wait that long. I could hear her voice calling me and I knew I needed to get her inside me to take away the fear that had suddenly and unexpectedly begun to grow out of nowhere. I knew once she was in my hands, once that cap was unscrewed and the familiar scent of that intoxicating kerosene hit my nose, everything would be all right, just like it always was. I got to the door and the addict put out his hand to open it. Everything was going to be just fine. The voice came out of nowhere, the memory still too vivid.

"Open the door and everything will be fine. Just fine. . . . All you have to do is open the door."

It was locked. I suddenly thought my heart was going to explode.

I walked back down the hallway, toward the entrance of the store. I figured the hallway door must have been locked because it was late. I didn't want to think about why it looked so dark inside because the fact that it was late didn't seem like the time that anyone would want the lights off in a store. I didn't think about any of that; I wanted to get something to drink. I made my way through the store and could tell before I even got there that the doors leading into the liquor section weren't open. It was dark inside; the place was closed. Panic was overwhelming me and I started to look for the beer aisle but soon realized that everything with alcohol was locked up and put away for the night. Someone must have known I was coming.

I stopped some poor guy pushing a cart down the juice aisle.

"Hey, is the liquor section closed?"

He looked at me and I swear he took a step back. I must have looked as desperate as I felt but I didn't care. He'd never see me again and I needed a drink.

"Yeah, it's a state law." He was almost stammering. "You can't buy anything past eight."

I stepped toward him. "You mean there's nothing open? Anywhere?"

He stepped back again and turned around with his cart. "I guess you could drive to Wisconsin."

I stood there, scared of the addict and wondering how long the drive was but I knew it wasn't an option. As I made my way out of the store and tried to remember where I had parked the car, I was hit with the realization that I was going to go through a night without alcohol, and thoughts of the thirtieth came flooding back to me. I saw the faces looking at me out of the window, heard the woman softly calling my name, felt the fear grip me and start to strangle the very life out of me. Sweat was suddenly pouring out of me. I had no idea what I was going to do and suddenly I also had no idea of where I was. I found my car, sat inside, started to shake uncontrollably, and felt the tears begin to well in my eyes. I was in trouble. Very big trouble.

In time, I collected myself as best I could and called Mark.

"Hey, bro," he said when he answered the phone. "Where are you? We've been waiting for you."

I looked around the parking lot. I had forgotten the name of the store. I had forgotten just about everything. All I knew was that Wisconsin was somewhere off to the east and it couldn't be that far.

"I'm, I'm," I squinted to see the Byerly's sign, "I'm at the Byerly's over by Laurisa's house."

My voice was shaking. My body was still shaking as well. It wasn't the violent shakes that I'd had a few minutes earlier but the kind of shakes I'd get in my hands at ten at Millhiser when the morning buzz would wear off and the addict would start letting me know that he needed to be fed. Not bad, but apparently noticeable, even over a cell phone.

"Byerly's? What are you doing over there?" He paused. "Hey, bro. You okay?"

Now I paused. "No, I'm in trouble," I said, surprised to hear those words come out of my mouth and then immediately backtracking as best I could. "I mean, I'm not sure how to get to your house from here. You know, I'm having trouble figuring out how . . . you know . . . how to find you."

He didn't say anything for a few seconds, and I was thankful he didn't press me about what I was doing in the middle of the parking lot at the Byerly's that was nowhere near where I should have been. He had to have known that I went there for a reason because it certainly wasn't on the way to his place. I don't know what lie I would have told him if he had asked but I know I would have come up with something. I always did.

He gave me the directions to his house and I scribbled them on a piece of paper that I pulled out of the glove box then hung up and tried to get my bearings. All of the exits out of the parking lot looked the same and I had no idea where I was supposed to go. I looked at the directions and thought about calling Mark back and having him come and get me. I thought if anyone would understand my desperation, he would be the one, but there was something . . . a sick sort of pride maybe . . . that kept me from making the call. I finally crept out onto the nearest road that ran by the mall, squinting at the road signs, looking for something that I either recognized or had written down. It took me a long time and more than one wrong turn before I finally found Mark and Meta's townhouse and parked in the driveway wondering how I was going to get through the night.

I thought about simply going in and telling Mark I needed a drink. By then, it felt like he was the only friend I had left and I figured he would understand what I was going through. But in the end, I knew I couldn't do it. The addict wouldn't let me because if I admitted that I had lost control and needed alcohol to make everything right, then he, the addict that had come to take complete control over what was left of my life, would be found out and it would be over for him. I *had* lost control, and as much as I had come to despise him, I felt that I couldn't live without him anymore.

I grabbed my bag out of the car and made my way to the door. As I raised my hand to ring the bell, I saw how badly it was shaking. I placed my bag on the ground and held up my other hand and saw that it was shaking as well. It wasn't the violent and uncontrollable shakes that I'd had earlier in the car but there was no hiding the fact that I had a serious problem. At that moment, I wanted to leave; I wanted to get in my car and drive to Wisconsin and keep going and never come back. I could hear the addict telling me he thought that was a great idea and even though I knew I couldn't really do it, I bent down and picked up the bag and turned away from the door just as the light came on and Mark's voice hit me from behind.

"Hey, bro! It's good to see you. I was getting worried about you."

I took a deep breath, unsteady and shaking with fear, and turned to face him, forcing a smile. "Yeah, well, it's been a long time since I've been here, man. I had completely forgotten where you live."

He stepped out and held his arms out to hug me. I thought of how he might feel me shaking but then realized it was cold enough out to justify it and since I wasn't wearing my coat and didn't know how to explain myself not giving him a hug, I stepped into him. It felt good to be held and I found myself letting him pull me in close. We stood there for a minute, neither of us saying anything. He was crying softly, sad for what had happened to me and to my family and no doubt feeling a little of what he knew I was going through. It was hard when he finally let me go.

"Sorry about that, bro," he said, smiling and wiping his eyes. "I'm so sorry about everything that's happened. How are you doing?"

He held the door for me and I walked into the townhouse. I could tell there was a fire going and I was hoping the heat and the flames would relax me and make me stop shaking.

"Oh, you know, I'm doing okay," I said as he took my bag from me and motioned to the couch in front of the fire. "It's been pretty hard, losing my job and all." And I added, almost as an afterthought, "And not drinking . . ."

Honesty, even if a bit misguided, seemed so strange coming out of my mouth. After all, I hadn't had anything to drink yet that day. That *was* pretty hard.

He put my bag on the floor and then we both sat down.

"How long's it been? Not drinking, I mean."

I looked at him and then turned and looked into the fire. I thought I saw the face that had been looking out at me from my living room window and then closed my eyes for a minute as if counting the days. I finally looked back at him.

"It seems like forever," I said as I moved my hands under my legs and sat on them so he wouldn't see them shake. "It feels like it's been a really long time." Still being honest. It felt like it had been forever.

"Can I get you something?" he asked. "Coffee? Soda?"

It hung there and I waited for the addict to ask for a brandy or some Irish Whiskey in the coffee, or a vodka, neat, with an olive, or a glass of wine, or a gallon of gas and a match. I waited and was surprised to hear my own voice. "Yeah, something cold would be nice. Ginger Ale or Seven-Up if you've got it."

"Sure, no problem; wait here and I'll be right back."

He stood to go and said over his shoulder on the way to the kitchen, "Meta went to bed. She's got to get to work early but she said hi. She'll see you at breakfast."

"Cool," I said, knowing he didn't hear me. I don't even know if it was my voice or not. I held up my hands and saw the tremors and knew Mark would see them too and suddenly wondered how I was going to drink whatever he brought out. I looked around the room to see if there was anything . . . a bottle of brandy on a bookshelf, an opened bottle of wine in a wine rack . . . anything . . . but there wasn't. The people at Byerly's must have called and told him I was looking. I needed a drink. The addict was screaming for a drink.

Mark came back and sat down and we talked for a long time about what had happened and what I was going to do. He kept telling me that I wouldn't have any trouble finding a job because everyone knew me and I had a lot of contacts. I remember thinking those were the very reasons why I knew I would, in fact, have a *terrible* time trying to find a job. I would look at the fire while we talked, thinking it would relax me, but I kept seeing faces in the flames and I'd have to look away. I didn't drink any of the soda he brought in and I don't even know what it was. I kept sitting on my hands and thinking of Wisconsin and how I should have driven there from the grocery store when I had the chance.

We talked well into the night and that was fine with me. I wasn't all that anxious to go to bed because I was afraid of what might happen in the downstairs guestroom where there wouldn't be any vodka bottles hidden under the bed.

I learned from Mark that he had, shortly after my sister had divorced him, contemplated suicide, figuring he was worth more dead to his kids than he was alive. He said he had even picked out the place where he would do it. It was sad to hear him talk about things like that but I soon found myself thinking about how much life insurance I had and wondering if Wisconsin had any tall buildings from which to jump. I shook my head at the thought and realized it was only the addict putting those dark visions in my mind because he was angry that he hadn't had a drink all day.

We finally went to bed around midnight, Mark telling me we would all have breakfast in the morning before Meta went to work and that he had to run to his office for a couple of hours. He started to tell me what we were going to do when he got back but I didn't hear him. All I heard was that I was going to be alone for two hours. Two hours! Even though I had no idea where I was, I knew that … in the light of day … I should certainly be able to find a liquor store. That thought alone gave me some hope for the long, cold night that I faced.

After he showed me where everything was downstairs, Mark went up to bed and I went into the bathroom and washed my face then looked at myself in the mirror. I looked old … tired. My eyes were red from the drive and there were dark circles hanging like suitcases underneath them. My skin was dry and had a gray and yellow hue to it. I wanted it to be the lighting in the bathroom but I knew that wasn't it. I was sick and I found myself thinking that I wasn't doing anything to make myself get better. I knew I needed to stop. I knew I wanted to stop. There wasn't a single reason to keep drinking and there were a million reasons to stop. I thought of what I'd already lost and what I had yet to lose and knew that I could hang on to what I had left if I would only stop. I hadn't had anything to drink all day. Maybe I could do it. I knew I needed to. I also knew that I was going to go out and find a liquor store as soon as Mark left in the morning.

I was up all night. I left the lights on because I was afraid of the dark and I sat in bed wrapped in a blanket to try to stop shaking and kept waiting for that woman's voice to tell me everything was going to be fine.

"Open the door and everything will be fine . . . just fine."

I was starting to believe that things weren't going to be fine ever again.

CHAPTER 14

Found Out

THE NEXT DAY, FEBRUARY 22, 1996, I got up and took a cold shower and went upstairs to the sounds and smells of breakfast . . . bacon, eggs, English muffins, hot coffee . . . and all I wanted was one of Dad's Bloody Marys. One with more vodka than tomato juice, a squirt of lemon, Worcestershire, some Tabasco, salt and a dash of pepper, that special dollop of horseradish he always put in, and a dill spear. That's all I wanted for breakfast but all I saw was a carton of orange juice. There wasn't a jug of vodka to be found anywhere.

We sat and small-talked while we ate; I don't remember much of what we talked about, concentrating instead on making sure my hands weren't shaking and that I wasn't saying anything I shouldn't. I had been telling everyone I wasn't drinking and didn't want to give myself away this close to feeding the beast. Meta left when she was done and Mark and I cleaned up the kitchen, had a last cup of coffee, and then he left as well, telling me he'd be back in a couple of hours. It was ten; I was on my own until noon.

As soon as he left and I knew he wasn't coming back, I went out and got in my car and headed out to find someplace to buy my vodka. I tried to keep track of where I was going because the last thing I needed to do was get lost. I didn't have to go far until I found a liquor store and went in, bought two fifths of Gilbey's, and got in the car to head back. I wanted to wait until I got to Mark's before I had a drink but couldn't. I uncapped a fifth while I drove and then, when I knew no one would see me, took a long pull and immediately felt the warmth and security of my lover. She was back and the addict finally seemed satisfied. By the time I got back to Mark's, five minutes tops, a third of the bottle was gone.

For the next two hours, I sipped from my bottle and relaxed. I felt that I'd been in a war zone for the past twenty-four hours and was now back in the security of my base. The vodka was like a sedative; nothing mattered in my world. My lost job was a distant memory and my family didn't even exist at that moment. There was nothing but me and Gilbey's and I realized that it was all I needed in my life anymore. Nothing would be too difficult to handle as long as she was with me. I never wanted to be without her again.

Around eleven forty-five, I went downstairs to get cleaned up a bit before Mark got home. I hid the bottle, only about a third full, under the bed, put the other one in my bag, and went into the bathroom to throw some cold water on my face. I looked at myself in the mirror as I was drying off and stared at the vacant and blurry eyes looking back at me. I thought for a moment about what was happening to me and what the addict was doing but never once allowed myself to make the admission, even in the solitude of that lonely bathroom, that we were one in the same. He was someone else to me. He was the one who demanded to be fed; he was the one who had cost me my job; he was the one who made me lose my mind; he was the one who was killing me. I felt that I should make him stop but knew I couldn't. I was afraid of him. He had complete control over me.

Mark came home and we went downtown and had a bite to eat. I didn't eat much because I didn't want to ruin the buzz but managed to get half a hamburger down. We wandered through town for a while and then he went to his barber and got a haircut and even had the beard he had worn forever shaped into a goatee. We had a good time together; the weather was nice for late February and the sun was shining. Everything was so much better than when I had gotten there the night before. I smiled as I realized that everything was always nicer when I was drunk.

I started to crash around four and we got some coffee and then headed home. I was tired and went downstairs and stretched out on the bed for a bit while Mark started getting dinner ready. I slept for a while, and when I woke up, it was almost six and I could hear Meta upstairs in the kitchen with Mark while the smell of something . . . I don't know what it was . . . made its way to my room. I was hungry but as soon as I thought about food, the addict reminded me that it was time to feed him. I reached under the bed and pulled out what was left of the first bottle and took it into the bathroom and got cleaned up while I drank the rest. There was a full fifth tucked away in my duffel but I didn't want to open it yet. I knew I would need it for later and there was no way I was going to go through another night like the last one. I was going to go over to my sister's for a while after dinner and figured I'd need a lot to drink when I got back from there. I didn't want to be too lit up when I went, given how she and Arnie weren't all that crazy about me being there in the first place, so I knew I'd probably want to drink a lot when I got back. Life was so much more enjoyable when alcohol was a part of it, especially when the addict was happy.

I was giddy at dinner, much more talkative and amiable than I had been at breakfast. I was drunk and, because of that, I was relaxed. Mark was planning on driving me over to Laurisa's after dinner and even though I wasn't looking forward to it, the dread didn't seem to loom as large with my system full of vodka. My relationship with my sister, sown at an early age, had never really blossomed as we journeyed through adulthood. We didn't go out of our way to avoid being around each other or anything like that. We always did holidays together at our parents' whenever we had the chance, mostly so our kids could all get the experience of being a family. But when we were together, our conversations were pretty superficial. Most of that was my fault; I'll be the first to admit that, but I was like that with pretty much everyone. It was as if I didn't want anyone to get too deep to see all the junk that was going on inside me. It was especially hard to open up at all around her. She was smart and was seeing through me long before I started seeing through myself. Because of that, as I sat at the table with Mark and Meta, a completely different person than I had been when I sat up with Mark the night before, sitting on my hands and seeing faces in the fire, I was happy to be drunk. I needed to be at the top of my game when I was with my sister.

I was still drunk when Mark took me to Laurisa and Arnie's. I think the plan was for Laurisa to bring me back when we were done "visiting," but I don't remember. I was so focused on trying to get through my time with my sister that I didn't pay much attention to the details of how I was going to get back. I only knew that I had a full fifth waiting for me in my bag and that the addict would be much happier than he was the night before. That fact alone made me feel better; if he wasn't happy, my life didn't seem to go as smoothly.

When we got there, I went upstairs with Laurisa and Arnie and found myself sitting uncomfortably on one of the couches in their living room. Laurisa and Arnie sat on the other couch, talking to me about all that had happened in the past few weeks. I was doing my best to make sure they knew that no matter what had happened, things would be better somehow because I wasn't drinking anymore. I was at ease talking to them, mostly because I was drunk, but also because I knew I was going to get drunker before the night was over.

Everything was going well until the phone rang. Arnie disappeared into the next room to answer it and then came back to tell me that Mary wanted to talk to me. It was either the look on his face or the sound of his voice that was telling me that something wasn't quite right. I suddenly found myself wishing I was back at Mark's tucked away alone in the room that I was too afraid to stay in the night before and that the warm poison that I had come to depend on so much was wrapped comfortably in my hand, the addict lifting the bottle to my lips, the fear being washed away.

I went into the other room and picked up the phone.

"Uh, hello?" I said with as much confidence as that woman with no arms trying to juggle machetes.

There was silence on the other end except for the sound of someone trying to control her breathing before she was going to say something she didn't quite know how to say. I knew her well enough to know that she was angry. That didn't seem like such a good thing, especially since she hadn't seemed so angry at me when I left home the other day. She finally took one last unsteady breath and then spoke.

"I found your empties, Steve. They were under the chair, under the couch, they were everywhere."

She paused a minute while my mind raced to the chair, the couch, everywhere, and I tried to see myself putting them there, but I couldn't remember seeing myself doing anything, so chances were pretty good she was right. Still, I knew I had to deny it. Of course I had to deny it. She was trying to trap me and I *had* to deny it. I took a breath, trying not to sound as afraid as I was beginning to feel, but before I could say anything, she spoke again.

"It's over, Steve. When you come home . . . and I want you home tomorrow . . . we're going to deal with this once and for all. I mean it . . . this is going to end."

And with that, she was gone.

I stood there for a minute before I hung up and tried to slow down the jumble of the million things that were suddenly running through my mind. I wondered if Arnie had anything to drink in the house.

What had she meant?

It's over, Steve.

What was over? The marriage? The drinking? The belief she had shared with me that everything was going to be all right? That was only . . . what? . . . two days ago?

This is going to end? What was going to end? The lies? The denial? Me being a little too lax in how I disposed of my empties?

And the coming home tomorrow part . . . I didn't see how that was going to happen. Not now anyway. Things had suddenly changed and I needed time to think. I needed a drink.

I took a deep breath and went back into the living room and saw Laurisa and Arnie sitting on the couch. They didn't say anything; they just watched me and I wondered how much they knew of why Mary had called.

Laurisa spoke first. "Is everything okay?"

What, another test? Did she know everything wasn't okay and was just trying to see if I was going to lie again? Of course I was going to lie again.

"Yeah, everything's fine. The girls just missed me and wanted to say hi for a minute."

And with that . . . with that single mention of my two little girls and the sudden realization that my life with them would never be the same again if I were to lose them . . . I broke down. I made my way to the couch I'd been sitting on and I lost it. I sobbed uncontrollably until my sister came to me and sat next to me and put her arms around me and kept asking me over and over,

"What's going on? Please, talk to me. What's going on?"

I tried to tell her how sorry I was about everything that had happened but was aware that I needed to be careful about not saying too much. I hung on to the lie about my drinking . . . or rather, not drinking . . . the way a man would hang on to the anchor that was pulling him down to the bottom of the lake. I wasn't going to let go, even though I knew I was drowning. I couldn't let go, even though I felt that there was something inside me telling me that it was time to do just that.

I took comfort in her comfort and tried to compose myself, afraid of what was going to be waiting for me at home but suddenly overcome with the intense desire to get back to Mark's and immerse myself in the very thing that I had allowed to create all the fears in the first place.

Just let go.

I couldn't do it. All I needed to do was look at my sister, put "Moon River" aside once and for all, and tell her that I was sick and I needed help. It was time, and somewhere deep inside, I think I finally knew it but I also knew I couldn't do it. I just needed to get out of there. I needed a drink and didn't know what to say so I sat there and let her hold me and thought of how good it was going to feel when I would lay down in that bed and feel the familiar warmth overtake me and make everything right in my life again. It was all I knew anymore.

I was vaguely aware of hearing the phone ring again and Arnie leaving the room for a minute and then coming back and looking at me, anger mixing with . . . pity? I could tell that something wasn't right. Nothing seemed right anymore but I didn't know what to do or what to say so I continued to sit there and let my sister hold me and fought not to hear the voice inside me that kept telling me,

Just let go.

I sat there with her for another five minutes or so and finally composed myself and got up to go get a tissue and when I came back, Laurisa was sitting on the other couch and Arnie was standing beside her and there was a sudden and strange silence surrounding us. I sat down and looked at them and waited for them to say something, anything, but there was silence until Arnie glanced out the window at the driveway and looked at Laurisa before he headed to the front door. I suddenly didn't like what was going on even if I had no idea what it was. I only knew it wasn't good.

CHAPTER 15

One Honesty at a Time

I HEARD THE FRONT DOOR open and then the sound of too many feet coming up the stairs. I looked toward the top of the stairs leading from the front door and saw Arnie, followed by Meta and then Mark. None of them looked at me and no one looked very happy. They all went to the couch where Laurisa, who didn't seem to be as sympathetic as she had been a few minutes earlier, was sitting. They all sat down and looked at me, the silence in the room suddenly deafening. I felt like a contestant on *To Tell the Truth* and they were the panelists, all looking at me, knowing I was one of the guys that had lied through the whole show pretending to be someone they now knew he wasn't. It was a bad feeling and I didn't think there were going to be any consolation prizes worth writing home about.

Mark was the first one to speak. He hesitated because I think he knew, even if I didn't at the time, that what he was going to say might possibly change my life forever.

"Steve, Meta's here because she cares about you and I'm here because I love you."

I looked at the rest of the panelists. They all had me now. The addict was starting to feel agitated. Something was going horribly wrong.

"I went downstairs after I dropped you off and I found the empty bottle under the bed. You're drinking again."

It wasn't a question. They knew. I opened my mouth to protest, to say something, but I was cut off. The voice sounded exactly the same as Mary's when she had said it on the phone.

"This is going to end."

It was my sister.

There was silence for a moment and then people stood up so I stood up too.

What do you mean, this is going to end? That's what I wanted to say, to stand tall and defiantly challenge them, but I think all I got out was, "What. . . ?"

My sister moved into the kitchen and I followed her, my fear and anger building, and watched as she pulled out a thick phonebook from one of the drawers and started flipping purposefully through the pages.

I turned and saw Arnie and Mark hovering behind me, not right behind me but close enough to look like a couple of Secret Service agents who weren't going to let their man get out of sight. I turned back to Laurisa, who had settled on a yellow page and was now running her finger down the numbers. Whatever she was looking for, she was zeroing in on it.

"What are you doing?" asked the addict, sounding a lot like me.

She didn't look up from the page. "Finding someplace to take you."

"What do you mean, someplace to take me?"

She still wouldn't look up and seemed to ignore my question.

"I said—" I started, but she suddenly looked at me. I thought I would see anger in her eyes but there wasn't any there. What I saw instead was more like a deep sadness and an acceptance that this had now fallen into her lap. She spoke and I suddenly found myself wanting to hear "Moon River" again, to be swept away from the lies that were crumbling down all around me and taken back to doing the dishes and being a kid again.

"You're drunk and you're not staying here. I'm going to find a place to take you until you get sober."

She went back to what she was doing and found a number and dialed it. She looked at me as she waited for someone to answer the phone and I stood there, frozen in fear and more anger than I had felt at any other time in my life. I started to speak, but she held up her hand to cut me off and I heard her say,

"Hello, my name is Laurisa Sellers and my brother is an alcoholic. He's intoxicated and we've reached a point where we're not willing to keep him in our home. He lives out of town and we're trying to find a facility where we can take him tonight. Are you able to help us or do you know of a place that can help us?"

Or something to that effect. I didn't hear much of what she said after she said I was an alcoholic. I had never heard that before.

The addict was telling me to stop her, to reason with her, and to make her stop. *Tell her you just need some rest. Tell her you're fine. Tell her something!!"*

But all I could do was look at her and scream, "*I hate you for what you're doing to me!!!"*

She covered up the receiver and looked at me and laughed.

"*What are you laughing at???"*

"That's the first time you've been honest with me in years." She spoke back into the phone. "Oh, I'm sorry . . . yes . . . I see. . . . Sure, do you have the number?"

I didn't wait around to hear the rest. I turned and walked out of the kitchen, past Arnie and Mark, and headed for the steps that would take me downstairs. The Secret Service followed me down and into the family room where Brian, my nephew, then fourteen, was lying on the couch, watching television and crying quietly. He knew what was going on. Everybody knew what was going on. I was still the only one who was trying to pretend like it was nothing.

I looked at him, his tears flowing, and thought back to my own children, the vision of Katie standing at the front door with Mary, the empty bottles in her hand and the tears running down her cheeks and I, too, began to cry softly. I walked over to the couch and looked down at Brian.

"I'm drinking again, Brian," I said. "I'm so sorry."

It was the first time I had been honest with anyone, and it was to a poor fourteen-year-old kid who didn't need this kind of stuff in his life, but he somehow knew it was a big deal for me to tell him that . . . him of all people . . . and he stood up and put his arms around me.

"I know," he whispered to me as we cried together. And then, the words that I will never forget because I think I felt I'd never hear them from anyone ever again: "I love you, Uncle Steve."

It broke my heart to hear it and I said it to him as well in case I'd never have the chance to tell anyone ever again. "I love you, too."

I stood there for a few minutes because, next to being alone with my bottle of Gilbey's, it was the most comfortable place I had been in a long time. I finally stepped away and looked at Brian for a minute, the tears still in his eyes and a quiet smile on his face as if to say, *It's going to be all right and I'll always love you.*

I don't know if that's what he was saying or not but I found myself needing to hear it. I smiled back at him and then turned and walked past Arnie and Mark and went back upstairs where my sister was hanging up the phone.

She saw me but looked past me and spoke to everyone who was now standing behind me.

"I've found a place. It's over on East Lake Boulevard."

"That's close to our place," said Mark from behind me.

And the planning began.

I walked aimlessly around the house from one room to the next, Arnie and Mark never far behind me and Laurisa and Meta never far behind them, the four of them plotting their logistical strategy while I was trying to figure out how to make a run for it. The anger was still there, boiling under the surface, but I knew I needed to be in control so if the opportunity to run came up, I'd know it.

And then, it hit me. I didn't even have my car there. Where would I even go if I could manage to slip away from the two thugs that followed me everywhere I went? Reality was slowly beginning to drape itself around me and I realized at that moment that one of the reasons I had always wanted to drink was so I wouldn't have to deal with reality. I felt then that drinking had always been the wiser choice. I hadn't dealt with reality for a long time but knew right away that I didn't like it much.

The four of them decided that I would ride with Arnie and Mark in Mark's vehicle and Laurisa and Meta would follow behind in Laurisa's. I'm sure there was some sort of logic involved in all of this but I couldn't help but think that it was nothing more than to have a second car in case I opened the back door of Mark's car and rolled out onto the highway to try to get away. This way they would have something with which to run me over and put everyone out of his or her respective misery.

Arnie and Mark actually had the audacity to chitchat while we went to wherever we were going. I was sitting in the back with the addict, trying to hear what they were saying; I thought I was mad but it was nothing compared to what he was feeling. He was screaming at me to do something and the sound of his voice was making my head hurt and I found that it was getting hard to breathe back there. I thought of what it would be like to jump from the car and what it would feel like to be run over. I knew my sister was driving and could imagine her singing "Moon River" as she aimed her car at me, smiling at finally putting us all out of our agony.

I don't remember how far we drove but became aware of stopping at a forbidding looking place where, in a few hours and completely unknown to me at the time, my life would change forever. Bethel Relief Detox Center: the worst of my nightmares and the last hope I would ever have all rolled up into one.

But all I was thinking about was the nightmare part. At that particular moment, I didn't think any hope existed for me anymore. All I wanted to do was die—and that was, in fact, what was about to happen.

CHAPTER 16

Alone

WE PARKED BOTH VEHICLES AND everyone went inside, the heavy glass doors closing and locking behind us. I was locked in, and that fact alone sent a wave of panic through me. It wasn't so much the part about being locked in but rather the realization that I wasn't going to get out. I had always been able to get out of everything in my life, always been able to lie or deny my way out of anything that had come up, but with the sound of those heavy glass doors closing, I didn't feel that there was going to be any way to get out of this.

The only person that was in the large room with us was a heavyset nurse in a less than crisp white smock and blue jeans. She smiled at Laurisa and then looked at me, the smile vanishing, before sticking a clipboard in my sister's hands and then reaching under the counter and pulling up a now familiar object. The first thing she made me do was blow and, because of my experience at Sedlacek when I relapsed, I blew with much more confidence this time and, surprisingly given all the time that had passed since my last drink, I was still way over the limit.

While my sister went inside the confines of the nurse's station to get the paperwork started, Mark and Arnie prepared to go back to Mark's to pick up and deliver my bag to me. I realized a fairly serious issue with that prospect and took Mark aside. I'm certain he must have thought I was going to plot a major breakout or something but I wasn't even thinking about that anymore. All I was thinking about was my bag.

"Hey," I whispered to him, suddenly ashamed at what I was about to admit. "There's a full bottle of vodka in my bag. I don't think . . ." He pulled me close for a minute and gave me a hug. I think he was grateful that for the time being at least, my anger had subsided. I guess it had; there wasn't anything that being angry was going to accomplish now. All I wanted to do was have someone I know be the one to dump out my vodka. Plus, I figured if the ominous-looking nurse who was filling out the paperwork found it in my bag, I could end up being in that place forever.

Mark and Arnie left while Laurisa continued to fill out the paperwork. Meta stood next to Laurisa, avoiding eye contact with me, and, since no one was watching me, I thought briefly about making a break but knew I couldn't get out. Looking around, it didn't seem to be a good place to be trapped.

The room we were in was large, almost like a cafeteria in college. There were fifteen or so round Formica topped tables with six metal chairs with the uncomfortable vinyl seats on them surrounding the tables. There were long tables lined up in a row at the far end of the room, almost like an all-you-can-eat buffet. A few couches were spaced around the tables, none of which seemed very inviting. At the opposite end of the room was the nurse's station where Laurisa, Meta, and the nurse were filling out the necessary forms to put me away. The station was circular with a wooden counter surrounding the filing cabinets, fax machine, copier, computer, and a single telephone that would, on occasion, ring and, since the nurse was busy, would send the caller to what I assumed was an answering machine. I wondered why Laurisa's call couldn't have gone unanswered; at least that way I might have ended up somewhere where escape might have been a more viable option. Behind the nurse's station were two doors, both with the same sign: Office Personnel Only. I felt like someone behind at least one of the doors had a gun on me and was just waiting for me to make a move. The thought flashed through my mind that maybe a bullet wouldn't be such a bad thing right about now.

The one thing that struck me as odd was the large tin of loose-leaf tobacco that sat on the counter next to where my sister was filling out forms. It was surrounded by packages of Zig Zag rolling papers and next to them was a single Bic lighter on a chain that was nailed to the wooden counter. It apparently had tried to escape from this place once and I needed to keep that in mind if the urge to flee got too great. They were apparently pretty serious about keeping everything that was supposed to be in here, in here.

I kept waiting for my anger to subside but it never did. I didn't yell or scream at anyone but I knew ... I could feel it ... that I was still as angry as I had ever been in my life. To compound matters, there were some pretty significant questions about how and when I was going to get out of that place. I had assumed I would get out the next day but it didn't turn out to be that simple. Laurisa and Arnie were leaving early the next morning for Wisconsin, a bit of irony that seemed far too out of place given that I was locked up in a detox facility. I thought when I heard that, that if I would have only bitten the bullet and driven to Wisconsin the night I got there, maybe none of this would have happened at all. Maybe if I asked them nicely if they'd bring me back something to drink ...

When I heard about the little glitch in the plan to have me discharged in the morning, I blew up at Laurisa again.

"What do you mean, you're leaving in the morning? You have to get me out of here!"

She smiled that smug smile of hers and I half-expected her to start singing to me.

"Arnie and I are going to Wisconsin in the morning. It's a trip we've planned and we're going."

I looked at her, my eyes losing focus because of the sudden rage flowing through me. I had to blink hard to see her and took a couple of deep, unsteady breaths not so much to calm down as to simply be able to get the words out. "You can't just bring me here and leave me. You've got to get me out of here."

There was a moment of silence that was long enough to give the nurse enough time to force herself into the conversation.

"I'm sorry, but there isn't a guarantee that you'll be released tomorrow. You're from out of state; we simply can't let you go. There are procedures—"

I didn't let her finish, my eyes still focused, somewhat, on my sister. "You have to get me out of here. This whole thing was your idea. You can't just leave me here. You have to get me out."

She looked at me and I could tell that what she wanted to say was, *We don't have to do a thing for you. You're right where you belong and you'll stay here as long as you need to.* But all she did was smile and turn back to the nurse, no doubt telling her that if I gave her any trouble, all she had to do was sing.

I was suddenly scared, the fear overtaking the anger. I was in real trouble. For all the years I drank, consequences existed, even if only in the deep recesses of my clouded brain. I think I had always believed that someday, if I wasn't careful, something horrible like this might happen, but I also think I had believed more that it couldn't possibly happen. I realized now that I was surrounded by my consequences and felt that there were a million more of them lining up all the way back to Cedar Rapids that were going to have their way with me once I got out of this place. Suddenly, I wondered if staying there forever wasn't such a bad idea after all.

Mark and Arnie came back, the duffel now as devoid of vodka as was my foreseeable future, and the four of them all congregated around the nurse's station while I paced the room and looked closer at where the addict had brought me. The Formica table tops all had burns in them from the countless cigarettes that had been smoked, and the tile floor was dirty and looked to be faded a dull yellow. There was a television hanging on a wall, an old black and white movie playing, the sound being drowned out by strange and distant noises coming from somewhere down one of the darkened hallways. Screams. Somewhere in the dark, a man was screaming. It was frightening yet there was an odd comfort about it; I think somewhere inside I felt good knowing it was going to be okay if I screamed in the darkness of what was going to be a long night.

I was too angry to say anything when the four of them turned from their conference and made their way to the door. I waited for someone to say something but no one did, and if someone did, I didn't hear it. I think Laurisa's lips were moving but all I heard was the screaming from down the hall and remember wondering if it might not be the addict who was screaming from somewhere deep inside my mind. I didn't hear a word she said as they all turned while the nurse lumbered out from behind the station and made her way to the door to unlock it and let them out.

Mark turned before he walked out, sadness painting his face, his eyes wet as they met mine. I waited for him to tell me he was sorry and then realized that he didn't have to tell me. I knew he was sorry, sorry that the addict had run me into this wall and sorry that I hadn't been able to do anything about it. It was as if he knew something I didn't know yet, but his eyes spoke only of the sadness he felt.

He turned and walked out the door and they were gone. The doors were locked behind them, the nurse lumbered back to her station, and I was alone. I had never felt more alone in my entire life.

CHAPTER 17

The Visitor

THE NURSE PICKED UP THE phone and punched a couple of numbers and then, as soon as she hung up, a skinny man came through one of the doors behind the station. He grabbed the clipboard out of the nurse's hand and looked at it for a minute, occasionally glancing at me and jotting something down on the chart. He put his pen in his pocket and then walked around the counter to where I was standing.

"Hi, my name's David. How are you feeling?"

He seemed non-threatening.

"Pretty upset," I said.

He smiled and said, "Yeah, most people are when they come in here. Other than that, are you feeling all right? Any withdrawal symptoms yet?"

I thought immediately of the thirtieth and the voice that kept calling my name, the faces that kept looking at me, the police, the fear.

"Uh, no, I think I'm okay. Why do you ask?"

"Oh, we just want to make sure you're as comfortable as you can be in here. Acupuncture's available to help you through withdrawal if you need it. We don't have any meds here so if you need some help, that's what we have for you."

I shook my head. I'd need a lot more to drink before I let someone stick a bunch of needles in me, and the prospects of getting a
drink in this place seemed pretty remote. "No, I'm fine for now;
I mostly just need to get some sleep." I realized how tired I was.
Anger tends to take a lot out of a person.

"Yeah, well, okay, why don't you grab your bag for me. I need
to take a look through it if that's okay."

I handed it to him and he rifled through it; he even opened my
overnight kit and took out my razor and aftershave. They were
pretty serious about all of this. He set my things on the counter
behind him and then handed the bag back to me.

"Great; why don't you follow me and I'll show you where you
can try to get some sleep."

I followed him out of the cafeteria and through one of the two
heavy doors that led down a dimly lit hallway. The smell hit me almost
immediately. Vomit and beer. The sounds followed. Loud snoring and,
occasionally, voices crying quietly in the darkness. In the distance, from
somewhere down the other hallway, I heard the same scream I had
heard when I was in the cafeteria. This wasn't a pleasant place. I felt like
I'd been put in a prison and my sister had walked out with the key.

David stopped at the door of a room that reeked of warm, stale
beer. I peered in through the darkness and could make out six cots,
five of them filled with men I imagined to be exactly like Otis
Campbell from Mayberry. They all looked big and bald and they
were all sleeping and snoring and had the worst breath I had ever
smelled. I felt my stomach lurch slightly as I looked around the
room and then looked at David.

"This is where I have to stay?"

He nodded but didn't say anything.

I looked back in the room and saw the empty cot in the far
corner. I was going to have to walk through all of them to get

back there, a thought that didn't appeal much to me. "Isn't there anyplace else I could go?" I asked. *Daytona Beach? Hungary? Anyplace would be better than this.*

"No, I'm sorry. This is yours. If things get too loud for you, you know, with the snoring and all, we have some ear plugs up front."

I thought back to all the nights in all the beds through all the years where all I had to do was reach under the bed and pull out a bottle and drink myself to sleep. The bed was comfortable, there was no noise, and there were even vague memories of someone lying next to me, but all of that was gone. Now all there was before me was a time and a place I'd been afraid of in my mind but one that I never thought I'd see. One I never imagined in a million years but one that now made it feel like it would be a million years before I ever saw anything else again.

David patted me on the back and turned to walk away.

"Oh," he said over his shoulder as he shuffled down the hall. "The bathroom's the second door on the left toward the end of the hall. It's late so it's not as clean as it'll be in the morning but it should be all right. And don't forget the ear plugs if you need them."

I watched him make his way down the hall and through the heavy doors that led to the cafeteria, and then they closed behind him and all that was left was me and that wretched smell that wouldn't leave me alone. It was going to be a long night.

I made my way toward the bathroom, walking by three other rooms on the way. Normally, if I'm driving down the road, I'll look into the windows of the cars I pass. If I'm walking down the hall in a hospital, I'll look in all the rooms to see who's in there and see how sick they are. Not tonight. I kept my eyes fixed on the second door on the left toward the end of the hall, having absolutely no desire to see what nightmares might come crawling out of the darkened and foul-smelling rooms. I felt as if I were in hell. When I got to the bathroom, I knew that I was.

It was dirty in there. Not the kind of dirty you see in most houses where there are a couple of loose hairs on the carpet or a hint of a ring in the toilet bowl. This was dirty. This was someone-couldn't-make-it-to-the-toilet-in-time dirty. I could hardly walk in the place without stepping on . . . or in . . . something. I felt my stomach lurch again and for a moment thought I was going to be sick and then realized I may have been the only person in the place that hadn't been yet. I tiptoed to the row of sinks and turned on the hot water to wash my face, and as I waited for the water to get hot, I looked at myself in the mirror.

I looked like I was ninety years old. My skin was gray and the bags under my eyes looked like they were going to pull my face off. I had dry patches on my face where the skin was flaking and peeling, and when I stuck out my tongue, it looked yellow.

I closed my eyes and wondered what was happening to me. I wondered how I ended up in this place with all these sick people and how I was going to get out. I wondered how far I'd get if I could somehow manage to make a run for it. I had my bank card with me. I could clean out my . . . our . . . account and take a bus or a plane and just go and never come back. I didn't think anyone would miss me. I knew my roommates wouldn't, and my sister wasn't that concerned since she was going to Wisconsin and all.

I threw some hot water on my face and then grabbed some of the rough brown paper towels out of the dispenser and wiped myself off and looked back in the mirror. I still looked bad and decided that instead of making a run for it, what I really needed to do was sleep. I didn't think I'd have to be too sharp to deal with the losers in this place in the morning, but I knew I wanted to be rested enough so they'd know that I wasn't one of them.

I made my way back into my room and was again hit by the smell of failure that surrounded me. I tiptoed through the maze of cots that spread out before me, hopeful that no one would wake up and see me. The last thing I wanted to do was talk to anyone. I got to my cot and thought for a minute about taking off my shoes, but after being in the bathroom I decided that I didn't want to touch them. I lay down on the cot and knew immediately that I wasn't going to go to sleep. It wasn't the discomfort of the cot that was only about a foot too short, nor was it the snoring or the stench that hung like the summer haze over a garbage dump. What was going to keep me from sleeping was the realization that the addict had taken complete control over my life and maybe, despite all my public and private rantings to the contrary, he and I were the same person.

I didn't stay in the room long before I knew I had to get out. A feeling of panic was beginning to press itself upon me and I knew that I needed to get out of the darkness that, along with the stench, was beginning to suffocate me. I got up and tiptoed back through the drunks scattered about the room and headed down the hallway toward the heavy doors that led to the cafeteria. As I pushed through them, I saw that, aside from the overweight nurse who was reading a newspaper at her station, there was no one else in the room. She didn't even look up when I walked in nor did she acknowledge my presence when I made my way to the big coffee maker that sat on one of the long tables on the far wall. As I walked by the television, I noticed that the movie was over and there was a preacher evangelizing to a large congregation; the only word I heard was *salvation*. I smiled and thought, *Yeah, right.*

I filled a Styrofoam cup with coffee and went to a table and sat down in one of the metal chairs with the vinyl seats, the nurse never looking up at me from her paper. I sat at the table and sipped my coffee; it was bitter and lukewarm and I felt myself longing for the comfort of a familiar pull from a bottle of Gilbey's. I knew that if I ever got out of this place, I was going to drink and never stop again. Anger and shame and frustration and fear were battling deep inside me, each emotion crashing over my soul like a wave and then rushing out for something else to wash over me. I was as miserable as I had ever been in my life. I closed my eyes and tried to picture myself sitting in my car after work, driving down the interstate, jazz on my stereo, vodka in my coffee cup, life as good as it gets, and I wasn't even aware that I wasn't alone at the table anymore. My eyes had been closed so I hadn't seen him; the jazz was running through my head so I hadn't heard him; but when I opened my eyes, he was there.

I was surprised to see him, but more than that, I was frightened. His hair was matted and caked with mud and a long gash cut its way from his left eyebrow, down his cheek, and ended just above his jaw line. It was deep but he hadn't had any stitches. He looked as if he was suffering. He was trying to roll a cigarette with the tobacco he had gotten from the large bin that sat on the counter at the nurse's station. Even if he succeeded in getting the cigarette rolled, and his shaking hands indicated that it would be difficult at best, he would have to leave the table where we sat to go back to the counter to use the lighter. He was determined though, and eventually he produced what looked like a poorly rolled joint and was excited at his accomplishment.

I tried not to look at him as he got up to go to the counter to use the lighter and I found myself hoping he would find somewhere else to sit. As I looked around the room, I realized that probably wasn't going to happen. Aside from the duty nurse who was now also smoking at the counter, completely oblivious to the man standing before her lighting his cigarette, we were the only ones in the room.

I turned and looked at the large clock that hung above the television and noticed it was almost two o'clock; the second hand appeared not to be moving. I had tried not to look at the clock at all, but looking at it now, I couldn't help but notice it teasing me with its inactivity. It was taking its own time passing time.

I again saw the preacher and thought for a moment that he looked familiar but I couldn't figure out who he was. I know that I found myself staring at him, but my mind was miles away from being able to grasp what I was hearing. I was surrounded by the reality of my failure and found myself wishing there was a way to get up and run into the darkness that enveloped the world outside the locked doors beyond where the Bic, too, found itself chained, unable to move.

I found myself thinking of death, wondering what it would be like. I thought of heaven and hell and thought that hell for me would be small spaces and feelings of suffocation. Heaven, it seemed, was far beyond my grasp. It was the longest night of my life.

Out of the corner of my eye, I saw him come back to the table. There were other tables in the room, but I was the only other person that was up. I was hoping for some kind of distraction, but the volume on the television was turned down, almost too quiet to hear, and the snoring and screaming that was coming from down the hall nearly drowned out what little sound there was.

He sat down and I finally allowed myself to look at him and saw that he was staring back at me, his eyes red, a crooked smile on his face. He was inhaling deeply on the limp cigarette and smoke encircled his head. His hands had stopped shaking. I tried to look away, but he held my gaze and I found myself unable to take my eyes off of him. He sat silently for a moment, the ash from the end of his cigarette growing, drooping toward the black plastic ashtray that sat before him. The brown scars on the table were testament to the thousands of times that no one had really cared if the ash trays were there or not, but the man across from me made a point of carefully tapping the ashes into the tray.

He took another deep drag and inhaled slowly, his eyes closing briefly and that same slight smile creasing his dirty face. I thought about getting up and leaving while his eyes were closed but didn't know where I'd go. I couldn't go back to my room and I certainly wasn't going to go hang out in the bathroom. There was no place to hide, no one else to talk to. I again thought of small spaces and suffocation and thought for a moment that maybe I was already in hell. Maybe death had come to me and I didn't even know it. I felt tired, but there was nowhere to go. Home seemed as far away as heaven and I felt that I would never see either of them.

He opened his eyes and I tried to look away before he saw that I was staring but I was too late.

"Nasty, isn't it?" he asked, slowly running his finger along the length of the gash on the side of his face.

I didn't want to be drawn into a conversation and sat silently for a moment, wondering if he knew that he was in hell. I wondered if he cared.

Finally I knew I needed to say something. "What happened?"

That seemed reasonable but it sounded strange to say it. I don't think I recognized my voice. It sounded like the voice of a man who was afraid of what was happening even if he didn't know what it was.

He smiled. "I'm not sure," he said, shaking his head. "The last thing I remember is that the cops were chasing me and I was in a car . . . someone else's car." He shook his head and closed his eyes again, chasing the fragments of the memory that were tumbling through his mind. He opened his eyes. "I think it was stolen. Yeah, yeah, I remember. It was stolen."

I was suddenly hot and was finding it hard to breathe through the smoke from his limp cigarette. I coughed, but he ignored it.

"Yeah, it was stolen. And . . ." He was reaching now, ". . . and I remember that I crashed the car into a tree, a big tree. I swerved to miss a car that was parked on the side of the street and I hit this big tree."

He smiled slightly and bowed his head and was silent, and I became aware of the voice on the television but still couldn't understand what it was saying.

I wanted to get away from him. I found myself wishing that I could find a tree to run into just to get away from him.

Suddenly, the smile was gone from his dirty face. He had found something up there that had been running loose and catching it didn't seem to be a good thing for him.

He slowly raised his eyes and looked back at me, shaking his dirty head. "I'm going to jail when I get out of here tomorrow. I'm going to jail. My time's up." He looked down and laid what was left of his cigarette on the top of the table and watched it a moment before slowly looking back at me. "My time's up," he said again, deliberately this time as if to make sure it registered with both of us.

I looked at him and shook my head. The screaming from the rooms down the long hallway had nearly stopped and I realized that maybe it was just the voices in my head that had been making the noise.

"You're sick, man," I said but thought I had only said it to myself.

He looked hard at me and leaned in closer, the smoke from his cigarette still encircling his head. "We're all sick, brother, and we all need to be saved," he said with intensity in his eyes that hadn't been there before. "We're all sick. . . ."

I sat there and watched him and shook my head. I couldn't help but think that he was a loser and I couldn't believe that I was in a place like this with a lowlife scum like him. I looked back at the table and watched what was left of his cigarette slowly begin to burn into the tabletop, creating another brown scar, and I began to become aware of a thought that was slowly forming in my mind. It seemed odd, out of place almost.

"*My time's up*," he had said. He was a lowlife and he was here and he said it.

As I watched the Formica top begin to melt and the scar begin to form, it all slowly began to fall into place in my mind. My time was up too. I was a lowlife and I was there, just like him. The scar that was forming on the tabletop was like the rest of them that had been there from who knows how many nights like this one. Nights where people like me who knew that they didn't belong there were suddenly hit alongside the head with the reality that they were there with the rest of the lowlifes because in this place, no one is any better than anyone else. All the brown scars on the table looked the same. Everything and everyone was all the same in this place. You aren't hauled into a detox center somewhere in the suburbs of Minneapolis screaming at the people who love you most and are sick of your lies and deceit because all is well in your world. There, in the midst of the vomit and the screams and the man who had no idea why he was running, my reality came crashing down on me. I was an alcoholic. I wasn't who I thought I was when I had kept telling myself that I could stop anytime I wanted. I couldn't stop. And now, my time was up too.

I bowed my head into my hands for maybe two or three seconds, no more, and then slowly raised it again to look at him.

He was gone.

I looked around the room and didn't see him anywhere and hadn't heard him walk away. I looked over at the duty nurse at the counter.

"Hey," I said once, and then again, a little louder. "Hey! Where'd that guy go who was just here?"

She slowly raised her tired face toward me, irritation washing over her. "Where?" she asked.

"Here," I said, spreading my arms out in front of me.

She shook her head and looked back down at her paper. "There hasn't been anyone in here but you and me. Why don't you go on back to your room and get some sleep."

I looked at her for a long time waiting for her to laugh and waiting for the man with the gash on his face to jump up from behind one of the couches. Neither happened. I looked around the room again and waited for David to come out from behind one of the pillars, dressed up like the man at the table, acupuncture needles ready to take me away from the odyssey in which I found myself. Instead, my mind was drawn to the voice that was coming from the television. I looked up and felt myself being drawn out of my chair and I walked slowly to where the TV was hanging from the wall. I stared hard and saw the preacher looking right at me with the same intensity I had seen in those eyes that two minutes earlier had been sitting across the table from me. He stared at me and I couldn't look away. The scar on his left cheek had frozen me. There was a fog around his head as he leaned closer to the camera and spoke to me because there wasn't anyone else in the room to hear him.

"We're all sick, brother, and we all need to be saved. . . ."

I sat, overwhelmed at the realization of what had just happened, and felt the tears begin to make their way down my cheeks, trickling at first, then streaming as I convulsed in sobs. God's Spirit had been there with me. My prayers had been answered. Not how I had hoped, but He had answered them nonetheless.

It was a Friday morning, a little after two o'clock, February 23, 1996. With the reality of the cigarette burning into the tabletop, I finally realized that I had scarred enough lives with my drinking. It was time to stop. It was time to finally admit to that notion that leaps out at all of us from the fifty-ninth page of that grand Blue Book:

> *We admitted we were powerless over alcohol and that our lives had become unmanageable.*

I don't know how a person could claim he was managing anything in his world while sitting in detox, his life and career in ruins, so I gave up. I knew, finally and thankfully, that my time was up. I was sick. I needed to be saved.

I had finally surrendered. He had saved me.

Part III

The Faith

Faith can move mountains, but don't be surprised if God hands you a shovel.

—U NKNOWN

CHAPTER 18

"I'm Done"

I DIDN'T MOVE THE REST of the night. I shut everything and everyone out of my mind, the nurse, David, even the preacher, and simply sat at the table by the television and waited for morning, replaying in my mind what had happened. I wanted to see everyone that would come in for breakfast, hoping in a strange way that I would see the man with the dirty, matted hair and the long, bloody gash on his left cheek. I wanted to see him, to know that he really had been there with me. If he wasn't there, then I knew that, like what had happened to me before, I had imagined the face and the voice, even if the fear had been real. Either that, or it really had been Him. I didn't think I had imagined Him; I didn't think it was the same kind of hallucination that I had experienced before. I was drunk when I had come in; I had never hallucinated when I was drunk, only when I hadn't had anything to drink. The fact that I had blown over the limit confirmed how drunk I was. I couldn't shake the feeling that something remarkable had happened, but if it had, I was having a terrible time understanding why. I figured I was the last person to deserve a visit like that.

At six thirty, men started wandering . . . staggering . . . into the cafeteria. Most looked at me as they walked past; some even nodded and smiled before heading to the coffee pot. I watched them all, looking for the long hair and bloodied cheek, even looking for someone who might appear as if he had washed his hair and cleaned up a bit from the night before, but I couldn't imagine anyone risking a trip into the bathroom to try to get clean. By seven, sixteen other men were in the room, standing and smoking or sitting at the tables sipping coffee. There was quiet conversation among a few groups of two or three men, but mostly there was silence that seemed to be mixing with the shame of the realization that we were all in a place that we had never expected to be. He was the only one who wasn't there.

I glanced to the counter where the duty nurse had been and saw David with his coat on, getting ready to leave. I got up from the table and made my way over to where he stood. He smiled at me when he saw me coming.

"How you doing today? It doesn't look like you got much sleep last night. Ear plugs didn't work out for you?"

I shook my head.

"No, I don't think I slept at all. Hey," I said as I turned to the group of men milling in the room, "is that everyone? I mean, is everyone in here that was in this place last night?"

"Why?"

"Just curious." I thought for a minute about telling him what had happened but I didn't want him to think I was crazier than he probably already thought I was.

He looked at me and then turned around and reached behind the counter and pulled out a clipboard.

"I can't tell you who anyone is, you know."

I nodded at him as he ran his finger down what must have been a list of names and then watched as he looked up and counted everyone with a slight nod.

"Yep," he said as he put the clipboard back behind the counter. "Everyone's in here. Some are leaving this morning, most actually.

How about you? You know what's happening with you yet?"

I shook my head. He had no idea how little I knew about what was happening to me. "No, I don't."

"Well," he said as he turned and headed for the door, "Wayne, he's the director, he'll be in around seven thirty or so and I'm sure he'll be able to tell you what's going on." He held out his hand. "Good luck to you," he said as he shook my hand. "I hope things go better for you."

"Thanks," I told him as he released his grip and turned to head for the door that led to the freedom beyond. "I have a feeling things will be different."

I watched him leave and then headed back to the table and glanced quickly up to the television. The news was on but all I heard was the voice that spoke to me the night before.

"...We all need to be saved."

: : : : : :

I don't know how it all got done, but Mark came at 11:30 to pick me up. Laurisa had talked to Mary and then to someone at Sedlacek, who in turn talked to someone in Bethel who agreed to let me go as long as a family member would pick me up. Mark was the only family I had up there given that Laurisa and Arnie were in Wisconsin, so he had agreed to come get me and drive me back to Cedar Rapids in my car and then fly back to Minneapolis that same afternoon. I don't know who was footing the bill for his flight but when I heard the story, I slowly began to realize how many people were working to get me out of there and back home where I belonged. There was no question that I was going back into Sedlacek, this time at the not-so-subtle urging of the Linn County judicial system, as Mary was going to have me committed, but the irony, to me at least, was the fact that I already knew in my heart that I was done drinking and nobody needed to force me into treatment. I knew I needed to be there, and after the night I'd spent, I realized that I wanted to be there.

Mark hugged me for a long time when he got to Bethel and we both cried. He cried no doubt for the guilt he was feeling about all that had transpired the previous evening, and I in gratitude for the same thing. There was a quiet voice coming from somewhere deep inside me that was trying to tell me that it all had happened exactly the way it was supposed to, but I think I was having a hard time making sense of it all. I was tired and more than a little scared. I knew what had happened to me but I had no idea what was going to happen once I got back to Cedar Rapids. All I knew was that for the first time since I had come to Minneapolis, I was ready to go home.

The trip home was long. I slept off and on and we stopped around one thirty or so for a sandwich and coffee and then talked most of the rest of the way. I didn't tell Mark what had happened to me; I was still struggling with how people would react and decided that maybe it would be best if no one ever knew. I had lied so much to so many people that I thought everyone would think this was another lie, more lunacy to make everyone think I had been miraculously saved from my addiction and that, because of it, I was never going to drink again. That's exactly what I believed had happened—knew in my heart *had* happened—but I didn't feel that my credibility was such that anyone else would believe it.

It was good to be with Mark. I could tell he felt terrible about what had happened and I kept telling him over and over that it was okay but I don't think he ever really believed me. Once, a couple of years later, when I had gone back to Minneapolis for the first time since that night, he and I went out to a restaurant and sat outside under an umbrella and I think he finally came to believe me when I told him how grateful I was that he had the courage to do what he chose to do that night. Without him, I wouldn't be here; it's as simple as that. When we finished our ice cream we stood and hugged right next to a table of two fairly elderly couples who were more than a bit uncomfortable to see two grown men hugging and crying in such a public setting. Mark and I both saw them and knew, without having to say a word to each other, what we needed to do next. We released from our embrace and then, his hand visibly in mine, we walked . . . skipped almost . . . past them and smiled at them as beautifully in love as we could. I think that day he finally came to understand that something remarkable had happened that night, even if he couldn't quite get his mind around it. He knew that I loved him, though, and that was the best part. Well, that and the looks on those four people who suddenly thought that life as they knew it had come to an end.

We got back to Cedar Rapids around five and went right to the house. I was more than a little afraid about what was going to happen, but when we pulled into the driveway, a sense of peace covered me and the fear vanished. Our neighbor, Kelly, the woman who had come over to our house on the thirtieth when I called the police, was there to watch the girls while Mary and I took Mark to the airport. Kelly gave me a big hug and it felt good but not as good as the hugs I got from Katie and Laura when I went inside. I cried when I held them because I knew that things were going to change and maybe some of the changes weren't going to be that good. I knew in my heart, though, that the biggest change was one they wouldn't understand yet but was a very good thing: their dad was back and he was indeed a different man. Mary was the only one who didn't hug me.

We drove Mark to the airport and Mary waited outside while I walked in with him. We said our goodbyes and hugged once more and then I turned and headed back out to the car while he made his way to the ticket counter. I got in the car, and Mary drove me to the hospital, the silence in the car louder than the snoring and screaming in the halls of Bethel. I thought for a minute about telling her what had happened but felt that it wouldn't make any difference right now. She was hurt, angry, and a million other things that I won't ever know. I didn't think I needed to add "disbelieving" to the list.

We got to the emergency room and I was immediately taken back to an exam room. I hadn't been in there for more than a minute when there was a knock at the door and the Linn County Sheriff and a deputy came in and served me with my committal papers. I think they were surprised that I wasn't angry. I had been around people who had been committed when I was in the first time and most of them were as mad as they had ever been in their lives, so I guess I could understand their surprise. I knew they were coming, but more importantly I knew I needed to be there, so it didn't matter to me that they were there to make it official.

A doctor examined me and, naturally, I had to blow, but this time there was no alcohol in my system. He debated about sending me up to the psyche ward because he knew that I wasn't drunk and, because of the medication they would put me on, there was little chance of any severe withdrawal, but he also knew that Sedlacek had their rules, so I ended up going back to the fifth floor for the night. I didn't mind; I was sick and knew that I needed to get better. *I am an alcoholic.* I remember telling that to the doctor when he was talking to me about having to go up to the fifth floor. It was the first time I'd said it and meant it and it was odd to hear it coming out of my mouth. It was cathartic in a way because I felt that by saying it, it would become easier to say to others and then it would also leave no doubt in my mind that it was true. *I am an alcoholic. I will always be an alcoholic.*

I got to go down to the fourth floor the next morning. I tried to call Mary but the line was busy so I tried calling Laurisa but her line was busy as well. I figured they were talking about what had happened and didn't know how I should feel about that but then realized it didn't matter how I felt because it wasn't going to change anything. I knew that whatever was going to happen was going to happen; the only thing I knew I needed to work on was getting better. The rest would take care of itself.

The counselors that were there on that Saturday weren't all that surprised to see me back at Sedlacek. I talked briefly with Andy Peterson, one of the few I hadn't worked with or talked to much when I was in the first time, and he told me he was going to work with me this time around. Andy's a good guy; he's older and you can tell by looking at him that he's been through some pretty rough times in his own life. He's got an eye disorder of some kind and I was never able to tell if he was looking at me or not, but I made a point of looking at him when I spoke to him so he would know, or maybe I would know, that things were going to be different this time around. I didn't tell him that because I didn't figure he'd believe me.

That's the funny thing about lying. A person does it so much and everyone knows he's doing it, but when he finally does decide that it's time to tell the truth, he won't because he knows that people won't believe him anyway. Sort of like Chicken Little with the sky falling and all that. I caught myself many times early in my recovery when I would be talking to people and about to make a point about something, saying, "Now, to be perfectly honest with you . . ." It was like I had to announce my impending honesty so it wouldn't be missed by anyone. I was also reminding myself that what I was about to say was the truth because for so many years, I wasn't telling the truth about much. I don't preface much of what I say now with that verbal prelude. Honestly, I don't.

I got moved into my own room on the fourth floor on Saturday. I thought it was nice to be alone but also figured they didn't want me around anyone else. There was a Sedlacek reunion going on downstairs in one of the big meeting rooms and I got to go down and eat a cookie and listen to Bill Martin talk to the fifty or so recovering graduates who were there. I thought it was strange at first to so publicly announce that you were an alcoholic but realized as I stood in the back corner and listened to Bill that these people viewed their disease no differently than a cancer survivor who is celebrating five years of being cancer free.

I've come to wonder through the years why there aren't more public displays of support for alcoholics and alcoholism awareness. There is the "Race for the Cure" and it's a wonderful gathering for awareness of breast cancer. I'm blessed every year to go to the "ARC March" to support those with cognitive disabilities. I've seen walk-a-thons for juvenile diabetes, telethons for muscular dystrophy, and dance-a-thons for multiple sclerosis. However, I have yet to see the "Drunken Dash" or the "Run Against Relapse" to support awareness and treatment of alcoholism. I guess the fifty people I saw that day, celebrating what I hoped would someday be something I could share—a healthy and sober lifestyle—was as good as it was going to get. Still, I've often wondered if the "Drunken Dash," were it ever to be run, would have a "staggered" start.

By the first of the week, I knew in my heart that things were going to be different, even if nobody else in the place believed it. A lot of the same people that were in when I was in the first time were still there, and not many of them seemed too surprised when they saw me walk into our self-esteem class on Monday afternoon. The group of in-patients were all new and I ended up having a room-mate on Monday, a guy named Phil, who was significantly messed up with cocaine and alcohol and a worse attitude than I'd had when

I was in the first time. He was only my roommate for Monday night; Tuesday and Wednesday night he stayed up in the lounge watching television and sleeping on the couch, and Thursday night he tried to strangle himself with his pajama pants. Even with my renewed sense of purpose to getting it right this time, it was still hard to see everyone else struggling as much as they were.

Phil ended up leaving the program and I didn't see him again until a couple of weeks before I graduated out of the center when someone wheeled him into our afternoon group session in a wheelchair. He was cut up pretty badly and had broken a lot of bones in a car accident that he caused under a variety of influences. I remember that he cried and told everyone he was done and was never drinking again. He was out of the program again less than a week later.

It's no wonder people doubted my sincerity; not many people left because the staff felt they were ready to be cut loose. Most left because they felt they would never be able to adjust to a life without that noose that they kept tightening around their own necks.

: : : : : :

The first day I was in, during afternoon group when I got to be "reintroduced" to everyone, Andy, who was running the group, made me tell everyone what had happened and why I was back and how things might be different for me this time around. I thought about telling everyone what had happened in Bethel but, like every other time the urge started to creep into my thinking, I chased it away. I was not only struggling with not having anyone believe me but also wondering if I could believe it myself. The whole experience was surreal to me, and I began questioning if it hadn't simply been my mind playing tricks on me. Mostly though, I struggled and continued to struggle for a long time with the idea of worthiness.

At the time, I knew nothing about how unworthy all of us are for something like that to happen and that it happened because of a kind of love that most of us can never quite get our heads around. I couldn't understand it and still carried the feeling that not many people were going to believe much of what I was going to tell them anyway, so I decided not to push things too much.

Instead, I looked at Andy and said, "Something happened to me; I can't quite explain it, but I realized when I was up there that I'd caused enough damage to everyone who cares about me and that I need to stop drinking before I lose anything else. I'm an alcoholic; I'm sick and I want to get well."

I remember that after I said that, no one said anything for a minute. I sat there, trying to look at Andy, which never got any easier through the years, and watched as he nodded his head and smiled at me. It was one of the best feelings I'd ever had in that place because, for the first time, two things happened: I told the truth, and someone believed me. A lot of people had believed a large number of lies in my life, but this time someone who had a lot of experience being around liars and could probably see through the lies even with bad eyes believed the first truth I had ever uttered in that place. It was a great feeling and one I wanted to hang on to for as long as I could until,

"Steve, I hear what you're telling us, but I don't know, man. It seems like what you've just said is the same line you told everyone the first time you were here. I don't believe a word of it."

It had come from Dan, an intern, a practice counselor who had just started near the end of my first stay and someone, because of his inexperience, I had blown off at the time because I knew back then he was no match for me. I suppose his point could have been interpreted as being valid; everything I'd said the first time in *had* been a lie and he had every right not to believe any of what I had to say.

Still, it irked me a bit that he responded the way he did. I mean, it's one thing to have someone say he doesn't believe you when you know you're lying, but, as I found out for the first time in my life, it's a different story when he doesn't believe you when you're telling the truth.

"You know what, Dan?" I said as I looked away from Andy. "I don't care what you think or what you choose to believe. I'm not in here to please you or make you like me or get you to believe everything I'm saying. I'm in here because I'm tired of drinking. I'm an alcoholic; I don't want to drink anymore. The first time I was in, all I wanted to do was to make people like you happy; I wanted to make you believe me and like me and think that I really had it all together. Now, I couldn't care less about what you think. I'm not in here for you, Dan. I'm not in here for Andy. I'm sure not in here for my job, and it may even be too late to be in here for my marriage. I'm in here for me. I'm in here because I'm sick and I want to get well. You don't believe me? I couldn't care less."

I looked hard at him, and for a minute you could have heard a pin drop in that room. I waited for him to say something but he didn't; he just looked at me for a minute and then lowered his eyes to the notebook in his lap. I looked at the top of his head and ended the conversation.

"I'm not drinking anymore. I'm done."

No one said anything. Andy waited for someone to say something but nobody said a word. I got up and walked out of the room. Class was over.

CHAPTER 19

One Thing Left to Lose

THE NEXT DAY, TUESDAY, I had just finished breakfast and was back in my room getting ready for my committal hearing. I was going to meet in one of the conference rooms with my court-appointed attorney, Andy, Bill Martin, Mary, her attorney, the doctor who checked me in on Friday, and the judge who would ultimately decide how long I was going to be in Sedlacek. Andy had told me that there was a possibility that, because I had been kicked out once already, the judge could send me to another facility but he didn't think that was very likely. It was strange to find myself hoping that I would be allowed to stay in the very place that, two weeks ago, I would have done anything to escape. I had finally come to feel comfortable over the weekend knowing that I was going to stay there. I was comfortable with the routine, the people, the system. I couldn't imagine being anywhere else. I never thought I'd feel that way but I knew I needed to be there.

I was in brushing my teeth when I heard a knock on my door and someone calling my name.

"Steve? It's me, Joe O'Connell. Can I come in?"

I swallowed my Crest.

Joe O'Connell was in my Thursday morning Rotary Club. This was going to be interesting.

I wiped my mouth and stepped out of the bathroom. "Joe. Wow, what a surprise. You draw the short end of the straw?"

He tried to smile but, being an attorney and all and knowing I didn't have any money, I'm sure it was a pretty hard thing to do.

"No, not at all. I saw your name and figured you might be more comfortable with someone you know. Hope that's okay."

"Yeah, sure," I said as I waved him in. "I just wasn't expecting to see you."

"Well, I have to admit I was a little surprised to see your name on the list too."

I felt like quizzing him about that to see if I really had fooled everyone at all those Thursday morning breakfast meetings when I was too drunk at seven to even cut my eggs but thought I should probably let it pass.

"So," he said as he came in and put his briefcase down on my bed. "Have they told you anything about what's going to happen at the hearing?"

"Andy's told me a little but not much. He said that there's a chance the judge could send me somewhere else but I'm hoping that's not going to happen."

Joe smiled that smile that you don't like to see on a lawyer. The smile that looks like he's got more than his arm up his sleeve. "Actually," he began, "I think there's a pretty good chance I can get you out of here and not have to go through any of this."

I looked at him, not quite certain as to what he was saying. "What do you mean? I don't think I understand."

"Well," he began slowly as if he knew he was talking to someone who had been systematically destroying large portions of his brain over the past few years. "I think that since there really isn't a good 'legal' definition of alcoholism, there's a good chance we can argue that without that definition in place, the court has no legal right to force you to stay. It's been done before."

He looked at me and waited for my response. I think he knew in his heart that he had told me exactly what I wanted to hear. I was the death row inmate on my way to my hanging and he was the governor offering me a chance for clemency. I could walk away; he was trying to make me believe that he could make it happen.

There was a time, not all that long ago, when I would have taken him up on his offer and been indebted to him forever, but when I heard him, I heard an even more powerful voice in my head, one that was beginning to sound familiar to me even if I had only heard it, audibly at least, five nights before. It spoke as clearly to me then as it did the first time I heard it and as clearly as I've heard it in my mind the thousands of times I've heard it since.

. . . We all need to be saved.

There was no doubt what I needed to say. No question that it was going to be the right thing to say.

"Joe, I appreciate the offer, but all I need from you is to make sure they keep me here. I need to be here. I'm an alcoholic. A loophole isn't going to change that. All you need to do is to make sure they don't send me anywhere else. Will you do that for me?"

I could tell he wasn't happy about it but he agreed. As it turned out, I didn't even need him at the meeting because everybody was in agreement that I needed to stay at Sedlacek, and the court mandated that I stay, first as an inpatient and then in the intensive outpatient program I had failed at so miserably the first time. It was a pretty uneventful meeting but a couple things stuck out in my mind.

The first was that the "testimony" Mary gave through her attorney, a rehashing of the events that led to me being put in Bethel, stated that I was intoxicated when I got to Mark's. I think if I had been intoxicated, none of this would have happened and, as I've looked back on the episode from the spiritual angle God wanted me to eventually see it from, it was this very reason that I kept driving by the liquor stores on the way up.

The second thing that stuck in my mind is what happened after the meeting was over, after it was determined that I would in fact remain hospitalized until the staff deemed me "ready" to be discharged and then in the IOP until . . . well, until whenever. This second thing shouldn't have surprised me really. It seemed like it should be the next logical event that was going to take place in my life, but it still caught me off guard.

Mary came to me after all the decisions had been made and everyone, except Joe, of course, agreed to what the judge dictated. She asked me to step out into the hall, alone, with her. I leaned against the wall and looked at her; I knew what was coming but it still hurt to hear it. It's one of those things that you can spend a million years preparing to hear, but when you hear it, it takes all the wind out of you.

"I've contacted an attorney; I'm going to file for divorce."

I glanced over to the door where the meeting had been and saw Andy come out of the room. He saw us, or at least I think he did, and he stopped as I turned back to look at Mary.

"Is this final?"

I knew it was final, kind of like I knew it was final when I got fired, but I think you're expected to say something even if it's asking for clarification.

"I can't do this anymore, Steve. We . . . the girls and I . . . need to get on with our lives. I just can't do this anymore."

I think I wanted her to cry or something but I'm certain that there weren't too many tears left. I know it had been a hard thing for her to decide to do this; telling me might have been the easiest part of the process.

I didn't say anything as she turned and walked down the hall, away from the door where Andy stood. He hadn't heard what she had told me but his years of experience told him what had happened. He came to me and put his arm around my shoulder.

"Let's go into my office for a minute, okay?"

I didn't say anything and let him walk me down the hall and into his office. He closed the door behind me and I sat down in the chair across from his desk. It then hit me what was happening. The feeling I'd had when I hugged Katie and Laura when I got back from Minneapolis came back and I knew that things would in fact never be the same again. I broke down; the tough guy who would never let anyone see what was going on inside was exposed as the broken man I had become. I was angry. I somehow felt cheated, like I had made the huge admission that everyone had waited for, confessed to my inability to control my drinking, vowed in my heart to change, and somehow had expected that because of that, everyone would jump up and down and say, "Yes, good for you. All is forgiven. Let's get on with our lives now."

Maybe I had even expected the old boys from Millhiser to walk in and give me my job back, with a nice raise to boot, but there are no such rewards with admissions of this type. All we're really doing is admitting to God that we need His help to do this and will do whatever He asks us to do no matter how hard it may be. He had told Mary what she needed to do and she did it. Still, that didn't make things any easier for me.

Andy sat there for a few minutes until I had composed myself as best I could and then he spoke. "You're not really surprised by this, are you? You had to think that this might be coming."

I wiped my eyes and tried to look at him. "I guess not; I think I was hoping it wouldn't happen, but why now? I mean, the timing is perfect, don't you think? I sit in there and . . . and then this.

Why now? That's what I don't get. Why now? Wasn't that enough for one day? Why did she have to do this now?"

I felt the tears come again as I thought back to her words.

"I just can't do this anymore."

What made her think *I* could do this? Why was she leaving me now, right when I thought I needed her the most?

Andy reached out and put his hand on my shoulder. "Steve, you've hit rock bottom. That's where most people need to find themselves before they're willing to admit that alcohol has become something more than they can handle on their own anymore. Mary's going to be fine; your daughters are going to be fine. They're going to start focusing on their lives and doing what they need to do to get better. Now is the perfect time for you to do the same thing. Now is the time for you to be selfish and think of getting better if for no other reason than now you're able to do it for you. You're not doing it for anything or anyone but you."

I looked up at him and, as much as it seemed to be my nature to disagree with anything anyone told me in that place, I knew he was right. I was in here to stay for a while; even if I got out, I didn't have anyplace to go. I thought back to what had happened in Bethel and thought of how sincere I was to quit and knew that the only way I was going to be able to do it was to not have anything else standing in my way. I had lost my job and now I had lost my family. I thought back to what I had told Dan in our group about being in here for me and realized that's probably the only way anyone ever made it out of this place the way he was supposed to. I had been selfish all my life, doing whatever I wanted without regard to anyone else's feelings. There was no one left to hurt; I was the only one left and I only had one more thing to lose. I didn't feel that I was ready to lose it.

I didn't say anything to Andy but he knew that I was ready to do this. I was ready to try to make a go of life in a sober world. I felt that I was all alone, except for Andy, and I had no idea how I was going to do it. But I kept thinking back to that man and that voice and that feeling that something wonderful had happened to me in Bethel and thought that maybe I wasn't going to be alone after all.

We all need to be saved.

CHAPTER 20

Starting New

TREATMENT WAS DIFFERENT THE SECOND time in. The food was the same, some of the people were the same, even the video of the woman with no arms was the same. But as much as nothing had changed, everything had changed.

The biggest change to me was the feeling I couldn't shake that the counselors sensed that things were different for me. Andy went where Dave Robertson tried to go my first time in, but I was more willing to hold the door open for Andy. Part of it was the fact that Mary wasn't there for any of the sessions and there was obviously nothing to hide anymore. I found myself talking freely about my past: the lies, the infidelity, the fears, the fact that I had become totally dependent upon alcohol in every aspect of my life. Nothing stayed inside except for the episode in Bethel. I was still trying to come to grips with the concept of worthiness; I think it's hard for anyone court-ordered into treatment, fired from his job, and divorced by his wife to feel worthy about anything.

I made friends with a group of people in treatment the second time through. There was David, the son of a successful car salesman in town who had a little bit of me in him . . . the me the first time through that thought he could blow through treatment and get back to life as he knew it. He was a decent guy and I'd like to

think he learned something from me even though I never preached
to him about what he should or shouldn't be doing. I wasn't one
to preach to anyone since my failures were held up for all to see.
There are no secrets in treatment unless they're the ones you're
trying to hide, and everyone seems to find out about all of them
anyway. My first time through was always being brought up when
there would be lulls in the conversations in group.

"Uh, Steve," Andy or Dave or Bill or whatever counselor on duty
would ask, "how did you see yourself accepting treatment the first
time you were in?"

I would always get asked something like that whenever silence
filled the room and everyone was looking at his feet.

"I guess I was a lot like David here," I'd say. "I never recognized
the need and had to go out on my own and push the wall a little
farther back so I could pick up a lot more speed before I hit it."

David would always look at me and roll his eyes, and Andy or
Dave or Bill would smile at me and then look at David, who would
look back at his feet, but I knew he was thinking about what I said.
I know for a fact that David did eventually hit the wall again. One
day, after we were out and involved in the IOP, he was gone. I only
know that he relapsed; I don't have any idea where he ended up.

Theresa was a woman of about fifty whose husband had "vol-
unteered" her into the program but she hadn't been hospitalized,
and I got to know her through the IOP in the afternoon and evening. She was pretty flighty and I think part of that was because it
seemed like she had been drinking a long time. She never denied
her abuse; she mostly just denied that it was a problem for her. She
was there for her husband, an older guy you could tell was tired
of dealing with her, but he was never able to get away from work
much to be at anything other than the after dinner group. I never
got to know him very well. Even after we all got out, Theresa
had everyone over to her house for a little reunion and he wasn't

there. A week after the party, Theresa got drunk and fell down the basement stairs and ended up in the hospital and then, after she got out, I never heard from her again.

Matt was a younger guy, probably around twenty-five. He was married and had a couple of young sons. He was a good guy and was struggling with cocaine but I could tell that he really wanted to get things right, mostly, it seemed, for his boys. Matt always wore a seed corn cap and flannel shirt and his cheek was always full of some kind of chewing tobacco because he was trying to quit smoking. He'd sit in group and spit into a Styrofoam cup and I always admired him for trying to overcome two addictions at once, but, unfortunately, I think the only one he got a handle on was the smoking. He was sent home one night because he was high when he came in. He made a point of coming over to me before he left and giving me his Zippo lighter with the serenity prayer on it. It's the only tangible memory I kept from my times in Sedlacek and I still have it on my desk. I can't look at it without seeing Matt's face, the cheek full and the greasy hair tucked under the DeKalb hat, the eyes determined but too tired to really believe he was going to make it.

Janet was three years younger than I and I know this because she grew up across the street from me. I was sitting in self-esteem one of my first days in, sitting right up there in the front row because I felt that's where I needed to be, when I heard someone behind me.

"Steve? Are you Steve Sellers?"

I've never been very comfortable when someone says that to me. My first instinct has always been to say something like, "No, sorry, I get that a lot. Whoever that guy is, I sure do feel sorry for him looking so much like me."

What with my new-found honesty and all and especially since I was in treatment with whomever it was behind me who knew me, I thought it would be best to just go ahead and admit it. I turned around and saw an attractive woman with brown curly hair and a bright smile who said,

"It's me, Janet Gillman. I was Janet Miles when you knew me. I lived across the street from you in Newton."

It had been years since I'd seen her and she looked nothing like the snot-nosed little fifth or sixth grader she had been before her parents moved to the other side of town. It was odd seeing someone from that far into my past, but as time went on, it was fun having her around. She was in for alcohol abuse and told me how her family had intervened in an attempt to help her and had taken everything out of her house that had any alcohol in it at all. They took the cooking spray, the mouthwash, perfume, anything and everything that she would have been able to get into her system to satisfy her own addict. She still couldn't make it and they put her in the IOP and she ultimately couldn't make it in there either.

She got involved with another patient, a guy named Craig who had lived in Pittsburgh, and they both showed up in our group session one night and announced that they were in love. They were both drunk too but they didn't really have to announce *that* since it was a pretty hard thing to overlook. They told everyone that they were going to move to Pittsburgh when they were done with the program and Bill Sackett, the counselor that night, pretty much told them they didn't need to wait that long. Neither one of them ever came back.

Amanda was a nurse's aid at the University of Iowa Hospitals who was hooked on morphine. I suppose that was bad enough, but the fact that she would steal it from the hospital to appease her addict made things especially tough. She was in treatment because it was the only way she would ever be allowed to go back to work again. She became a good friend and seemed like she had enough support from her husband and motivation from her two little children to make a go of it. I think morphine might be a little harder to get your hands on than most anything else. I don't think you can just walk into a pharmacy and ask for some without something from a doctor and I'm thinking Amanda probably didn't have many doctors who were willing to prescribe anything for her. I'm not saying it was easy for her, because it was an addiction and no one has an easy time dealing with an addiction. Still, if I'm addicted to Parisian escargot and I have absolutely no way of getting to Paris, it's a little more realistic that I may have to learn to cope without them. Gilbey's was in every store in town; I couldn't escape it. Morphine was a little harder to come by for Amanda. I think the thing she was working hardest on in treatment was putting her marriage back together and trying to save her career. The sad part is, those were the same reasons I was in the first time and I didn't stand a chance. Amanda, though, was able to do it. Like the rest of the people I was in with, I lost track of her, but there's no reason to think she didn't make it.

One of my favorites was a guy named Loren. He was in his early sixties, and he was in because his wife thought he'd been drinking too much wine. There was no threat of divorce, and since he'd already retired, no pressure from anyone at work to quit. He was there because his wife thought he needed to have a better handle on how much wine he drank. She wasn't even after him to stop drinking wine; she just wanted him to learn how to better control how much he'd have. He and I talked a lot about alcoholism and we both agreed that he probably wasn't an alcoholic. He didn't intend to stop drinking wine when he finished the IOP; he was only going to drink more responsibly. I liked Loren because his was the philosophy I had secretly wanted to adopt my first time in but the difference was I didn't have anyone at the time that was willing to support me in that endeavor. I ended up going to Loren's house for dinner one night after he got out of the program and he told me everything was going fine. Out of respect to me, he didn't have any wine that night, but I couldn't help but notice that the iron wine rack sitting next to the china cabinet was full. I think Loren went into treatment because his wife asked him to, and if it made what had already seemed like a pretty good marriage even better, then my hat's off to Loren. Personally, I would have opted for a weekend retreat of some kind, but this seems to have worked for him.

My best friend, the guy I got closest to at least, was a young guy named Robbie. He was twenty-six with alcohol, pot, and cocaine issues. He was married and his wife and his parents had all encouraged him to go in. He was a happy-go-lucky guy, good-looking, fun to be around, and the kind of guy that was everyone's friend. We hit it off because he didn't want his marriage to end up like mine and I think he spent time with me to learn how not to let that happen. He was on the phone every night with his wife, and after most of the conversations he would be in tears. We would go find someplace quiet to hang out and I would try to help him through the night. The hardest night for him was the night he had to spend in jail to satisfy a judgment against him for a driving offense. He left Sedlacek in the afternoon acting like a kid going to a circus, but when he came back the next morning, he looked like he had been through the worst night of his life. You could tell that it had scared him but it didn't scare him enough. I went to Robbie's a few times after I got out and he still did coke, still smoked pot, and still slept with a gun under his bed because of too many drug deals gone bad. I got to know his parents and tried working with them in helping him any way I could, but eventually he disappeared as well. He was a good kid; I still think about him a lot and pray that things have somehow gotten better for him.

We all hung out together in the afternoon and evening sessions. We were like a high school clique that would sit by ourselves and make fun of everyone else mostly to ease the tension we were all feeling, except for Loren of course. We all shared things with each other that most of us weren't too willing to share in a group, but as time went on, we all were eventually able to encourage each other more and more to talk in the group sessions. We challenged each other and forced one another to be more honest about what we were feeling and what was going on. It was probably the most productive time any of us had had in quite a while in terms of actually getting some of the junk out that had been building up for all those years. The good feelings only lasted a couple of weeks as people slowly began to disappear from the program, but even when we all got together at Theresa's for our reunion, when Loren and Amanda and I got out of the IOP, it was still good to talk about what we had gone through and what most of us were willing to admit we were still going through.

Loren and I used to hang out together outside after dinner because he smoked a lot and, I have no idea why I did it, but one night I bummed a cigarette off of him and the next thing I knew, I was a smoker. I had smoked before, years ago and not very much, but all of a sudden I was smoking like there was no tomorrow. It was strange because smoking is what killed my dad and I had vowed never to smoke after losing him. Plus, I always used to make fun of the smokers the first time I was in. They would all dash to the "Smokers Room" on the fourth floor and suck down as much nicotine as they could during breaks, and it was the very reason that we all had to sit through those "How to Quit Smoking" films the first time I was in the hospital. Now all of a sudden, here I was, one of those same guys, taking on a new addiction while trying to overcome another. The only saving grace was that I got to use the lighter that Matt had given me. I don't think I was too serious about smoking because while Loren would stand there after dinner, sucking down his Marlboro Reds, I was there next to him puffing away on my Salem Lights, remembering that they were the same cigarettes my Aunt Betty used to smoke when I was a kid.

I moved through treatment at a pretty good clip. I think the counselors sensed that things had changed for me, and even though I still had issues to work through, trivial things like honesty and my history of shutting down and closing up when someone tried to get too close, things like that, they all seemed to think that even if I wasn't on the right track yet, I had at least bought a ticket for the train. I asked questions of the counselors during class and group sessions. I challenged people who I felt were a bit too much like me. I don't think I was trying to impress anyone or anything like that. I think I was mostly trying to identify myself in the people who were there. I was trying to see what I had been like. I wanted to understand where they were coming from to get a better handle on where in the world I thought I was coming from the first time I had been in.

Andy pointed out to me that part of the reason I was more open about things was that Mary wasn't there. I supposed he was right. There wasn't the feeling that I had to look over my shoulder to see who was there listening to me and making sure it was what I was supposed to be saying. There wasn't any pressure to have to lie to anyone about anything anymore.

I was genuinely sorry about the way I had behaved throughout most of my adult life and knew that if I was ever going to change, the groundwork had to be laid. Treatment can be a pretty good place to do that kind of work.

: : : : : :

The week went by much more quickly than the first week the first time I was in, and the main concern when they were getting ready to discharge me was where I was going to go that night. Sedlacek couldn't discharge anyone unless he had someplace lined up, or at least until everyone knew what options were available. Andy called me into his office the afternoon when I was supposed to get out.

"Well," he said as he settled into the cracked leather swivel chair, "are you ready to leave this place?"

I thought I was but was kind of curious as to what he thought. "Yeah," I said. "How about you? What do you think?"

Most of the time if you asked a counselor a question like that, he would lean back and pick up your file and pretend to be looking through it to see if there was anything in there that would jump out and make him change his mind. What he was really doing was trying to figure out how to answer a question like that. Most of the time they might not have felt that you were ready but had to let you go anyway because your insurance wasn't going to pay for you to stay any longer. With Andy, though, he didn't even hesitate. He didn't even bat an eye because that would have taken way too long.

"No question you're ready, but we're just concerned about *where* you're going to go."

I was kind of concerned about that too because I really didn't have much of an idea.

"So," he continued as he reached for another file on his desk, "I want to share some of this information with you." He opened the file and put on his glasses and then bent down really close to his desk so he could read what was in front of him. "The YMCA has rooms available. They're not very expensive and they have showers and you can get meals at the café down the street. It's . . ." He adjusted his glasses and bent down even more. ". . . it's twenty dollars a night for a maximum of five nights. You know where it's at, don't you?"

I'd been in the Y in Cedar Rapids a couple of times, and when I was in college, I had even stayed overnight in the Y in Mason City. The dorms were closed over the holidays but we still had basketball practice, so our coach made arrangements for the players who lived out of town to stay at the Y for nothing. Nothing was too much to spend at that place, staying with a couple of kids I played ball with and far too many "less than fortunate" men than I could even count.

"What else?" I asked. I shouldn't have been so picky given the last place I had stayed with a bunch of men. No Y would have been that bad, but still. . . .

"Well," said Andy, squinting at the file in front of him. "There's the Dodd Center; we can probably get you in there but it's a pretty rough environment. Clean, but they've got some pretty hard men in there from time to time. It doesn't cost anything though."

I barely had any money. I went from having quite a bit of money to having hardly any in just a few days and it hadn't really hit me yet that I was broke. Plus, I had no viable means of having more money anytime in the near future. Like the ex-con who holds up a store just to get back into prison, I was wondering what it would take to get me back into treatment. Oh yeah, I remembered. I didn't want any part of that.

"Is that it?" I asked.

Andy looked up at me. "Yeah, I'm sorry, but that's about it. Why don't you take a while and think about it and then let me know what you want to do. We can't let you out unless you've got someplace to go but we can't keep you here any longer because your insurance has run out. I'm sorry; there just aren't any more options."

It had been a while since I had read *Catch 22* in college, and back then I'd had a hard time understanding what it meant. It finally hit me.

I headed back to my room and, on my way, walked through the lounge where Robbie was sitting at a table writing a letter to his wife. He asked me to read it but I told him I wasn't up to it and then told him what Andy had said. I needed to go lie down for a while and think about what I was going to do but I promised him I would look at it later.

I went back to my room and lay down on what in two or three hours wasn't going to be my bed anymore and thought about why so many people failed, realizing that a lot of times it was because of things just like this. Here I was, struggling with the idea that I had been saved, seriously approaching treatment, and beginning to establish thought patterns that were supposed to help me take the first steps toward a meaningful recovery, and now, I was facing a night spent . . . where? I understood why people just got in their cars and drove away and went back to whatever it was that got them in trouble in the first place. It was the easy way out. It was the way I had always taken, the choice I had always made, and now, despite my good intentions and the miracle that suddenly seemed so far away, I found myself wondering if I was going to make it. I closed my eyes and searched out the face I had seen at Bethel, listened for the voice, and heard myself quietly asking for help. I realized I hadn't prayed since those nights I would lie drunk in bed beside Mary asking for any kind of help He would be willing to give me. I also realized that He had helped me; I was praying that He would do it again.

I ended up falling asleep and when I opened my eyes, Robbie was in my room, sitting on the chair by the small built-in desk. He had that same cocky smile on his face that he always had when he wasn't talking to his wife.

"What's up?" I asked.

Usually Robbie would joke about whatever it was he was going to tell you. Kind of like the night he went to jail. He had joked about it and even thought it was going to be an adventure, but whatever it was that had happened in there, he never told me about it. He wasn't going to joke about this; he came right out with it. "I took up a collection from everyone. I got almost fifty bucks. It's yours. Go get a room or something someplace. You don't need to stay over at Dodd. You deserve better than that."

He tossed a wad of bills and some coins on the bed and I looked at the money and then looked at him. I started to say something but he stopped me.

"Look, man, you've come too far to have to go spend a night where all you're going to be able to do is think about all the junk going on. Go get a room somewhere. Watch TV. Get something to eat. Get through the night and then work on getting through the day tomorrow. Go on. Take it. Go tell Andy you're ready to get out."

I sat on the bed for a minute or two, just looking at him, trying to think of why I shouldn't take the money, and then I realized that God had again answered my prayer. I was starting to get a little freaked out about all of this.

"Thanks, Robbie," I said as I got up and went to the chair. He stood up and I gave him a hug and I know we both started to cry. That's one of the many things about being in a place like Sedlacek: crying came easy and no one ever held it against you. Most of us had a lot piled up inside and it was nice to let go and let it out once in a while.

Two hours later, after saying my goodbyes and hugging more people than a pastor's wife at a Pentecostal church on Sunday, I was at the Red Roof Inn on 33rd Avenue on the southwest side of town. After I checked in, I went back out to my car and drove to the convenience store across the street because it was too cold to walk. I bought a two-liter bottle of Mountain Dew, a bag of nacho cheese Doritos, and a pack of Salem Lights. By the time the sun came up, everything was gone. I hadn't slept at all, the lights and the television both on all night, and every thirty minutes I went outside on the balcony to smoke a cigarette and look at my car and find myself being thankful that it was too cold and that I didn't have any more money with me. I realized that it would have been too easy to leave if I could have, and it hit me that staying sober was probably going to be the hardest thing I had ever tried to do in my entire life.

CHAPTER 21

"I'm an Alcoholic"

I REALIZED PRETTY QUICKLY THAT day that I didn't have any place to stay. There were those people who had so graciously opened their homes to me the week I had been asked to leave my house, but none of them appeared to be viable candidates, especially Mary's brother given the divorce thing and all. Most of my friends were in the process of divorcing me as well so none of them seemed worth the phone call. I could have gone to Mom's but I'm certain she was having enough trouble dealing with everything that was going on; plus, she was three hours away. There weren't many options so I took the only one that was there: I called Laurie and ended up staying with her.

Ours was an interesting relationship. She was everything I needed her to be when I was drinking but I was learning a very important lesson about *not* drinking even in the short period of time in which I had not been doing it. It takes a lot of energy and focus not to drink. The ease with which I had had a relationship with another woman when I was drinking had disappeared, my attention now being placed squarely on staying sober.

I stayed with Laurie because I didn't have any other place to stay; no one else would have me. I know she believed that we would work through all that was going on: the now very public "scandal" of our relationship, the even more potentially public fall from whatever professional pedestal on which the people at Millhiser had placed me when they first hired me, all sorts of things. I knew that it probably wasn't going to happen.

As I worked my way through the IOP classes and started paying attention to the same things that I hadn't listened to the first time through, I realized that some of those things wanted to stick to me like an uncomfortable covering of Post-it Notes, each a reminder that this trip was going to be about a lot more than not drinking. As I watched Janet and Craig get kicked out of treatment and drive drunkenly off to Pittsburgh, I remembered Bill Sackett talking about how important it is not to be involved in a new relationship for at least a year into recovery. It was the same thing I could hear Dave Robertson say when I was in the first time. The only thing I was focused on then was how to get out. So how to live once I got out . . . how they were encouraging us to live once we got out . . . was the furthest thing from my mind. Consequently, I didn't listen to it.

Another Post-it that started to stick was the one about "enabling." I sat in one of the evening group sessions, the one where everyone was there, spouses and parents mostly, and watched them all hang their heads when Bill Martin would talk about how they, with "unknowing willingness" as he called it, had enabled us by making excuses for us. He talked about how it hadn't really been encouraging us to drink but rather allowing us not to have to face the consequences of the drinking.

"Oh no, Mr. Smith, my husband can't come to work today. He's got the flu. I think he picked it up from our daughter who must have brought it home from her daycare. There's quite a bug going around there."

"I'm sorry, Mrs. Jones. My wife's been called out of town today to visit her sick aunt in Montezuma and won't be able to help with the choir practice tonight."

Laurie was, with the same "unknowing willingness," my greatest enabler. She accepted me, flawed as I was, and never held me accountable for my destructive actions. It was what I wanted and needed from her then. It was why I had sought her out in the first place. And it was the same reason that I knew a meaningful relationship wasn't ever going to amount to anything now. I had a feeling that I was going to need to devote all my time and energy into staying sober, not nurturing a relationship that had gotten started for all the wrong reasons in the first place. At some point, I needed to be held accountable for my actions; right now, I needed a place to stay.

My life settled into a routine. I would go to the IOP during the afternoon and evening and would spend the mornings trying to begin thinking about finding a job. I hadn't looked for a job since I had interviewed at Millhiser. My resume was . . . I didn't even know where it was, and I knew my list of references would need to be seriously updated. Bill Osborne and Steve King had indicated that they would put in a good word for me, but I had a feeling that as secret as I had hoped my downfall had been, there were more than just the three of us in the conference room that knew what had happened. Millhiser was a prestigious place to work; nobody up and left on his own accord, especially if he didn't have any other place lined up to work.

I knew that I was going to need some help finding work so I ended up calling the same recruiting firm that I had contacted before I went to work at Millhiser. I had worked with a woman named Cathy Lammers; when I called, Cathy passed me off to someone named Marilyn Jones. I couldn't help but think that Cathy had talked to Steve, since they were pretty good friends and knew what was going on. But it didn't matter much to me who I talked to; I needed to find work.

My first meeting with Marilyn was uncomfortable for me. It was one of the first times I had been out in public and met with someone not associated with alcohol abuse for a long time. I wore dress pants and a sweater because I thought the bulkiness would make me look heavier. I had grown a beard to hide my pale gray skin, but when I stopped in the men's room to check myself out before I went in to the meeting, I realized I still looked terrible. People really take a beating physically with alcohol. I was in terrible physical condition and hadn't even begun putting on all the weight I had lost. Plus, I was smoking, mostly to keep myself from drinking, and that wasn't doing me any good. I was a wreck. As much as I was committed to doing this, I think I would have killed someone at that moment for a drink. If nothing else, I needed it to calm me down and boost my confidence before I went in to meet with Marilyn. I wasn't used to not having confidence. I wasn't used to not drinking.

Four weeks later, I was still unemployed, still staying with Laurie, but still sober. None of these things was easy and two of them needed to change. I'd had a couple of interviews, cursory visits with a life insurance company and a farm implement dealer; neither appealed to me and I wasn't offered either job. I was starting to feel that I was going to end up doing something I didn't want to do before it was all over. The questions focused on why I left such a good job with nothing planned and no real income to tide me over. I struggled with how to answer them. I talked to Andy about it one afternoon during a break and he said I wasn't obligated to say anything. He said that while some potential employers would admire my honesty, they would also probably look at my history as not being very conducive to good team building on the job. I was starting to get nervous. I needed to find a job.

I also needed to get out of Laurie's house. She was good to me but I was not in the frame of mind to work on building a relationship, and that was hard for her given what we had been through before I had my breakdown. I think she continued to believe that we were going to become a couple but I knew I wasn't going to be able to do it. Even though I was committed to staying sober, there were days I didn't even know if I could do that.

I also started going to AA. There was a big building in town on First Avenue and 32nd Street called the Fellowship Club and I decided that I needed to go. Andy had been encouraging me to go so I picked a Sunday night meeting that ran from eight to nine. The first night I went I introduced myself to a couple of guys that sat on either side of me. I couldn't really see anyone else; the smoke was so thick in the place I kept waiting for the fire department to come. I sat and smoked with the rest of them, playing with my lighter to calm me down. It was strange being in there. Other than the reunion at Sedlacek, it was the first time I had ever been so public with my alcoholism. When it was my turn to speak, I took a deep breath and said it. It was the first time I had said it in a room full of strangers.

"Hi, I'm Steve and I'm an alcoholic."

"Hi, Steve."

I didn't say much that first night. I told them I was just there to listen, but it was a big deal for me even to do that. While others would talk, I kept thinking back to the night I bought the fifth and the package of poker chips and rode around until I went home to Mary, stumbling into the kitchen waving my chip and telling her I had surrendered. That night, when they handed me my white chip, I cried a little because this time I knew I really had. It was weird in a way because there wasn't anyone to share it with except for a room full of strangers who all came up to me after the meeting and hugged me and told me they would be there for me if I ever needed them. Even though I didn't know who any of them were, I knew that they were all telling me the truth.

CHAPTER 22

Lesson from a Spider

A COUPLE OF WEEKS LATER, I finally got a call from Marilyn telling me she might have something for me.

"I don't know if it's what you had in mind," she said as I sat on Laurie's porch smoking a Salem Light with another burning in the ash tray. "It's a small local company and they're looking to expand their business. When I told them you were getting divorced . . . I hope you don't mind that I mentioned that . . . it seemed appropriate when I heard of their expansion plans . . . they were very interested."

"What is it?" I asked, putting out one of the Salem Lights.

She hesitated. "Oh . . . it's a sales position. Inside sales mostly."

"It's not retail, is it?" I couldn't see myself selling shoes at the mall but was starting to feel that something like that may be all that was going to be available.

"Oh, no," she said, sounding somewhat relieved. Whatever it was, it was only slightly above brown pumps and spiked heels.

"Well . . ." I said.

"It's hearing aid sales," she said quickly, as if by doing so it would seem like she hadn't said it at all.

"It's what?" I asked, not because I hadn't heard her; it was more because I *had*.

"Oh, that's funny," she laughed nervously into the phone. "I'm guessing people in this line of work hear things like that all the time."

"Hearing aid sales?" I asked again. "Where?"

She cleared her throat. "Well, as I said, it's a small local company, and they're planning to expand to Davenport and I thought, with your experience, that you would be a good candidate. They're very eager to meet with you."

"What do you mean, very eager?"

"Well, the owner . . . partner actually . . . the one heading up the move to Davenport . . . his name is Mark Raske and I think he would like to meet you in my office tomorrow afternoon at two if that would work for you."

I took a long drag on my cigarette, closed my eyes, and shook my head. *Hearing aids.* "Yeah, sure," I said, blowing out the smoke. "I'll be there."

Mark was a decent guy; typical hearing aid salesman I guess. He talked fast and loud and only got quiet when he quizzed me about why I left Millhiser. It was the same old thing and by now I sounded so confident with my answer I almost believed it myself.

"Well, Mark, I left Millhiser because I felt I needed a new challenge." Staying sober was a big challenge so I didn't feel like I was too far off base by saying that. Andy had told me not to volunteer anything about my treatment but if anyone asked me, I should go ahead and tell them. Mark never asked. I got the feeling he was as desperate to hire someone as I was to find work. I had a second interview with the actual owner of the business the next week but I knew by then that I was going to be a hearing aid salesman. *I said I was going to be a hearing aid salesman!!*

There's nothing like hearing aid humor.

: : : : : :

I got the job and even though I couldn't believe I was going to sell hearing aids, I was glad to finally be working again. Livingstone Hearing Aid Service was owned by Don Livingstone, a quiet, unassuming man in his sixties. His son, Derrick, worked with him, and Mark Raske had come on board when he had been let go from his sales management position with a farm implement company. I wondered when I heard that if that was why I had interviewed with a farm implement company but never asked him about it.

The first couple weeks on the job were spent learning how to run the otoscope, a machine with a tiny camera on the end of a tapered tube that was stuck into someone's ear. The image was then displayed on a small television screen so the patient could see what was going on inside his ear canal. Since most of the people who came in for a hearing test were older, it was amazing the amount of hair, wax, car keys, and all sorts of other things you would see down there. It was no wonder people couldn't hear, with their ear canal stuffed full of an entire year's worth of *National Geographic*.

Most of the time, we'd pour this stuff called Debrox into the ear and it would foam up and whatever it was that was plugging the ear would break up and everything would be fine. When that didn't happen, that's when the real sales part would come into play. We would test their hearing to identify which frequencies were giving them the most trouble and then put headphones on them to simulate what "normal" hearing would be like. After that, it was simply a matter of convincing them that $3,400 was a pretty good deal for a pair of hearing aids. The only part about the job that I was going to like was that I got to wear a starched white lab coat just like a real doctor. I halfway expected Amanda to call me looking for some morphine.

Since I was working until five, I was allowed to miss the self-esteem class. Andy thought that would be okay since I had been through the class about six times. My self-esteem had improved but mostly that was due to the fact that I was working again. I would leave work at five, right after I changed my clothes in the back room of the shop, and head to the hospital to eat with Loren and whoever else was still in the program. Amanda was still there but usually left to go have dinner with her husband. Theresa was there early on but you could tell that something wasn't quite right with her. She was really struggling with a lot of things; most of the issues were with her husband and she cried a lot. Robbie was still there but would leave right after dinner to go use the phone. David, Matt, and Janet were there at first but one by one disappeared and never came back. Loren was the only one who would be there every night, and after dinner he and I would go stand outside and talk and see who could smoke more cigarettes before it was time to go to group.

After group, we all headed to the gym to play volleyball; I was much better this time around. I think most of that had to do with the fact that I'm six-and-a-half feet tall and the net was only about five-and-a-half feet off the ground, so I would just stand there and spike the ball whenever it came to me. Loren started calling me Chief, from that Indian guy in *One Flew Over the Cuckoo's Nest* and it was kind of funny in a way. If I hadn't been locked up on the psyche ward and legally committed to complete an alcohol abuse program, it might have been funnier. As it was, it hit a little too close to home, but since Loren and I were the only ones who knew who Chief was, I didn't worry too much about it.

The hardest part about my new job was the realization that I was going to have to move. While I was ready to move out of Laurie's house, I didn't know how ready I was to move out of town. I already felt like I was a million miles from my daughters; I didn't see them as much as I wanted, and when I did, Mary wouldn't let me take them anywhere. She wouldn't let them ride in the car with me and I guess I can't blame her for that. I can't even begin to count the number of times I had driven drunk and had them in the car. We had all been blessed that nothing had ever happened, but I found myself suffering the consequences for my actions, even though they were never the consequences I would have imagined when I was drunk and behind the wheel. I've learned that's the way most consequences are: you rarely expect they'll affect you, but when they do, they're usually not the ones you hadn't been worried enough about in the first place.

I took a Saturday and drove over to Davenport to see about finding an apartment. It was a strange thing, thinking about looking for an apartment. It's one of those things that when you're in high school would have been the coolest thing ever. I mean, living in an apartment, having the freedom to eat what and when you want, come and go as you please, be the boss of yourself—what an appealing thought. But I was almost forty-two years old, trying everything I could think of in an attempt to stay sober and facing the prospect of selling hearing aids for a living. Living in an apartment didn't sound like such a big deal to me at that point in time.

I ended up finding a place that wasn't too far from where Mark said our office was going to be. It was a newer building and I took a place on the third floor, mostly because it had a gas fireplace and I had never lived in a place with any kind of fireplace. It was a pretty small apartment but had two bedrooms for when Katie and Laura would be allowed to come spend the weekend with me. In time, Mary loosened her restrictions about them riding with me and I think a lot of that had to do with the fact that the divorce decree she was working on with her attorney was going to allow me to see them every other weekend and she probably wasn't too keen on driving them over herself.

My new place also had a deck that overlooked the asphalt parking lot and beyond that, the parking lot of a lawn and garden center. It was flanked on the left by the parking lot of a muffler shop and on the right by the parking lot of an auto stereo installation company. As I stood there on the deck before I went to sign the paperwork, I looked out at the asphalt landscape sprawling before me and counted a total of two hundred thirty-two parking spaces shimmering in the sun. They were going to become the first thing I would see in the morning and the last thing I would see at night and I again realized how much my life had changed. I had a feeling that the changes were just beginning.

It was lonely living in Davenport even though I had known the place as a kid and still had relatives living there. Growing up, I had hung out with my cousin David, who now, at forty-four, still lived at home with my Aunt Betty. As kids we had always had a great time together, but we had drifted apart through the years. He had been married at least three times and was, like me, a pretty significant alcoholic. He had no job and hadn't been able to drive legally for a number of years. He hadn't acknowledged his illness, and because of that I would not allow myself to be around him.

I had another aunt and uncle who lived across the Mississippi River in Taylor Ridge, Illinois. My uncle Bob was a successful chiropractor and his wife, Patty, was my mom's youngest sister. They had three kids, and Judy, the daughter who was going to take over her dad's business when he retired, was my first and only friend in the area. She had been dating a guy long-term and he and I had nothing in common so we didn't end up doing all that much together. The whole family was big into hockey so we would on occasion go see the minor league team play, but other than that I opted not to do much. I had forgotten how to socialize without alcohol.

My life consisted of going to work in the new office Mark and I had set up and testing people when they came in to see us. For the first month or so, Mark was there pretty much full time and then, after we felt comfortable with how things were going, he would go on the road to the small towns around the area in our mobile unit, which was nothing more than a pull-behind camper with portable electronic testing equipment. He would park the unit in the parking lot of the local drug store and offer free hearing tests to anyone who wanted one and then try to sell them hearing aids. I would stay in the office and do the same for anyone who came in, but Mark's goal was to have me go on the road and he would eventually hire someone else to work the office. I was not excited about any of the possibilities being presented to me but kept at it because I had nothing else to do.

After work I would head home, stopping at the Cub Foods store to buy whatever I felt like having for dinner that night. The liquor section was at the far end of the store and I made a point of never going any farther than I had to in order to buy food. That meant I always ended up eating pretty much the same thing: boxed spaghetti dinners, which I ate two or three times a week. I got tired of it after a while but I didn't want to go to the frozen food section because it was too close to the place where I knew my ex-mistress sat on her shelf and I didn't know if I was strong enough yet to turn my ear to her if I heard her call me. I suppose I could have gone somewhere else, but usually by the end of the day I was tired and just wanted to go home. I hadn't worked without alcohol for years and it really wore on me during the day.

When I would get home, I would make dinner and watch television and then go out on my deck and smoke cigarettes and usually have a cup of tea. I didn't like tea much at the time but would battle these pretty significant urges to drink something at night and tea seemed pretty safe. There was a spider that would spin a huge and intricate web in the corner of the deck wall and the overhang, and one night, out of sheer boredom more than anything I suppose, I lit the web on fire with the lighter that Matt had given me and got some sort of odd satisfaction out of watching it slowly melt away. The next morning, I went out with a cup of coffee and a cigarette and happened to look up and saw that the spider was up in the corner, spinning away, trying to rebuild from the damage I had caused.

That night, when I got home and went out on the deck after dinner, he had spun his web again and I, for no good reason, burned it away again. This went on for a couple of weeks, him spinning his web, me burning it down, and him out again the next morning, building it back up again. One day, it hit me what I think someone was trying to tell me. One, there were probably a lot of people, Mary and our daughters especially, who were trying to rebuild from the havoc I had continued to create in their lives and, no matter what I had done to tear it all down for them, they were going to persevere. The other thing I kept hearing was that I needed to do the same. I needed to rebuild my own life, one day at a time, no matter how much work it was going to be or how much I would have to tear away to get it done.

One afternoon I came home early and went out on my deck and watched the spider at work. He didn't seem to notice me and if he did, didn't seem to care. He simply kept working at putting things in his life in order after some idiot with a lighter kept burning it all down. I told him thanks for the lesson he had taught me and realized that, next to my cousin, he was now the best friend I had. I also told him that since we were such good friends now, I was going to quit smoking and stop burning his house down every day.

CHAPTER 23

The Dry Drunk

I STRUGGLED WITH THE URGE to drink. It was pretty ironic in a way because I couldn't shake the reality that if I did drink, no one was around to know. However, the other reality that far outweighed the first was that I would know, and more importantly, the same God that sent His Messenger to save me in Bethel would know as well. I started to treat my sobriety as a gift, something that I had prayed for and that countless others had prayed for me as well, and began to feel that I would be doing a real disservice if I gave it back.

My noble thinking didn't take away my urges at all, but it did make me a little more creative in how to deal with them. One night, when I was cold and tired and depressed and about ready to give in and go back out to Cub Foods, beyond the frozen vegetables, and back to the neighborhood where my old lover was waiting for me, I was hit with an odd inspiration. I took off all my clothes except for a pair of shorts and a bad T-shirt and then went out on the deck and threw my car keys into the bushes next to the edge of the parking lot where I parked my car. I figured that if I was going to go out and buy something to drink, I was going to make it hard to do because it was dark in that parking lot and I was fairly certain that I didn't have the energy to get dressed again and go downstairs to root around in the bushes looking for my keys. I started doing this every night and thought it was a great plan even though I would still have to go out in the morning and find my keys so I could go to work.

Everything was going well until I woke up one morning and it had snowed. It took me forever to find my keys but eventually I did and knew that I was going to have to depend on my own strength until spring. I figured that was kind of the way this whole journey was going to be. You do something until you feel that you're ready to take the next step and then you take it and hope—or pray—that you'll always find yourself on some sort of substantial footing.

On weekends that I would have Katie, now thirteen, and Laura, nearing seven, I would leave Davenport on Friday after work and drive the hour and a half to Cedar Rapids and get them and then do the same thing on Sunday nights when I took them home. It made for a lot of driving, but there was never a time when it wasn't worth the trip. We crammed a lot of life into the short time we had together, but it was some of the best time I'd had with them in years. Katie was always a little tentative around me at first, but I think that was because she was still scared about all that had happened and maybe more than a little concerned that it could all happen again. The more time she spent with me, though, the more comfortable she got.

They both got into hockey and we would go to games whenever we could and really enjoyed being together. Our first Christmas at my place was nice, right down to the real tree I bought that fell over on Christmas morning after we had opened presents. I slowly began to feel that I was getting my girls back and it was the best feeling I'd had in a long time. It was always hard leaving them at Mary's on Sunday nights, so I would usually go to see my AA group before I went home to keep connected with everyone and let them know that so far, everything was going okay. It was hard when I'd go though; there were always people who had disappeared and no one seemed very confident that they were going to come back.

The one major highlight was the Sunday night when I picked up my one-year medallion at my AA meeting. The people who were still there that had been there from the first night I came all hugged me and sang "Happy Birthday" to me, but the best part of the night for me was when I went back to Mary's before I left for Davenport. I wanted to share part of my night with my girls but didn't quite know how they would take the celebration. Laura was in bed when I got there but Katie was still up, so I went to her room and sat down on her bed. I looked at her a long time and tried hard not to cry. It was difficult to be there knowing that I had allowed the addict to take all of this away from me. I had allowed him to be more important than this young woman who hadn't done anything to deserve this kind of thing happening to her. I suddenly didn't know what to say to her but knew that I somehow needed her to know that more than anything, I just wanted to be her dad again.

I took the medallion from my pocket and, as I pressed it into her hand, told her, "If there ever comes a time in your life when you come across something that you think is too much for you to handle, I want you to take this and hold it tight and remember that if God can give me the strength to go a year without drinking, He will give you the strength to do anything." I didn't know how it would sound to her, but it was all I could think of to say. My prayer continues to be for her that she has remembered that night and has never come across anything that the Lord hasn't given her courage to overcome.

Laurie would come over on weekends when I didn't have the girls, but by then, our relationship was about over. When it did finally end, it ended because I told her something I don't think I had ever told her before: the truth. I told about her enabling and how I had come into the whole thing for every wrong reason there was and how I needed time to deal with my sobriety without the guilt that was weighing me down over what had happened in my marriage. I was not in the place I needed to be with her, and I knew it was hard for her to hear what I had to say, but it all needed to be said. It was a big step for me, one I hadn't been able to take with anyone before without the crutch that alcohol used to give me. It was hard knowing that I caused her so much pain because she still believed that we could make things work, but I knew that it was not going to happen. I needed to change so many things about myself and knew in my heart that one of the things I needed to change most was to let go of something that had, unknowingly at the time, wreaked so much havoc in the lives of so many people.

I was also beginning to experience some significant financial issues, something I hadn't expected but, like all consequences, something that was a direct result of what I had allowed drinking to do to me. I had made a good living at Millhiser and when I got fired, Mary's attorney had drafted the divorce decree and child support payments based on the money I had made my last year there. The problem was, the following year, I made just over $12,000, not having worked for about half the year and learning how to sell hearing aids the other half. I hadn't paid Laurie anything while I was staying with her, so moving to Davenport really added to my expenses. My rent was $450, my child support was $800, plus I was now paying utilities and expenses, not to count the gas money it was taking to drive back and forth to Cedar Rapids. Needless to say, my money disappeared fast the first day of the month; I was usually out of it around two thirty in the afternoon.

There weren't many options for me in terms of relief. I was allowing my guilt to accept the $800 in child support payments and that would be the first check I would write. There wasn't any other source of income available to me and I knew no one in his right mind would loan me any money, so I turned to the only viable source I had: credit cards. Every week I'd get credit card checks in the mail telling me to take a vacation or transfer balances or put a hot tub on my deck for me and my spider, but all I'd do with them was write one to my landlord, another to the electric company, one to the phone company, and on and on. It wasn't a healthy way to live, but until things straightened out at work and I was able to start selling something, it was all I could do.

At work, I finally started to go on the road with our mobile unit, but it wasn't the glamorous life I had thought it would be. I didn't have a vehicle that would pull the thing, so on Sunday nights I would switch with Mark and take his diesel pickup and go hook up the camper and head off to whatever town he had arranged for me to visit for the week. If it was close enough, I would drive home at the end of the day, but more often than not, it was far enough away that I would have to spend the week in a motel, usually something far less substantial than the Red Roof Inn where I had first waded into a sober world. As much as I tried to put a positive spin on those weeks, I hated everything about them. The rooms were cold and empty at night, the food, fast and greasy. During the day I would sit in the camper, an empty one-gallon milk jug for a urinal, the baseboard heater running, and test the hearing of any unfortunate souls that would wander in. The locals were fascinated by the process, the big-city electronics that I flashed in front of them. Most, not surprisingly, were amazed at the pictures of the small third world countries that were developing in their ear canals.

Few of the people who made their way into the trailer needed hearing aids; all most needed was irrigation and many found that they had lost about twenty pounds when the process was completed. However, for those that were hard of hearing, I found it difficult to try to convince them that $3,400 was a fair price to pay to accomplish that goal. I was finding that I didn't have it in me to take that kind of money from people who didn't have it to spend with no guarantees that the problem would be solved and, after three days, no money coming back to them if it wasn't. For people like Mark, it was easy; I couldn't do it.

I was becoming increasingly dissatisfied with not only my job but also what wasn't going on with my life. I was lonely, a fact that I had addressed one weekend with my daughters there. They promptly convinced me that I needed a pet so I ended up that same day with a light blue parakeet named Larry. He and I bonded immediately and I started to enjoy the knowledge that I wasn't going to come into an empty apartment on that first Sunday night. However, much to my dismay, he was dead when I went into the kitchen to uncover his cage on Thursday morning. I held a brief service for him prior to work that morning before interring him in the dumpster in the parking lot.

Finances continued to create a big problem for me and I turned to the only man I felt I could trust, my good friend Jim. Years ago, when money was not a problem, I had invested in some annuities with him and he now suggested that I cash in a couple of them and use the money to get back on my feet. I hung on to two smaller ones, figuring that I may need them someday. Cashing in the other two seemed reasonable at the time and I went ahead and did it. I opted not to have taxes withheld, figuring that by the time taxes would be due on it the next year, I would have made enough money to pay them.

About that same time, I had heard from Jim that there was a potential opening with an insurance agency with an office in Davenport. He asked if I would be interested and I knew I had seen enough wax clots to last for a lifetime, so he said he would nose around a bit for me. Even though I was a little apprehensive about the prospect of getting back in the business, it was what I knew and felt that I needed to get back into a more familiar work environment.

: : : : : :

One Monday, I was in my office working on the ear of an elderly widow who was there more for the company than for anything else. We were chatting in the exam room about the land mass in her ear when I heard footsteps coming down the stairs into our office. I turned my head and saw the letter carrier toss mail on my desk and knew that my life was about to take a significant turn. I didn't know at the time how significant or in which direction the turn would take me, but there was definitely a turn coming.

Melanie had been working for the post office for seven years when I first met her. I had asked for her phone number the next day but my nerves kept me from calling her. But when she came in on Friday, she told me it was her last day as a substitute on that route and that if I didn't call her that night, I shouldn't bother calling her at all. For a long time, she thought I was a doctor and that was the first reason she showed any interest in me, but, in time, she got to know all about me and still decided to stick around. She was eight years younger than I and had been divorced for a couple of years after a ten-year marriage that ended when she and her husband couldn't agree on whether or not to have children. Oh, each was having an affair as well, but it seemed that the marriage may have survived that in the past, so I think it was more the children thing that drew them apart.

We went out about a week after we first met and I was nervous. I had yet to tell her about my drinking past and knew from my conversations with her that alcohol was an important part of her life. That and men. She prided herself in the fact that she was just coming out of relationships with two men simultaneously, something that should have been a red flag, but at the time, I was blinded by the fact that someone as lovely as she, an observation shared by the two of us, would be the least bit attracted to me. That fact alone did wonders for my self-esteem, more than the six rounds I had made through the class at Sedlacek.

In the early part of our relationship, I had begun meeting with the owner of a small insurance agency, Core-Vens and Company, in Clinton, Iowa, and his sons. They had a branch office in Davenport and were looking for a commercial producer. Jim knew them and had told them about me, and the meetings had gone well. Prior to Christmas in 1997, I had accepted their offer to join them, told Mark I was leaving, and with Melanie by my side had come to believe that life was really beginning to turn around for me. However, there was a feeling I couldn't shake that there was something missing.

Melanie and I moved in together in the spring of 1998. We lived in half of a large duplex with the owner, a younger guy and friend of Melanie's brother-in-law, living in the other. The house was really four floors, with a basement, first floor with living room, dining room, and kitchen, three bedrooms and a bath upstairs, and a large walk-up attic beyond that. It was nice when the girls would come to visit, as each would have her own room, and Katie, in June of the year, would turn sixteen and would be able to drive over on her own.

Work was going okay for me at Core-Vens and life was better for me than it had been in a long time. I felt that I was comfortable in my sobriety but was dogged by the fact that even though life seemed better, I wondered at times if I was really any different than I was when I was drinking. I was starting to struggle with the kind of man I was and beginning to realize that maybe I was the same man but just not drinking.

I had heard Bill Martin talk a lot about the "dry drunk" when I had been in treatment but had never really understood the concept, and there were times I would have given anything to know what in the world he was talking about. I wasn't at the point yet where I was comfortable praying about a lot of things but knew from my limited experience that it wasn't such a bad thing. So I began praying for an understanding of why I was feeling the way I was and what could be done to change things. Again, I was waiting for the thunderbolt; instead, I got David Jeremiah.

I didn't know anything about Christian radio. My only experience had been years ago when Mary and I were driving back to Iowa from Florida and it was about five in the morning and we were crossing the Mississippi River into Iowa. This was before FM radio or at least before our Pinto station wagon had an FM dial, and I was looking for something on the radio to keep me awake while Mary slept in the back. All I could find was a station that was playing hymns so I listened to it. It was the first and only time I had heard Christian radio.

Anyway, one day, I was driving in Davenport on my way back to my office struggling with the idea that as good as I thought my life was getting, the more I felt like I was struggling with it. I had pushed the "seek" button on my radio because I still wasn't all that familiar with all the stations in the area, and all of a sudden my radio stopped on a station where I heard a man saying,

"That's what they mean when they talk about the dry drunk."

I turned the radio up as another man spoke.

"So, let me make sure I understand this. You're saying that if a person has given up drinking but really isn't doing anything to address the issues in his life that were impacted by his drinking, then he's what you call a dry drunk. Is that right?"

"Yes, basically, that's what I'm saying. For example, if a man's spirituality has been impacted by his alcoholism, pushed aside and forgotten, and if that man, when he stops drinking, does nothing to restore or *recover* that spiritual relationship with the Lord, then he is a dry drunk. He is not *recovering*; he is only not drinking. . . ."

I was listening to David Jeremiah and his Turning Point ministry on the local Christian station, but at the time I didn't know who he was. I had been led to listen to that station on that day at that time because, as was coming to be a significant fact of my life, God had again heard my prayer and again He had answered it. It was, in reality, a turning point in my life.

When I got to my office, I closed my door and found the station on my own radio, and while I listened to whatever was on at the time, I thought hard about what I had heard. I knew that I was exactly at that point in my life that David Jeremiah had been addressing and he was telling me exactly what I needed to do. I was having a hard time getting a good grasp on just what this all meant but suddenly found myself compelled to take a blank piece of paper. I drew a line across the paper about a third of the way up from the bottom, and under the line, I wrote one word: *alcohol*.

That was my addiction although I figured at the time a person could write anything under there: food, sex, gambling, drugs, anything that had impacted a person's life in any way. Above the line, I wrote the word *spirituality*. I think it was pretty safe to say that every aspect of my life with the Lord had been pretty severely impacted by my addiction. Given what I had come to believe had happened to me in Bethel, the Lord seemed willing to forgive me of all of that if I would simply make the move and come back to Him, or, more likely in my case, come to Him for the very first time.

I went further and began to write above the line everything else that had been negatively impacted by my disease: *family, marriage, career, friendships, finances, physical, mental, and emotional health,* and even the intangibles like *honesty, communication,* and *integrity.* I wrote anything and everything I could think of that I had as of yet done nothing about to improve upon the kind of man I was.

When I was done, I realized that I had done a nice job of being sober, but I had done absolutely nothing to recover from my disease. It hit me that day how much work I had to do, and I knew where I had to start. Right there in my office, for the first time in my life, I dropped to my knees and thanked the Lord for His forgiveness and all He had done for me. Then, with the words I still offer up to Him every day, usually more than once, I asked for the wisdom to understand His will in my life and the courage to pursue it. It was time to start my recovery. Like being sober, I had a feeling it wasn't going to be easy, but at least I knew I wasn't going to be doing it alone.

CHAPTER 24

On the Right Track

WHERE DOES ONE START A spiritual recovery? I started with my Bible. It was an old one, a gift from my sister on Christmas Day, 1960. I had used it a lot through the years but hadn't really read it much. It had become a storage place for scrap paper odds and ends mostly because it zipped open and closed. I did have a tatted cross my grandmother had made and a purple bookmark for scriptures to read when one would find himself in one spiritual crisis or another, but everything else was mostly junk. I talked to my mom one day and told her that I was going to start spending more time with my Bible, and two days later I got a copy of *The Upper Room* from her Methodist Church. Thus began my daily wanderings into the Word.

I don't know that I was expecting anything miraculous to happen just by reading and studying, but then I realized that some significant miracles had already happened. Mostly I didn't know what to expect but soon came to understand that if you're going on a journey, a map is a pretty handy thing to have.

Life with Melanie continued to provide what I thought at the time I needed. However, it soon became apparent that even though she professed to understand my struggles with alcohol, she was going to do very little to move me away from having it be a significant part of our life together. Melanie liked to drink. Alcohol had become an important part of her life and played a big part in the troubles she had encountered with men through the years. Even though she gave me the impression of a desire to settle down, she didn't appear to be too willing to settle without alcohol.

Twice a year, once in the spring and once again in the fall, we would go downtown to the "Pub Crawl," an event that would allow us, for about eight bucks each, to go from bar to bar and mingle with her friends, all of whom got really good drink deals for their eight bucks, until everyone had decided they'd had enough to drink and turned to me for a ride home. While I didn't mind playing the role of designated driver to everyone, it was hard to realize that the woman who by then had become my fiancée was usually the one who most needed the ride. I know I had the right to put my foot down and say no, but at the time I simply wanted to give her what I thought she needed. It's ironic in a way. I had, with my own "unknowing willingness," become the enabler that Sandi, Mary, and eventually Laurie had become in my life. While I had spent my marriage tending to my needs first and foremost, I had thought it was time to give everything I had to someone else. In doing so, I had become exactly what Melanie needed me to be; I was allowing her to continue to drink to excess with little fear of the consequences. I had slipped into the role of enabler without even thinking about it and had discovered how easy it is for people to do. I knew that needed to change and I also knew it didn't bode well for our relationship.

I tried to learn to adapt to a new kind of life, catering to the needs of a woman and doing it in two ways I hadn't done it before: soberly and faithfully. While I had struggled in my marriage, alcohol running hand in hand with my infidelity while I never felt satisfied with what I had and always wanted more, it was different with Melanie. For the first time in as long as I could remember, I was coming to believe that maybe I had finally met the woman who would be the last one I would have to look for. And, without the alcohol, I now had someone who could become the most important thing in my life and then I would realize that life was good and I was recovering and . . . and . . . and . . .

One day it hit me. I was reading in *The Upper Room* about the same kind of life some unknown man in India was living, where he had come to believe that his Indian princess had become the most important person in his life. He talked about how he almost idolized her and would do anything for her.

I remember reading that and thinking about all the ways I was idolizing Melanie and all the things I would do for her. I thought about all of her girlfriends and how they'd smile at me when I'd hold the door for them and how they'd wish they had someone in their lives to idolize them. I thought about how wrong it seemed that Melanie would drag me to the Pub Crawl but how I would keep right on going along with her. I'd think about how every night she would sit on the couch and have two or three glasses of wine and how I would keep getting up and refilling her glass. I kept thinking that there was something wrong with all of this, but I'd keep on doing it because I was trying to convince myself that she was the best thing that ever happened to me.

All the while, the thought persisted that there was something trying to tell me maybe that wasn't the case. I kept trying to convince myself that she had to be the best thing for me because I was learning that it's really better to serve someone than it is to serve myself. I mean, that's what I'd been doing with alcohol for all those years. I'd been serving myself and satisfying my desires and making my needs more important than those of the people around me. Certainly this was a sign that I was improving; I was focusing my attention on someone else for a change and doing it with the belief that she was the answer to my prayer; she was the woman of my dreams.

But it was *The Upper Room* and the story about the guy from India that made me think I might be wrong. More specifically, it was the scripture that he referenced when he realized that his Indian princess had become the object of his affection and attention, the sun around which his world was spinning. I knew I had never read the scripture before because there wasn't any scrap of paper stuck between the pages in my Bible. It was the first time I had ever seen it and I'm pretty certain it was supposed to be that way for me. Psalm 118:8: "It is better to trust in the Lord than to put confidence in man" (KJV).

It hit me that morning as I sat in bed and read it again and again and again that I was missing the point with Melanie. As important as I was making her in my life, the Lord was telling me that for me to make any kind of progress, He had to be the focal point in my life. Not alcohol, not Melanie, not even my kids, who, despite the miles between us, were getting closer and closer to me every time I saw them. He had to be the one. That morning, I finally felt that I had taken a step in the right direction. It would have been nice if I could have shared my revelation with Melanie, but I knew she wouldn't take her fall in the polls very graciously. I continued to read and study but did it alone in the quiet of the early morning either before she would get up or after she had left for work. It became the most important part of my day.

I also started to pray more. I thought a lot about how prayer had impacted my life and started to come to an understanding that if what I prayed wasn't too far from God's desires for me, there was a pretty good chance He would hear and maybe even answer me. With that understanding came the realization that I was beginning to grow in faith because I don't think you can really pray with that kind of expectation if you don't have any faith. I would pray after I read my devotional or after I read the scripture but more often than not, I would pray when I got in the car and was on my way to work. I found myself thanking God for all He had done for me but was also beginning to ask for direction as to what it was He wanted me to do and for the courage to do it when I finally understood what it was. Through my prayer and study of the Word, I was starting to come to grips with some of the things that had happened when alcohol was really starting to take my life from me, but, like my night in Bethel, I didn't feel I was quite ready to share them with anyone yet.

: : : : : :

While a part of me wanted to share my growing spiritual awakening with Melanie, there started to be a stronger desire to somehow find a way to move back to Cedar Rapids. I never voiced this to Melanie because I never really believed that it was possible for a variety of reasons. Because my faith, though growing, was not yet as strong as it needed to be, I tried to push the feelings aside and figured they had to do with the emptiness I was feeling every other Sunday night when Katie and Laura would back out of our driveway and I would stand in the street and wave at them as they drove off, knowing I wouldn't see them for another two weeks. There were even occasions in the winter, when the weather would step in, that I would go three weeks without seeing them, and those times apart were almost too much to take.

I didn't have many friends in Davenport. Most of Melanie's close friends were single women, all about the same age, and none of them dated anyone. The closest I came to having a friend was Melanie's brother-in-law, Eric, a dentist who was married to

Melanie's younger sister, Mandy. Eric and I had nothing in common but he provided companionship at family functions when Melanie's parents from Minnesota would come down. Doug and Kris would always come for a week in May and then come again for a week between Christmas and New Year. I liked them a lot and always had a good time with them, but as time went on, especially during the week after Christmas, I found myself more and more wanting to be with my own girls. There was one Christmas where my sister and Arnie came from Boston, and along with my mom, Katie, and Laura, we all had as close to a true "family" Christmas as I'd had in years. It was nice but it fueled my desire to be closer to my daughters.

While Melanie and I continued to try to make each other believe that everything was going well between us, I knew that we were beginning to have some problems. She was selfish and I was starting to see a lot of how I used to be. It wasn't a pleasant sight. That, combined with my ever-increasing desire to get back to Cedar Rapids, was starting to put a strain on our relationship. I never told her about it, but it was a pretty hard thing to ignore. There were a couple of times when we would be coming back from Doug and Kris's home in Minnesota and driving through Cedar Rapids when Melanie would say to me,

"So, does it ever feel like home when you come through here?"

I probably should have thought about it more than I did, should have made her think it was more of a decision than it really was, but the answer would always come quickly and truthfully, "Yeah, it does."

"That's not good," she'd say, shaking her head.

"Why?" I'd ask. "You asked me."

"I know, but you don't live here anymore. This isn't your home. You live with me . . . in our home."

I wouldn't say anything. I know she wanted me to reach out and take her hand and squeeze it while I turned to her and smiled and said something like, "You're right; I'm sorry. Of course this doesn't feel like home. Home is where my heart is and my heart will always be with you."

I think not saying anything at all had more of an impact on her. I know it made me feel better, not lying and all.

Life went on at work and at home. I continued my daily walk in the Word and found myself praying more; every time I was in the car alone, I'd spend time with the Lord, continuing to ask Him for direction. Work wasn't going all that well. Core-Vens, while a big fish in a small pond in Clinton, Iowa, was a very small fish in a very large pond in Davenport. There was no name recognition and I had no relationships on which to build, and even though I was writing business, I wasn't happy with what I was doing.

The financial problems continued to worsen. Even though I was now back in the insurance business and I was selling, what I was selling wasn't generating enough income to keep up with my expenses, so I kept falling farther and farther behind. The annuity money, when it came in, totaled about $35,000 and was a true blessing. It was hard using it to wipe away some of the mounting debt, knowing that it was money that had initially been set aside for retirement, but that didn't seem to exist for me anymore. I kept telling myself that I needed to put some of it away to pay the tax on it when the time came but I also kept telling myself that I would certainly be making enough money by then to take care of it. Having the extra money helped ease the burden but by no means proved to be an extravagance for me. Even with the money, I was still making substantially less than I had made prior to my breakdown and my expenses were still greater than they had been. It was like a band-aid on a severed limb; it was a short-term fix to stop the bleeding but wasn't going to do anything to solve the problem.

Even living with Melanie and splitting the expenses, an idea that initially sounded like it would be a good thing for me, ended up costing me more money. She didn't make a lot and, like me, had a lot of debt, but she had about as much control over her spending habits as I'd had over my drinking. Extravagance got her in trouble; desperation put me right there beside her. She had spent because she wanted to; I was doing it because I had to. I continued to pay what I owed and never really talked much to her about my mounting concerns about where I was headed.

While all of this was happening, I continued to pray hard about it. I don't think I was praying for any kind of miracle. I wasn't praying to find a big bag of forgotten drug money lying somewhere under a bush and I wasn't buying lottery tickets looking for a quick fix. What I think I was praying for, though, was clarity about everything, and I realized one day that, even though I was in dire straits, for the first time in a long time I was actually aware of what was going on with me financially. It wasn't like that when I had been married. Back then, on payday, I would go cash my check and leave out enough cash to get me through the next two weeks and give the rest to Mary to put in the bank. She would take care of all the finances while I would spend my money, money she didn't know I had, on all the alcohol I needed. I didn't worry about the bills or expenses or anything else that I now found myself worrying about. I had left it all up to her.

Now I was paying my bills and I also knew every day how little money I had in the bank. What I had blown off in the past in regard to my finances was now a very real part of my life. The more I thought about that, the more I realized that I was, without knowing it at the time, addressing another one of my recovery is-

sues, one of those things above that line that I had neglected when
I was drinking. I was coming face to face with how my finances
had been impacted by my addiction. God had again answered my
prayer and, as I was beginning to understand, it wasn't answered
exactly how I thought it would be but rather answered the way
He knew it needed to be. Like everything else in recovery, this
was going to be a long process.

I continued my spiritual journey, immersing myself in reading the
Word and especially praying every chance I got. For me, 1998 was a
year of revelation in a way, mostly because I was beginning to understand more deeply the difference between sobriety and recovery.

Later in the summer, I went back up to Minneapolis to spend
time with Laurisa and Arnie before they moved to Boston and this
time I took Katie and Laura. It was the first time I can remember
that the visit was what a visit should be between a brother and
a sister. Laurisa and Arnie both knew that I had changed; I think
anyone who knew how I used to be could tell I wasn't that man
anymore. It was nice too for Katie and Laura to experience the
change in the relationship even though they probably didn't fully
understand the significance or appreciate all that had happened
two years earlier to get us there.

One night a friend of Laurisa's, Caroline Brown, and her husband,
old friends from Iowa, stopped by for dinner. They had been in
the Cities shopping and staying with family and they wanted to
stop by and say hello. Caroline is also a recovering alcoholic and
had been sober for fifteen years. We sat next to each other at the
end of the table and chatted during dinner, but after we ate, the
conversation turned more specifically to our recoveries. She shared
with me a thought that I have carried since that night and still
share when I speak with recovering alcoholics at the treatment
center here in Cedar Rapids.

She told me that an alcoholic will spend the first two years after drinking simply working on *not* drinking; he spends the rest of his life recovering. I thought about that and how, again, the Lord was working on me that night. I know He put the two of us together that evening as if to confirm to me that I was indeed going about this the right way. There is no easy fix; there are no miracle cures. There are only miracles. As much as I felt I was struggling with things at times, I was coming to believe that at least I was struggling with the right things. I was struggling with the things that needed to be fixed in my life and I was doing it, so far at least, without the help of the one thing that I had allowed to create all the problems in the first place. I haven't seen or spoken with Caroline since that night, further proof of my belief that God brought her there to share a thought with me that I had needed to hear: I was doing exactly what I was supposed to be doing.

It was also during this trip that I finally got to spend some time with Mark. It was the first time we had been together since the night I ended up in Bethel and it had been weighing heavily on him since then. We went out for ice cream and I think I was finally able to convince him that if it hadn't been for him and what he had done, I didn't think I would be alive. I didn't share with him all that had gone on that night; in fact, that was something I had yet to share with anyone, but I did tell him about my spiritual walk and I know that the time we spent together that day has cemented our relationship as brothers forever.

CHAPTER 25

The Chance to Go Home

WHEN 1999 ROLLED AROUND, THERE was a growing un-
easiness about a lot of what was going on in my life, but I think a
lot of that had to do with the fact that I hadn't made the money I
thought I would make. Tax time was looming and I had the feeling
that my bill was going to be pretty significant. By then, I had used
up quite a bit of the annuity money, most of it going to make up
the shortage for my expenses each month. Jim and I had figured
that I might be looking at about a $5,000 tax bill and, if it wasn't
much higher than that, I thought I'd be able to get by with one of
the annuities I had held on to. It was going to be close. I went to
Cedar Rapids on a Friday and gave Jim the info for my taxes, as
he had told me he'd do them for me to save me the money.

On Saturday morning, Melanie was at work and I was alone
when the mail came. I was surprised and more than a bit nervous
when I saw the envelope from Jim and knew that he had already
finished his work on my taxes. I tried not to think about why he
hadn't called to tell me he was done already and thought that the
reason he hadn't was because the bill was going to be a lot less and
he wanted me to be surprised. There was another possible reason
why he didn't call but I kept pushing that thought out of my mind
as I opened the envelope and pulled out the return.

I turned the pages slowly, looking at the numbers that meant nothing to me, yet still trying to put the most positive spin on them I could. I finally got to the last page and closed my eyes, said a quick prayer, and then looked at the number.

$11,073.

I looked again, somehow trying to make it $1,107, but no matter how hard I tried, it stayed the same. I owed over $11,000 in taxes.

I was sick. Physically sick. I felt that I was going to throw up and I ran upstairs to the bathroom but nothing happened. I just stood there and looked at the numbers in front of me and then, slowly at first, I was overcome with the biggest sense of surrender I had ever felt except for that night at Bethel when I had heard those words that changed my life.

"*. . .We all need to be saved.*"

With that, I dropped to my knees, tears in my eyes, and raised my hands and my face to the sky and said, "Lord, I give up. I don't know what to do. Please, please help me."

That was it. Again, I was on my knees, and again, I was crying out to God. As I knelt there, tears streaming down my face, for the second time in my life I felt His presence. He didn't come to me this time as He had the first time. I think He knew He had gotten my attention that night and didn't need to come to me that way again. But He knew that I had grown enough in my faith to recognize—and believe—that He was there with me in that bathroom. I felt a sense of peace come over me and the next time I looked at the numbers in front of me, even though they were still there, I knew that somehow, even in the desperate time I found myself, everything was going to be all right. I had no idea how, but I knew it was. I was learning, again, that an answered prayer does not always mean things will be easy; rather, in faith, things can be made right.

How does one pay an $11,073 tax bill when one hasn't the money to do so? In my case, I borrowed against another annuity and, with the money I had left from the first two I had cashed, I almost had enough. That is, until a couple of days later when Jim sent my Iowa return and I found out I owed another $2,512 to the state. All told, I owed $13,585 and had no choice but to cash in the rest of my future retirement income and pay it off. I was about $5,000 short until my annuities came in, so I turned to my employer and, out of the goodness of their hearts and knowing my desperation, they loaned me the $5,000 for thirty days (at only eight percent interest!) to see me through until my money came in.

I learned a lot about consequences during this time. Even though one could argue that I'd already had my fill of consequences, I learned that they will continue to come at you and there is really nothing you can do about it. I had no one to blame but myself for this whole mess; the thing I found interesting about all of it was that I never once found myself feeling bitterness toward anyone through the whole ordeal. In the past, if I had felt that I had been wronged, even if I hadn't been, I would react in anger and always point the finger of blame at someone else. There was nowhere to point this time and it was a pleasant surprise to me that I was so willing to accept the responsibility for all that was happening. I was where I was because I had put myself there. I was coming to realize that the prayers I had been offering up to become a new man, even though two years in the making, were bringing about the changes that needed to be made. Again, not in the ways I would want them to come to me but rather, again, in the ways He knew they needed to come to me. With trials comes perseverance; with perseverance comes faith.

The other thing I became aware of during this time was that there was never one moment when I thought I would drink.

Alcohol had always been my means of escape, the getaway car to take me far from any disruption in my life. While the disruption would always be there, having to deal with it would disappear as soon as the vodka would hit my system. The tax bill wasn't going to go away if I got drunk; it was only going to disappear if I dealt with it. There wasn't anyone around to cover for me and make my problem go away while I vanished into the world of oblivion I used to call home. I had created this mess; I knew that, with the Lord's help, I would have to make it right. As desperate as this time felt to me, I instead focused entirely on the peace that had descended upon me in the bathroom when I again surrendered to His will.

Another aspect of my recovery that needed to be addressed was my physical health. I had always prided myself in being fit. I used to work out a lot, running when I was younger and lifting weights as I got older. The alcohol abuse had taken its toll on me in a lot of ways, but it really hammered me physically. Even though I had tried to work out as I drank, I declined rapidly from a physical standpoint. Living in Davenport, I joined the gym that Melanie belonged to and began to start working out hard again. We both tried to eat better and started riding our bikes. The house we lived in wasn't too far from a paved bike trail that paralleled a creek running through town, and there were quite a few days when I would ride my bike to the trail and go from one end to the other, a total of about fifteen miles. It was during this time that I finally gained back all of the weight I had lost during the addict's reign in my life—over forty pounds. It was not the diet I would recommend to anyone looking to lose weight, and it felt good to be able to look at myself in the mirror again and not see the ghost of the man that I had seen for so many years. However, one of the things I've learned about recovery, much like life itself, is that there are setbacks, and I was just about ready to run into one that put a significant strain on everything.

: : : : : :

In early February of 2000, I woke up to an odd sensation in my left eye. It seemed as if I was looking through a screen door, and no matter how much water I threw in my eye or how hard I rubbed it, it wouldn't go away. There wasn't any pain and it wasn't all that much of an inconvenience. It was something that was there and, even though I knew it shouldn't be there, I figured that whatever it was would go away on its own. The next day, it did. Or so I thought.

On Monday, I was sitting in my office and noticed that every time I looked through my left eye, I would see a small, dark crescent shape at the bottom of my eye. When I would move my head up and down, it would shake, almost like jell-o. By Tuesday, the arc was bigger; Wednesday, it was taking the shape of a circle, and by Thursday evening, it had completely blocked out the vision in my eye. I could look peripherally and see things, but if I focused my vision straight ahead, it was like looking into a black hole. I know I should have done something about it sooner but, as with my alcohol abuse, I had to wait until it was almost too late to do anything. I was standing in the kitchen with Melanie, who was polishing her nails, while I was frantically trying to get in touch with my eye doctor in Cedar Rapids, an ophthalmologist named Lee Chalmers who had done my cataract surgery in 1995, also on my left eye. I finally got in touch with his answering service and, after explaining what was going on, hung up and in fifteen minutes got a call from Lee.

"You've detached your retina," he said, less calmly than how I wanted him to sound after I told him what was going on.

"How did that happen?" I asked.

"You're very nearsighted and that strains the retina. Plus, you've had cataract surgery and that strains it even further. It sounds like it's a significant tear. I need to see you first thing in the morning."

"Should I come tonight?" I asked as Melanie blew on her nails, frowning at the thought.

"No, but you need to come straight to my office first thing to-morrow. Please be there before eight if you can."

I hung up and told Melanie what was going on. She was angry that she was going to have to drive in the morning because it was her day off, but since her nails were done, she agreed.

I ended up first in Lee's office and when he decided the tear was too big for him to fix, I found myself at the University of Iowa hospitals. They initially tried to freeze the tear but, after a week, fluid continued to leak into my eye so I eventually had surgery in an attempt to repair the detachment. It was an agonizing surgery and the recovery, especially for someone already in recovery, was painful and slow. I had to keep my head down even when I slept and ended up wearing sunglasses mostly because it looked like I had beaten up someone's fist with my eye. It was black and yellow and purple and swollen and watered constantly. It was a long healing process that was slowed by an emergency surgery two months later when my eye began leaking fluid again. It impacted much of my life, especially the workouts at the gym, but, more importantly, the next step I had decided to take in regard to working on my career recovery.

I liked the people at Core-Vens, but it simply didn't feel that it was where I was going to stay. There was a yearning inside me that I could not ignore, and I had begun to focus most of my energy on trying to figure out if I was ready to find a way back to Cedar Rapids. I missed my daughters and was absent from so much of their daily lives. I knew that God hadn't saved me to recreate me as a father who was not a part of his children's lives so I'm pretty certain that the desire to return was placed there by Him.

I began praying in earnest for the opportunity to go home. I didn't share this with Melanie because I knew it wasn't something she would want to hear but did share it with my friend Jim because I knew he would be someone who would understand and pray for me as well. Every night, I would lie in bed and pray for the chance to get back the opportunity to confront my past and finally move beyond it, and every day I would force myself to haul out all of the things that had happened, things that I had stuffed away somewhere in my mind where I couldn't see them, and try to envision myself facing them. I soon came to realize that most of the things above my line—my recovery issues, like honesty, integrity, relationships with family and friends, and a deepening spiritual journey—were things that wouldn't be fully addressed until I was back in Cedar Rapids. I kept praying for the chance; I wanted to go back home.

I had decided to visit with a head hunter in a small agency in Moline to see what she might be able to do for me. Dee was in her early sixties and felt confident that she would be able to help me out, bad eye and all. True to her word, she quickly lined up interviews for me with a human resource company, the Boys and Girls Club, and two different insurance agencies. While the interviews went well, I could tell that the people talking to me were really freaked out by my eye. I had no real desire to take any of the jobs but would always walk out of the interviews feeling that I had done a better job of interviewing than the time before. I could feel my confidence growing, but my heart was still pulling me back to my prayers about going home.

One day, after I had interviewed with one of the insurance agencies and was getting ready for a second interview with the principals, pretty certain that an offer would follow, I got a call from Jim. I was at work when he called.

"Hey," he said, "are you still serious about wanting to come back to work in Cedar Rapids?"

I was floored. "Are you kidding? It's what I've been praying for."

"Yeah," he laughed. "Me too. I've got a friend, maybe you know him, Doug Robinson, he owns the Stanley Agency on the southwest side. Anyway, I was talking with him the other day and he told me he's looking to bring someone else on board. I mentioned your name. He's a Christian."

The thing I was learning from Jim about Christians is that they seemed to be a pretty forgiving lot. Jim had never wavered in his faith in me as a man, even through the worst times, and had forgiven me and, more than I knew until later, was praying fervently for God to continue His work in me.

"I know of him," I said, "but I've never met him. What's the deal?"

"He would like to visit with you. I don't know when you can come over but if you're able to find a time to get here in the next week or so, let me know and I'll arrange for the two of you to get together."

I sat there after I got off the phone with Jim and was struck again with how powerful prayer seemed to be. The thing I was learning most about it was that it seemed to work best if what a person was praying for was something that God wanted for him in the first place. I had prayed for freedom from my addiction and He delivered it to me personally. I had prayed for an answer to where I was going to stay my first night out of treatment and He had put money in Robbie's hands to throw on my bed so I had a place to go. It was beginning to look like if we pray sincerely for God's will in our life, pray faithfully and unceasingly for those things He wants most for us, they come to us. I had prayed for the chance to go back to Cedar Rapids; it looked like He was going to give me the opportunity.

Unfortunately, I should have been more specific in my prayer. I had asked for the chance; that's exactly what I got. I went to Cedar Rapids a couple days after I spoke with Jim and met with Doug. We had a wonderful talk; he is a good man and was running a good business. He was receptive to the idea of me working with him, but there was one issue that was going to keep us from moving forward. I was working for an agency that was providing me with health insurance; because I was going to be an independent contractor with Doug, there would be no benefits. And, because my alcohol treatment was significant and still relatively recent, I would not be able to secure health insurance on my own. Even if I did, my eye problems would have been excluded from coverage and I was still more than a bit concerned about what might happen there. The trip back to Davenport that afternoon was hard; God had answered my prayer and given me the opportunity, but my past—my own mismanagement of my life—was not going to allow me to see it through. It was hard to be angry; it was easy to be disappointed. Again, I learned a lesson about how the Lord works in our lives. He gives us a glimpse of what He has in store for us but reminds us that we still have to face the consequences for the decisions that we make that pull us away from Him. It's at those times that we learn to grow a little bit more in faith.

While there was a time in my life when the disappointment and anger would have been more than enough to send me to a liquor store to seek out my instant gratification, that day I simply gave thanks to God for hearing and answering my prayer and asked that He still keep His eyes open for a job in Cedar Rapids.

CHAPTER 26

A Hard Answer

DEE CALLED ME A COUPLE of days after I got back and told me she had an opportunity for me to work for Freedom Mutual, a large national insurance company with a local office in Davenport. It was a salaried position complete with benefits and a chance for growth with a company that had name recognition. I told Melanie about it and she was excited, mostly because she knew that it would keep me securely in place in Davenport. Even though she didn't know how hard I had been praying for the chance to move, she knew my heart wasn't completely where she wanted it to be. It was hard for me to accept the offer because I felt that I was giving up on my dream of moving back home. I prayed about it the night before I said yes to Karl Harold, Freedom Mutual's district sales manager, and waited for God to tell me no, but I didn't hear it. Instead, I kept thinking I was hearing Him say,

"Yes, this is what I want you to do. It's your decision, like all decisions will be, but it's something that I think you'll enjoy."

It was weird hearing that, given all the faith I'd had in my prayers to Him lately, but I believed, for whatever reason, that He wanted me to say yes. There had to be something I wasn't understanding about all of this yet, and while I felt I should have been thinking that I was giving up on my dream for myself, I couldn't help but think that maybe ... somehow ... I was yielding to His desire for me. The next day, I called Karl and told him I was ready to take the job.

In the insurance business, at least in the sales end of it, there really isn't such a thing as a two-week's notice, so I told everyone at work that same day that I was leaving; they told me goodbye. I think everyone's afraid that you're going to call all of your clients and tell them where you're going. They're afraid you're going to copy all of the client files and steal office supplies and make all sorts of long-distance calls to your family and chat for hours, so they pretty much just tell you, "Thanks for everything; now you need to leave."

When I left that next afternoon, I thought about how I should take a few days off and relax, but there was something telling me that I should probably start my new job right away, so I called Karl and told him I would be in the next morning. I got to my new office around seven thirty and was hauling in a box of my stuff. Karl was the only one in the office and he was sitting in my cubicle, on my desk, talking to someone on the phone. I could tell that he was talking to his boss out of the Chicago office, a guy named Les Barger, the man with whom I'd had my final interview. Karl was feeling pretty good about hiring me, not because he had hired *me*, but because he had hired someone to fill the empty cubicle and had no doubt met a corporate goal of some kind. He was doing the talking and I don't think he even knew I had come in.

"Yeah, Les, I'm real happy with Steve. I think we're finally all set here in the Davenport office. Now, we've just got to get things straightened out in Cedar Rapids."

He said more but I didn't hear anything after that. They had an office in Cedar Rapids. They were looking for people to work there. I could almost see God's smile.

Karl hung up a few minutes later and then turned around when he knew I was there. "Hey, how's it going?"

I didn't even tell him good morning. "You have an office in Cedar Rapids?"

He started to say something but I didn't give him the chance. "And you're looking for someone to work there?"

He nodded and opened his mouth but again I beat him to the punch.

"Why didn't you tell me that? I'm from there, you know."

He held up his hands so I'd give him the chance to say something.

"Yeah, we've got an office there. My territory is Davenport, Cedar Rapids, Des Moines, and Omaha. I thought you knew that."

"No, nobody told me that." And again, "I'm from Cedar Rapids, you know. My kids live there."

He nodded again.

"Yeah, Les and I talked about that but I told him I didn't think you had any interest in going back there."

"Are you kidding? I'd love to go back there."

I waited for him to say something to put an end to this momentary miracle but miracles—true works of God's will—don't end in a moment.

All he said was, "If you're serious about it, I'm sure we can work something out."

And just like that, I was again overcome with God's divine plan for us. I spent the rest of the morning getting to know the other guys in the office, guys I was only going to spend the next three weeks with while the home and district offices rewrote all the paperwork so I could start in Cedar Rapids the first of the next month. The rest of the day, while Karl was trying to train me on the computer, all I was thinking about was everything that had transpired from the moment I started praying for the chance to go back home.

I thought about how I had told Jim about it and how he was praying for it as well. I thought about how my eye surgeries had probably scared everyone else away from me. I thought about how I hadn't lost faith when Doug Robinson and I hadn't been able to work out the details. I thought about how I had decided not to take any time off between jobs and how that might have kept Karl from hiring someone else to work in Cedar Rapids. I thought about all these things and realized that God was again working in my life. I thought back to something else I had heard on Turning Point about how God is the Potter and we're the clay, and for the first time I could feel myself being formed into His creation, His desire for me. I was thinking about all of these things right until the moment I got out of the car at home and walked into the house and realized that Melanie wasn't going to be as happy about this as I was.

It was a hard thing that night, telling her about my decision. She got angry and cried about it; part of me wanted her to be at least a little happy for me but that was not to be. I know it hurt her, but I think it hurt her mostly because maybe for the first time in her life someone was choosing someone or something else over her. I suppose I would have felt the same way, but there was never a moment when I felt that I had made the wrong decision.

I realized something important about prayers and how God answers them for us. An answered prayer does not always mean that things are going to be easy. I thought about how I had prayed for freedom from my addiction and how that prayer had been answered. It had been a hard answer, coming to me in a hard place, but delivered in person. It came with no promises that it was going to be easy but came with the knowledge that everything was going to be my choice. My sobriety and recovery had been hard, but every decision had been up to me and every decision was now being made with the realization that it was part of the plan and design God had for me. Even though it was hard work, the knowledge that it was being done to satisfy His desire for me made it well worth the effort.

If I didn't understand that, the part about how answered prayers are often a lot of work, work that grows our faith, I was soon going to meet that realization head-on. I accepted the job with Freedom Mutual in early August and worked in the Davenport office until the first of September. During that time, I took a day and drove to Cedar Rapids and met the two people with whom I'd be working. Eileen was our receptionist and customer service rep, although she was really the one who was holding the office together. The other sales rep was Chad, a guy in his late twenties. He had been in the military and had a wife and a young daughter. Eileen and I went out for lunch that afternoon and then, when I left the office, I drove around Cedar Rapids a bit and thought about how long it had been since I had been there other than picking up or dropping off my daughters or driving through town with Melanie trying to make her think that the last thing I'd ever want to do is live there again.

On the way home, the reality of what was happening started to settle down upon me. I thought of all the demons I had left behind in Cedar Rapids and wondered how many of them were still going to be around. I thought about the blackmail, the boys at Millhiser, the pain I had caused so many people, the lies, the breakdown . . . I thought about all these things and wondered if I was really ready to come back and deal with all of it. I also knew that if I was sincere about my recovery, and so far it seemed that I was, I had to come back. Everything that I had not yet addressed needed to be addressed or I was going to spend the rest of my life as the dry drunk that David Jeremiah had told me about. I had done a pretty good job so far of getting my hands on some of the things that I had stashed away and pulling them back to look them in the eye, but there were so many more waiting for me back in Cedar Rapids. I thought about that a lot on the long drive home and then realized there was one more thing, unrelated to my past, that I hadn't thought about yet. There was going to be a lot of driving involved.

It was ninety-three miles from where we lived in Davenport to where my office was in Cedar Rapids. On one hand, it was all highway miles. On the other hand, there were ninety-three of them. It was a ninety-minute trip one way, and there weren't too many different ways to go. I got into the habit of getting up at four thirty and going to the gym and then going home and grabbing a quick shower and a quicker breakfast and then getting dressed and leaving. I would shave in the car and then, for the rest of the trip, I got into the habit of spending time with the Lord.

It was some of the best quiet time I have ever experienced in my life. Thirty minutes into my trip to work, I was done shaving and I would turn off the radio and talk with the Lord. It wasn't prayer as much as it was conversation. And I say conversation because it was during these times that I truly felt I was hearing what the Lord was saying to me. I was hearing that I was doing the things He wanted me to do. I was hearing that He was happy that I had grown in my faith and that I was learning to trust in Him, even if I didn't understand what I was doing at times or why I was doing it. I was hearing that He was happy that I had stayed sober; my sobriety had been a gift from Him, delivered personally, and He was proud of me for making the decision every day to keep the gift. He told me He admired the great leap of faith I was taking by getting in my car every morning and driving back to the place He knew I needed to be. Even though it made for long days, I kept hearing Him tell me to remain faithful in the things He had given me to do. I also kept hearing Him remind me daily that it was always going to be my choice, but it seemed to be getting easier to make better choices.

: : : : : :

Winter came early that year; our first significant snow hit in early October and stayed around a long time. At the time, I was driving a 1989 Ford Probe that I had originally bought for Katie. Her mom had decided that it wasn't a safe car for her to drive . . . apparently she had no such concerns for me . . . so I ended up keeping it and letting Katie drive the Bronco I had bought myself when I had traded off my little piece of luxury that I could no longer afford. It took me about twenty minutes to get in and out of the Probe, and when I drove it, I felt like I was about six inches from the pavement. It would have been a fun car to drive if I had been a foot shorter and twenty years younger, but it was a terrible car to drive that winter. It handled poorly, and because it was so small and sat so low, it was an adventure driving it through the snowstorms that pounded us that winter. However, I never once regretted the trips to work in the morning. Driving into Cedar Rapids each day only served to reinforce that God indeed was continuing His miraculous work in my life.

I found myself not enjoying the trips back in the evening as much. Melanie and I were struggling, mostly because she was not able to accept the decision I had made. She kept trying to make me admit that it had been the wrong thing for me to do, that it was hurting our relationship and that I should come back and work in the Davenport office. There was no way I was going to do that. Like my sobriety, the chance to work in Cedar Rapids was a gift to me and I was not going to give it back. I knew it was what

God wanted me to do. It was not what Melanie wanted me to do. She made that clear to me each night when I got home, and even though I knew I was the cause of her unhappiness, I did not waver for one minute in the belief that I had made the right decision. It was hard; that's why I knew it was the right thing to do.

Work in Cedar Rapids went well and I finally started to believe that I was going to be able to address the financial issues that had dogged me. While it was expensive driving back and forth, I was starting to make enough money to feel that getting back on my feet financially wasn't going to be the impossibility I had thought earlier. Freedom Mutual had a program with large employers who would offer their employees the opportunity to payroll deduct their insurance premiums if they did business with us. Chad and I would go sit in the cafeterias at the companies involved with the program and people would line up to let us quote their insurance so they could have it taken out of their paychecks. We were writing business like crazy and pretty soon, our office, the smallest and least productive in all of Karl's territory, was writing more business than anyone else. I was getting ahead but still struggling with all the credit card bills I had racked up when I was in Davenport, so I made a decision to finally try to do something about it.

I ended up calling a guy by the name of Scott Bradley who worked for Consumer Credit Counseling and set up an appointment to meet with him one afternoon. He was a great guy and very was sympathetic to my problem. He told me that most people who are struggling with finances have had one of three things happen: they've either lost a job, gotten divorced, or had an illness. I had all three happen to me so it was no wonder I was in the mess I was in. He set up a program for me that put all my debt together and figured that if I would make payments of $874 a month for the next five years, I would be debt free.

Sometimes facing those pesky issues can be more of a struggle than others. That was a lot of money. I signed up anyway because I knew there was no other way.

There was another thing I did that I was really happy about: with Jim's help, I got life insurance on me for my daughters. Most people wouldn't think that was such a big deal, but it was to me. It was the first time in a long time that I did something smart for my girls that would at least protect them if anything were to happen to me. I had left them open and unprotected financially for too many years and I figured this was at least a small step to take to make sure they would be taken care of. It was a good feeling, doing something for someone else, especially for Katie and Laura. It made me feel that I had done something responsible for them after so many years of blatant irresponsibility as their father. As 2000 was nearing an end, I felt that my life was slowly getting back on track and that the Lord's plan was finally beginning to get a little easier to see.

I got into the habit of carrying a small tape recorder with me not just to help pass the time but also to simply get my thoughts on tape. I was having wonderful conversations with God on my trips and wanted to tape my reflections so I could listen to them on days when things didn't always go the way I thought they should. One day, I was sitting in my office, tying up loose ends before I headed back to Davenport, and I was suddenly hit with one of those unexpected bolts of inspiration that come out of nowhere. I had always enjoyed writing. In fact, as a child I remember having this dream where I was a famous author. I have no idea what I had written in the dream; I only knew that people knew who I was because of it.

I wrote a lot through the years. I had accumulated piles of poems, stacks of stories, and bunches of beginnings to novels that never quite got off the ground. My problem had never been the desire to write something; as with everything else in my life, the problem was finding the discipline to finish. Something . . . alcohol mostly . . . always seemed to get in the way. But that day, sitting in my office, I was hit with the idea that God had given me a pretty good story to write and maybe I should look into it. By the time I got back to Davenport that night, I had spent ninety minutes with my tape recorder and had outlined an entire novel. After I got home, I transcribed the tape into a very rough synopsis of what I wanted to write, and for the next eighteen months, except for a brief hiatus that was unknowingly looming on the horizon, I wrote.

Melanie had become increasingly more uncomfortable living in the duplex and, maybe as a way to force the issue of my commute, told me one day that she wanted to buy a house. I think her original intention was that I would continue to live with her but by now, late in the winter of 2000, I had grown weary of the three hours a day in the car and knew that I needed to do something different as well. I think it was the Lord again taking me to the next logical step in my journey if I was willing to continue to walk on the path He had laid out before me. Early in the spring of 2001, when Melanie finally found the house she wanted, I told her that I was going to find a place to live in Cedar Rapids. She was disappointed but not surprised, and while we both put the most positive spin we could on the prospect of maintaining a long-distance weekend relationship, I think we both knew that everything now was subject to change.

I found a place that appealed to me in Marion, a suburb of Cedar Rapids. It was a two-bedroom apartment in a very quiet and semi-secluded neighborhood and was privately owned by a guy named Ken Novak. I met Ken when he was painting the apartment and liked that he was a decent guy who took good care of his building. On the day Melanie and I loaded up the moving van at the duplex and unloaded her stuff at her new house, I took the truck on to Cedar Rapids and my coworker Chad and I, along with Katie and one of her friends, unloaded my stuff in my new place. I was officially back home in May and my life was better than it had been in a long, long time. I guess those can be the times when most surprises occur.

Chad and I continued to write a lot of business in Cedar Rapids, and I started to settle into a routine at my new place. I was happy to be back and noticed that there were some significant changes that were beginning to take place. First of all, my relationship with Mary improved dramatically. I think most of that came from the fact that she seemed to know what I had gone through in my attempt to get back home. She knew what I had left behind in terms of my relationship with Melanie, which I'm pretty sure she saw as an intense desire to get back to being a father to my daughters. I think she admired that, especially when I would meet with her and begin to share a little about the spiritual journey I was on. Mary had been brought up in a significant Catholic environment, but when everything had happened with me, she had left the church. She ended up at an Assembly of God church in Cedar Rapids where she felt she was healing from the pain I had put her through, so we were both on separate but similar journeys. I had even gone to her church a couple of times and couldn't believe that I would sit there with Katie on one side of me and Laura on the other and marvel at the power of the Lord.

Katie graduated from high school in late May of 2001, and it was so nice to be there and share the day with her. It was odd at times because it was the first time I had seen most of her family

. . . what used to be my family as well . . . since everything had happened. I didn't want it to be too uncomfortable and take away from Katie's day so I didn't stay long, but it was still nice to be home to be a part of the celebration.

CHAPTER 27

The Brick Wall of Debt

MY LIFE WITH MELANIE GOT into a weekend routine. On the weekends that I didn't have Laura, Melanie would usually come to my place, and when I had Laura, we would go to Davenport and stay at her house. It was odd in a way because the life I used to live with my girls, seeing them on weekends and then trying to do as much as we could when we were together, was now how my life was with Melanie.

During the week, I would stay in and write, working diligently on my book. I didn't do anything socially; most of that stemmed from the past and all that had happened to me, and even though I was comfortable with what I was becoming, I still hadn't reached that same comfort level socially. I soon came to realize that this was another aspect of my life that had been impacted by my disease. In Davenport, I went out because Melanie went out and nobody there really knew anything about what had happened to me. I mean, everyone knew I was a recovering alcoholic but nobody knew what that meant other than I wasn't supposed to drink and I could drive everyone else home. It dawned on me that there are many things that are impacted by our abuse, a lot of things that need work after we quit drinking. My desire to be alone wasn't healthy, but at the time it was all I knew and I was justifying it with my writing. It had become my reason not to go anywhere, which was fine with me. I continued to believe that God had given me the story to write and I needed to write it.

In September, a couple of weeks after 9/11, Karl emailed everyone and told us all that there was a big meeting planned for all of us in Des Moines the following Tuesday. Chad got nervous because there had been rumblings that Freedom Mutual was losing money in Iowa. He and I both knew that in the big picture, it made no difference what kind of success our office was enjoying. Business was business after all. So he wanted me to talk to Karl and see what was going on.

"Hey, Karl," I said when he answered the phone. "What's going on with the meeting? Everything okay?"

He lowered his voice and I suddenly felt like I was talking to Deep Throat.

"I can't really talk about it."

"C'mon, Karl," I said. "You can tell me. I'm not going to say anything."

"No, I really can't say anything," he said, quieter this time. He actually sounded nervous. Maybe something was up after all. "Listen," he finally said. "I'll tell you this much. Everyone's going to be affected by this, okay? I mean, I can't tell you what it is, but it's going to affect all of us."

"We're closing, aren't we?" It was pretty obvious to me even if he wasn't going to say anything.

"Look, Steve, I'm sorry but it'll be my butt if I tell you. All I can say is it's going to affect everyone, including me. That's all I can say. You're a smart guy; you can figure it out. I'll see you Tuesday, okay?"

"Yeah, sure. We'll see you Tuesday. Hey look, Karl. It's really no big deal, okay? Don't worry about it."

"Yeah, right," he said as he hung up.

It apparently was a big deal.

Chad and I drove to Des Moines on Tuesday morning, both of us dressed in suits and crammed like sardines in the front seat of my Probe. On the way, we passed a semi that was hauling eight new Chevy SUVs, a miracle in itself that the Probe could pass anything.

"Hey, look," I told Chad as we passed the truck. "I bet anything that's why we're going to the meeting. Freedom Mutual has bought all of us a new company car. Go ahead and take your pick."

He was moaning and groaning like someone had hit him in the stomach. "We're going to lose our jobs, man. Can you believe it? We're all going to lose our jobs."

I thought about that and knew he was probably right but wondered, if he was right, why it wasn't bothering me more than it was. I had been thinking about it ever since I had talked to Karl the week before and was pretty sure that's why we were all going to Des Moines. I knew the numbers. I knew that it was costing Freedom Mutual nearly $250,000 a year to keep each of the four offices open, and I knew, even though all the offices were writing a lot of business, there was no way that we were writing enough to justify a million dollars to stay open. Of course we were all going to lose our jobs. Freedom Mutual's name recognition didn't really exist for anyone outside the insurance industry who didn't live on the east coast. I had gone to two training sessions with the company, one in Nashua, New Hampshire, and another in Mystic, Connecticut. People out there knew the name. In Iowa, all we were was Mutual of Omaha; I think people halfway expected Marlin Perkins to show up at the cafeterias to sign them up for insurance. People here had no idea who we were. All we were, in another hour or so, was unemployed.

So, again, why didn't it bother me more? I had come to believe that Freedom Mutual must have come into my life for one reason only: it was the vehicle that God had used to answer my prayer. It was what brought me home. It wasn't where God had designed me to stay; it was only how He planned on getting me home so I would be able to take the next step in my journey. I'm certain that He had used the job as a stepping stone for everyone else as well, but those who didn't understand how He was working in their lives would never be able to see that. I saw it; I believed it and had faith that He had something better planned for me. I had no idea what it was, and at my age, a couple of months short of my forty-seventh birthday, I should have been more worried about it. I wasn't. I had faith that this was nothing more than another leap of faith that God wanted me to take. I had taken them before and they all seemed to take me exactly where He wanted me to be.

We all lost our jobs. Les Barger sent the HR people from the district office in Chicago to tell us that, effective immediately, all four offices were closing their doors. We were all given severance pay, an extension of our benefits, and then an HR person followed everyone back to their respective offices so we could clean out our desks, hand in our computers and keys, and, like that, it was over. All in all, I had about six weeks of pay but knew that I shouldn't wait until the last minute to start looking.

I thought for a minute about calling Marilyn Jones at the same recruiting firm that got me my hearing aid job but decided that whatever desire I'd had to look into people's orifices using a tele-vised camera was long gone. I figured I could do this without her help because He seemed to have a pretty good handle on what He was doing for me so far. All I had to do was keep listening for that voice that I had learned to recognize.

: : : : : :

One of the things I decided that I wanted to do during my "sabbatical" was go back to Sedlacek and meet with Bill Martin. My book was a fictional account of my own recovery. There was a character in the book who was modeled after Bill and there was something that was telling me I needed to go see him. Bill was a vibrant man, robust and funny and full of life, and of all the counselors who had spoken to us in treatment, his were the words I most enjoyed hearing. While I knew I wanted to see him, I'm certain there was a big part of me that wanted him to see me. I hadn't set foot on the fourth floor since I had graduated from the program over five years earlier and I suppose I needed to wander back through the halls so people could see that I had, in fact, survived.

I called ahead and made an appointment to meet with him and when I pulled into what had been a parking lot five years earlier, I was surprised to find that it was gone, replaced with a multi-leveled parking ramp. I parked and wandered by the spot where Loren and I had smoked so vigorously after dinner and paused for a moment before I went into the building. I thought back to all those days when I had reluctantly gone through the sliding glass doors, at first almost too ashamed to go in, and later, too drunk to care. I got to the elevator and hit the button for the fourth floor and rode in silence, wondering what it was going to be like when I got there.

When the door opened, old fear came out of nowhere and grabbed me. I couldn't step out of the elevator. I looked to the left and saw the nurses' station; off to the right was the hallway that led to the inpatient rooms and to the left of the hallway, the small lounge where Robbie and I used to sit up at nights and talk about what he needed to do to save his marriage. I stood long enough for the doors to start to close but I stopped them and then stepped out of the elevator and walked toward the nurses' station, the door closing behind me.

I stopped as I felt beads of sweat pop out on my forehead as the past rushed by me. It was all coming back to me: the days and nights stuck in the prison that the addict had built for me and yet would still scream at me to find a way to get out. I looked down the long hallway to my left, past the nurses' station, and in my mind I saw Sarah standing there with her hands on her hips calling me to come back and blow because she knew I was drunk. I saw Katie walking with me down the hall, holding my hand, more afraid than I was of what was happening to me.

It was all there in front of me and I stood, transfixed by the sights and the memories and all the reminders of what I had been, and then, as if He knew I needed to see one more thing, the elevator door opened behind me. I moved out of the way as I turned around instinctively and saw a man, maybe older than I but too worn out and scared for me to know for sure, standing between two men dressed in white. They had come down from the fifth floor where he had been locked up just as I had been. He had on his robin-egg blue and white striped hospital robe and was still hooked up to the IV they had given him for his detox. I looked into his eyes and they looked right through me, the terror in them giving him away. I felt a shudder deep inside and knew that I was seeing what I had looked like five years earlier and I knew . . . He was making sure I knew . . . that I never wanted to be like that again.

What's more, I felt that He was telling me that He was laying upon me a part of His plan for me that somehow, someday, I needed to make sure that people such as this, people such as I had been, knew that He was their last and only hope. I hadn't known that until He came to me. I felt, when I saw the terror in those eyes in front of me, that He was telling me it would now be my job to do that for Him whenever I could. As I watched the man shuffle down the hall to the right, through the double doors that led to the inpatient rooms, I knew again that He had been with me. He had brought me here for more than to meet with Bill. He had shown me a part of His plan for me.

I finally took a deep breath and gathered myself and went to the desk. I recognized the nurse sitting at the counter but couldn't remember her name. When I told her I was there to see Bill, she looked down at the schedule in front of her and then looked back up at me and smiled.

"My goodness. Steve Sellers. I almost can't believe it. I'm Marie; you might not even remember me but . . . my goodness. I can't believe it."

"I get that a lot these days," I said, reaching out and shaking her hand.

It was true. I had been places where people would look at me as if they should know me but believed also that the man they thought I was couldn't possibly still be alive, so they would just smile and nod and walk away thinking they had seen a ghost. Marie at least knew I hadn't died.

"I never would have believed I'd see you again, at least, not like this. I think a lot of people thought you'd be back but . . . oh, my . . . you do know what I'm trying to say, don't you?"

I laughed at her and told her, "Yeah, I understand. I wouldn't have bet a lot of money on me either, at least not after what happened the first time I was in."

"Well, it's good to see you," she said. "You're here to see Bill Martin, aren't you? Why not have a seat over there and I'll let him know you're here."

I took a seat against the far wall next to the row of payphones where Robbie called his wife every night, crying and begging for another chance. I wondered if he was still alive.

As I was reading about "The Ten Indicators of Abuse" and seeing my past in all of them, I heard footsteps coming down the hall and put down the magazine and stood up to turn and face Bill. I wanted to stand tall and proud so he knew how far I had come and how grateful I was that he had been a part of it. I smiled, hearing in the back of my mind the angry young man shaking the jail cell and yelling at his tormentors: *"You can't do this to me!"*

I didn't even recognize him. Cancer had eaten away at him; he was a shell of the man I remembered, tiny and frail, a straw in his mouth sucking loudly at the water in the plastic glass he held in his thin and bony hand. It appeared that perhaps his own abuse, whatever it had been, had caught up to him and taken much from him. But it hadn't taken his smile and he showed it to me as he took my hand. "It's good to see you. Really good to see you."

We went to his office and talked for an hour. We talked about my recovery and I told him as much as I felt comfortable telling him. I had yet to share in great detail all that had happened to me and still felt guilt at times for not doing so. It was almost as if I was denying that it had happened, but I knew that when the time was right with people that were the people He had put in front of me, I would do it. We talked instead about the difficulty of the journey, of staying sober, of lessons learned and learned again. When I told him about my current job situation, we also talked about something I hadn't expected.

"You know, Steve," he said, sipping from his straw. "Technically, by definition, you are considered disabled in the eyes of the State of Iowa. Your disease classifies you as such."

"You're kidding," I said. "Disabled? What does that mean exactly?"

He leaned back in his chair.

"One of the things it means is that the Americans with Disabilities Act can provide people like you . . ." He smiled. ". . . People like *us* . . . the chance to pursue a master's degree in substance abuse counseling at the University of Iowa at no cost. It's a government funded program."

"I didn't know that," I said. "How long does it take?"

He reached into a drawer on his desk and pulled out a file, and after thumbing through it, pulled out a paper and looked at it before handing it to me.

"It looks like two-and-a-half years full-time; five years if you do it part-time. Most treatment centers . . . the good ones anyway . . . require a master's degree now."

I thought about what he was telling me and realized that it seemed like the perfect opportunity to take the step but also knew that not having a job at the moment was probably going to keep me from doing it. It was a little disappointing and it was something I would have done in a heartbeat if there had been money coming in. We ended up talking for another thirty minutes before he had to head out for a meeting and, after saying goodbye to Marie, I got on the elevator and went downstairs. As I was driving home, I realized that even though the timing wasn't right for me to pursue a career in counseling, my desire to do something to help people like the man I had seen coming down from the fifth floor was intense. I felt the Lord telling me the same.

"*. . . We all need to be saved.*"

: : : : : :

The only real emotion Melanie showed over the job loss was the frustration that I wasn't including Davenport in my new search. The thought never entered my mind. Without question, I believed that coming back to Cedar Rapids was a gift; I wasn't going to give it back.

I spent time posting my résumé online and working on my manuscript. I was happy that the discipline was there to do both and that I never allowed there to be the kind of idle time in my life that had created so many problems in the past. While I kept thinking that it would be nice to find something before my severance pay ran out so I could technically have two incomes, it ended up being the full six weeks before I found anything.

One day, I got a call from a guy named Dale Moore, the district sales manager for a company out of Minneapolis called FSC Insurance. He was based out of Cedar Rapids and told me about a program they had that would allow me to run my own office. We met a couple of times and even though I had no real desire to work for them, I knew I had no choice; there simply wasn't anything else out there. The big downside to accepting the job was that there was a two-week training session in Minneapolis that would take me away from Cedar Rapids right before the holidays. I made it through the class and was even able to spend some time with Mark and Meta and got back to enjoy the holidays with Katie and Laura and, to a lesser extent, Melanie. We were struggling a lot, especially given that my decision to pursue the job I did made it pretty clear to her that I was not going to go back to Davenport. I had talked to her about the possibility of her moving to Cedar Rapids but she would have no part of that. We were fast approaching an impasse and I knew that there was going to have to be change of some kind. I had no idea what it would be but felt pretty confident that when the time came, the Lord would show me what to do.

I ended up recruiting Chad to come and work for FSC. He and I, along with another young guy, Roger Harken, ended up leasing some office space. After we spent all the money we had buying furniture, phones, setting up utilities, and paying for signs and advertising, we opened for business. While we were successful to a point in regard to sales, everything we made and then some went right back into our business. We were losing more money than we were making each month, and while both Chad and Roger had spouses who worked, I was on my own. I even had to call my credit counselor one day and ask him if there was any way I could miss a payment. He made the arrangements with my credit card companies but told me that nobody gets very excited about something like this. I needed to be careful that it didn't happen again.

For the early part of 2002, I felt that I had hit a wall in my recovery, and most of it was due to my finances. Spiritually, I felt wonderful. I was walking daily with the Lord, immersing myself in the Word and praying constantly for His direction. Physically, I was in as good a shape as I'd been in a long time. I was working out, eating well, and getting lots of sleep, and there were no urges to drink. I felt that I was heading in a great direction with my kids and there was even healing taking place with Mary. I was close to my sister again, even though she was now in Boston. We communicated regularly and it was open and honest, something that she hadn't gotten from me since early childhood. I even liked myself more than I had in a while. But it was now the finances that had become the biggest issue in my recovery.

CHAPTER 28

A Man's Godly Duty

IN JULY, KATIE WENT TO Minnesota with my mom to visit an old friend of the family who owns a home my family had vacationed in when I was a kid. I had decided to drive up with Laura on Friday and make a long weekend out of it, mostly to spend time with my daughters but also to be in the one place that I had always believed was my heaven on earth. It had been an old resort, hidden from the lazy state highway that ran north out of Brainerd by a one-lane dirt road and old pine trees that held more secrets than I used to. It was the one place I had always gone to get rejuvenated.

I was hoping that this time I would be able to hear the Lord talk to me and tell me what I could do to get over the hump and out of the rut in which I had found myself. It wasn't that I didn't like what I was doing; I had been in the insurance business long enough to know that it was where I felt the most comfortable. I simply couldn't shake the feeling that I still wasn't where I was supposed to be. As with my time at Freedom Mutual, I couldn't help but feel that my current job was a stepping stone to where He wanted me to be. I went to Minnesota hoping I would hear Him tell me that the next step wasn't that far away. I was growing increasingly frustrated, not with the money that I was making but rather the money that we were all spending to keep our business afloat. Chad was already looking to get into the mortgage business and Roger had talked about moving back home to go into business with his dad. The last thing I needed was to deal with all of the expenses myself.

It was a wonderful weekend, and on the way home on Monday, with Laura sleeping peacefully beside me, I got a call from Dale who told me that FSC had decided to increase production goals and he wanted to meet with me about it when I got back. It hit me when I hung up from talking to him that I was at a pretty significant crossroads: the Lord was going to let me know either that I was, in fact, where He wanted me or that His plan for me was about to unfold even further. I prayed the entire way home for the two things I had always needed the most from Him: wisdom to discern His will and courage to pursue it. I needed to know what step I was supposed to take next.

After my meeting with Dale the following day, I sensed that there was a significant change coming, even if I did not yet know what it was. I went to church the following Sunday, and when I got home Dale called me again. He wanted to meet with me that afternoon about the rumors that had been floating around about Chad and Roger and how he was counting on me to try to keep them there. He told me it was essential for the success of his territory that I step up and convince them that their future was with the company. I didn't really know what to tell him since I had no idea where my own future was, so I told him that I couldn't meet with him, that I was previously committed and that I would talk to him the next day. I remember sitting on my bed when I hung up from talking with him, suddenly overcome with this deep sense of failure. I felt that I was not going to get out of the hole in which I'd found myself; all the work I had done in my recovery was slipping away because I didn't know if I was going to be able to manage my professional life. I felt stuck, but mostly I felt afraid.

I didn't know what to do so I called Mary . . . Mary, of all people . . . and shared, for the first time in my life, my fears, my doubts, my struggles, everything that I should have probably shared with her five or six or ten or fifteen years earlier. She listened and offered what advice she could, suggesting that I call the pastor at her church and tell him that I needed to speak with him about what was going on. I didn't know the man at all other than from the sermons I'd heard at church but I felt that I needed to hear God's voice and thought that there wouldn't be a better way to hear it than to speak to a true man of God. I immediately felt a little better knowing that God again was guiding me exactly where He knew I needed to be.

I called the church office the first thing Monday morning and spoke with his secretary. "Hi," I said, a bit nervously. I had never been in a position to prepare to speak to such a man as this. He was the senior pastor of a congregation of nearly two thousand people. He knew God. Even though God had sent a Messenger to sit across from me at a table in a detox clinic to offer me salvation, I had not yet come to grips with the fact that I could possibly be as close to Him as the man was with whom I was seeking counsel.

"May I speak with Pastor David, please?"

"Who is calling please and what is the nature of your call?"

A bit more formal than I would have perhaps expected but nonetheless, "My name is Steve Sellers and . . . well . . . I guess you could say that I'm having a . . . well . . . I think I'm having a professional crisis. I really need to speak to Pastor David." I could feel myself start to break up a little. "It's . . . it's very important that I speak with him. Please."

I heard the flipping of pages through the phone and then, "Yes, he would be available to speak to you three weeks from Thursday between two and two fifteen. Shall I put you down?"

"No, wait," I said. "You don't understand. I need to speak with him now. Today."

She laughed. "I'm sorry; that's not at all possible."

She said something else but I had already hung up the phone and was calling Mary. I told her what had happened and she was silent for a moment. I think she felt she needed to tell me something, to direct me somewhere. I'm certain she was hearing the desperation in my voice. I needed to talk with someone.

She finally spoke. "There's a man who goes to our church. I don't know him at all but I think he works for an insurance agency in Marion. His name is Steve Wells. Like I said, I don't know him but I've heard many people say a lot of good things about him. I don't know, maybe if you called him, maybe he would talk to you."

She looked up his number and gave it to me. We hung up and I remember thinking that there was no way in the world I was going to call this guy. I had told the pastor of the church that I was in the midst of a crisis and he booked me for a month down the road. What in the world was this guy, an insurance guy like me, going to tell me?

I sat there for a long time and looked at the number and then closed my eyes. I thought back to all that I'd gone through, all I had *come* through, and knew that I had gotten to where I was at that moment because the Lord had taken me by the hand and walked with me. I remember thinking back to finding David Jeremiah on the radio and how his Turning Point had been my own and knew that everything that I had done from that day had been directed by God. I sat there and, even though I know I didn't consciously ask God what to do, I know He spoke to me, and what He said was simply this: "Call him."

So I did.

: : : : : :

I went to Steve's office on Tuesday wearing the best suit I owned; it was the only suit I owned. I remember thinking that it was going to be a strange meeting; I had no idea what I was going to say to him and less of an idea of what I was hoping I would hear from him. Like the call I had made to him the day before, I was going to see him because the Lord had told me to so I had to have faith that He was going to sit in on the meeting with us. I was pretty sure I would sense His presence if He were because I had sensed His presence before.

When I met Steve, he wasn't at all the man I thought he would be. I guess I was expecting an insurance man. I felt instead that I was with a true man of God, and as he took me back into the small conference room, I immediately felt that God in fact was sitting at the table with us. Steve was genuine in his friendliness and sincere in his words. He was a tall and good-looking man, dressed like me in a suit, although I was certain it wasn't the only one he owned. He had a very relaxed manner about him and I felt instantly at ease. He in fact owned the business United Insurance Agencies and had three other agents working with him as independent contractors. We drank coffee and I told him about all that had happened to me professionally since I had lost my job at Millhiser. I didn't share with him about my alcoholism nor about what had transpired at Bethel but shared with him instead about how I felt the Lord was leading me somewhere; I was simply having a hard time figuring out where it was.

I likened my situation to that of Peter and his struggle with getting out of the boat when he saw Jesus walking on water. I told Steve that I felt the Lord was telling me to have faith and get out of the boat I found myself in but I was having trouble knowing where to step.

He laughed. "I think I find that hard to believe, given what you've told me so far about your journey. It seems that you've had a lot of faith and taken a lot of steps. Why does this one seem so hard?"

I thought about it before I answered. "I think that before I had some idea as to what I was going to step into; right now, I have no idea what's there. I only know . . . feel, at least . . . that I'm supposed to take some kind of step."

He told me he'd done that a lot in his life too, taken steps when he didn't really know what he was stepping into, but he kept walking because he knew that the path, even if he couldn't see it all the time, had been laid out by the Lord.

We talked a little while longer and then he asked me the question I had been waiting to hear, I think.

"What is it that you're looking for me to do?"

I looked at him and didn't say anything, trying to figure out that answer for myself. I really had no idea. Then he said something that I hadn't really expected.

"I don't really have any place for you here right now. I don't know if that's what you're looking for but I need to tell you that I'm full here. We just hired a life insurance person and I just don't have the room."

"Oh, no," I said with some hesitation. I didn't know if that was why I had come or not but apparently he had thought about it. "I guess I was just looking for someone to talk to. You know, maybe someone who could give me a little direction. I don't know. I appreciate you thinking, you know, that you would consider me, but really, I wasn't expecting anything other than a chance to talk."

Then he said something to me that made me understand why I had heard the Lord tell me to call Steve in the first place.

"You know," he said as he leaned forward and looked hard at

me. "There are no coincidences. It's not a coincidence that you and I met today."

I looked at him and even though I had only met him that morning, I could see understanding and compassion in his eyes. He must have known I was confused about some things that were going on in my life; maybe there had been a time in his own life when he had been confused about the same things. I didn't know. I only knew that he didn't seem all that surprised that I was there, and when we were done, he asked for my cell number and I got his and then I left.

It was a strange meeting in that I had no expectations when I went to meet him and realized that, because of that fact, I wasn't disappointed when I left. I hadn't expected him to offer me a job; I hadn't even thought about that possibility and hadn't even taken a copy of what was becoming a fairly extensive resume. I felt good that I had talked to a good man who, even though he seemed to be a lot farther up the road than I was, appeared to be on the same spiritual path.

I continued to slog through work at FSC. Chad and Roger, both as unsettled as I was professionally, stayed as well and we all talked about how hard it was. Money was flying out the window and we all worked hard at trying to blow some back into the office to cover our expenses, but it was a struggle. I kept praying for direction and the strength to do what I felt was the work God had given me to do, but for a while I didn't hear His voice. I think there are times when He sits back and watches us, much like a parent watches a child when he thinks no one is looking, to make sure we're learning the lessons that are being taught and applying them to the life we're living. I never wavered in my faith during this time and never quit working at the issues that needed attention in my recovery. I just kept praying and waiting to hear Him again.

This time when He came to me, He came in a voicemail from Steve Wells. I had been out of town and, on my way back, got his message.

"Hey, when you get back and have a minute, give me a call. I'd like to get together with you when you can."

I called Mary and told her that he wanted to meet with me.

"What do you suppose he wants?" she asked.

"I have no idea. Probably just wants to see how I'm doing. I don't know. He's such a nice guy; I'm sure he just wants to talk some more."

She lowered her voice a bit. "You know, I think he's a recovering alcoholic. I've heard that from a couple of people at church."

"Really?" I asked. If that was the case, and one should never take what is passed on third-hand as being the truth, then I was beginning to understand a little more about why God had led me to him.

"Well, it's what I heard; I don't know for sure."

I thanked her for sharing and then called Steve to set up a time to meet. We decided to get together in his office again the following afternoon but he gave me no indication about what he wanted. I prayed that night, as had become my habit, to give thanks and to ask for understanding as to what might be happening; there was a quiet stir in me that seemed to be telling me that clarity may be only a day away.

The next day, wearing the same suit as I had the first time we met, I was back in the conference room with Steve. He brought me a cup of coffee and I couldn't help but notice his silver cup emblazoned with the words *In His Grip* and I realized that I was with a man who, like me, had come to believe that God really did have His hands on everything going on in his life. The big difference was that Steve had no problem proclaiming that, even in the way he drank his coffee. I realized that I wasn't there yet, at least not in the way that I should be. The fact that I had yet to share my experience at Bethel with anyone was evidence to that. I had so much to be thankful for; I thought briefly back to my visit to Sedlacek and the vision of the man coming off the elevator from the fifth floor and knew that if I was going to become the disciple that I felt God wanted me to become, I had to get to the point in my life where I could share what He had done for me. I thought back also to Steve's comment the day I had met him about there being no coincidences; it was beginning to become clear to me that God *had* brought me there for a reason.

We chatted briefly about the things that two men talk about when beginning to learn about one another, I all the while thinking about what I felt I wanted to say to him and wondering why he had called me back. I decided to take the initiative.

"You, know," I began, "we have more in common than you know."

He looked at me. "What do you mean?" he asked.

What I wanted to tell him was that we were both recovering alcoholics and, even though he appeared to be miles ahead of me, both were on the same path spiritually. But then it hit me that I was about to make a statement based on nothing more than speculation from my ex-wife who had maybe heard something from a couple of people in church whom she had never identified. I thought briefly of a man saying to a woman, "Oh, how exciting for you. When are you due?" and her decidedly less than enthusiastic response: "I'm not pregnant."

I realized that it was too early in our relationship to make those kinds of assumptions, so I skipped over the alcoholic part and went right into the journey. "We're both on the same path. I feel that I'm somehow being led by God to see you. I guess that's kind of what you meant when you talked about there being no coincidences."

He smiled. What he said next came out of nowhere. "I'd like you to come work for us. I prayed hard about this and the Lord told me I need to do this. I've already decided that, if you're willing, I'll take apart the break room and turn it into an office for you."

I didn't know what to say, and while I was thinking about it he excused himself.

"Let me go see who else is here. I'd like everyone to meet you."

He left and I was alone in the conference room wondering about what had happened. It was one of those things that don't really hit a person until later, but when it hit me, I knew that the Lord was again directing my walk along the path He had laid out. He knew I needed someone like Steve in my life. Yes, I was walking, but I was essentially walking alone. I didn't have the daily influence of a godly man in my life and Steve was going to be that man for me.

The fact that I ended up meeting everyone else and we all seemed to hit it off immediately was really no surprise. For the first time since I had left Millhiser, and probably for the first time ever, I was, professionally, exactly where God wanted me to be and knew I needed to be. I was in a Christian workplace; I would be starting from scratch in a commission-only job, but that consideration really never became part of the equation for me. I knew that every day I would have a mentor that would, in however the Lord intended, serve as an example of how I should live my life. When I left the office that day, I felt that my recovery, professionally, had finally taken a significant turn. I went back to see Dale and told him I was leaving and on Tuesday, October 1, 2002, I started at United.

I met Steve's wife, Debbie, that first night. I was home working on my manuscript, and Steve called to see if I would be willing to come up and move furniture. He had already torn into the break room. All the cabinets were gone, and the sink was out. New carpet was laid and he had bought new furnishings for me. When I got there, Debbie was directing the operation and I knew immediately that they were a special couple. They shared the same birthday and were even married on that same day. They had been married for over twenty years, each already having been married before, and it was obvious that the Lord had meant for them to be together. They were partners in their marriage and in every other aspect of their lives. As I got to know them both, I found myself praying that maybe someday the Lord would bless me with someone that He had designed especially for me, just as He had for them.

I also learned something important from Steve one day. It was the first lesson the Lord must have planned for him to teach me. Since I had been back to town, I had gotten into the habit of picking Laura up from her daycare after school on Wednesday afternoons and taking her to Mary's house. It gave me an hour with her, alone, and even though it usually only gave us time for a quick ice cream cone or a soda somewhere, it was an hour that I had come to cherish because of all the time I had missed with her when she was younger. I was standing in Steve's doorway one of my first Wednesdays at United and told him I was going to leave a few minutes early so I could go pick her up. I think I just wanted to make sure it was okay with him.

He smiled when I told him. He knew Laura from church and, like everyone else who had come into contact with her, he had a special place in his heart for her.

"You need to go. It's a man's godly duty to be a father to his children."

Those words still ring in my ears. A man's godly duty. I had failed miserably at that duty and realized when he spoke those words to me that it wasn't simply an opportunity that I had to spend that hour with Laura; it was another gift that God had given me. Another chance to be something that I hadn't been the first time around. I hadn't been a good father. The decision I had made to come home had been the first step to being a better one this time around, but I had never thought of it as a "godly duty."

Steve, with those simple yet powerful words, had pointed out to me that it was not just something that I would do when I could, but rather, if I was sincere about this part of my recovery, it was something I was bound by God to do. My children needed me to be their father again. It dawned on me that God hadn't only answered my prayer for me when He brought me home; He had perhaps answered the prayers of two daughters who had prayed to have their dad back as well. It was now my duty, God-given, to be the father they needed.

CHAPTER 29

Hard Lessons

THE FUNNY THING ABOUT LIFE, especially a life in recovery, is that just because something good happens, it doesn't mean that suddenly everything else is going to be okay. Yes, finally working in a place like United was starting to bring my professional recovery into focus. Not only was I back in Cedar Rapids, working in the insurance business again, I was doing it in an environment where the spirit of the Lord was present every day. But, because it was a commission-only job, the first month there, I didn't get a paycheck. That didn't mean I didn't sell anything; it meant that commissions weren't paid for thirty days and, as a result, I took home nothing that first month.

The immediate problem was that I didn't have enough money to cover all my expenses and I ended up having to decide what wasn't going to get paid. I had no choice; I went to see Scott, my credit counselor, and told him I couldn't make my payment. He told me that he didn't think that was going to be an option that would allow me to stay in the program; I told him there was nothing else I could do. We talked for a while about what I could do. By this time, I had been in the program for almost eighteen months, diligently paying my $874 every month, and slowly, well, almost imperceptibly, making a very tiny dent in the mountain of debt I was trying to overcome. After we had gone over the numbers, he looked at me.

"You should be proud of yourself, Steve," he said. "You've fought a good fight with this. You've done something for almost eighteen months that most people wouldn't have done at all and you've done it with very little to work with. I'm proud of you. I really am. But I think it may be the best thing for you right now to accept that you simply can't do this anymore and surrender. I think you should consider filing for bankruptcy."

I didn't know what to say. *Bankruptcy.* It was a stigma that didn't seem like one I wanted to carry around. I was already lugging *Alcoholism* around and I didn't know if my neck would support any more weight holding it down. It had such a dark and dreary sound to it. *Bankruptcy.* People lost everything they owned. And then it hit me; I didn't own anything. Aside from my car, I had nothing. There was no savings, no annuities, no property. I had signed off on the house when my guilt was allowing me to sign anything Mary had put in front of me. There was nothing to lose. Well, except for the pride thing. And the thought that somewhere I would be letting God down, walking away from my responsibility like that.

"I don't know, Scott," I finally said to him. "I've got to think about this. What's going to happen with my creditors if I'm off the program?"

"Oh, nothing for a while, until they start to catch up to the fact that you're not making payments anymore. Then they'll start to call you, or turn things over to a collection agency and they'll call you. It can get pretty nasty. Eventually, they'll serve you with papers; you know, sue you; take you to court. That's why I think you should really consider filing. Like I said, you've put up a good fight. You've been through a lot; maybe it's time to start over. Think about it."

"I don't even know who to talk to," I said. "I mean, you know,

I suppose I need to talk to an attorney about this but I have no idea who . . ."

He reached into his drawer and pulled out a business card and handed it over to me.

"Give her a call," he said. "You don't have to do it right away, but think it over and when you feel that it's time, go ahead and give her a call. She'll talk to you; the first visit is free. She'll answer any questions you have."

I looked at the card. Linda Merritt. Attorney-at-Law. Specializing in Bankruptcy. I couldn't believe this was happening.

: : : : : :

I got through the rest of the year and tried the best I could to put the finances out of my mind. I knew that was the wrong thing to do because that was one of the things that I was working on trying to change in my life. As had been the case with my alcoholism, I had waited too long and tried to pretend that the problem didn't exist until it got too big to handle. I knew that I should take Scott's advice and call Linda right away and start the process, as uncomfortably painful as it was going to be, but my pride was standing firmly in the way. It wasn't the first time I had allowed that to happen and, as I was about to find out, it was not going to be the last.

As the year drew to a close, I came to the realization that something had to change in regard to my relationship with Melanie. We still maintained our weekend relationship but I felt that we were at a crossroads in our life together. I knew that she had been hurt by my decision first to leave Davenport with Freedom Mutual and then with my decision not to look back to Davenport when Freedom closed. She knew I was happy in Marion and even happier at United and I'm sure she was no doubt discouraged by the direction we were headed. I was too. I found myself praying hard for some sort of resolution to everything. Like my prayers when I knew I had gone over the edge with my drinking and I would pray for deliverance, I wanted this to be painless and easy, unlike how my sobriety had finally found me. I think I wanted Melanie to pick up the phone one day and say, "Well, I've thought about it and I've decided to sell my house and give up my life here. I'm going to move away from my friends and family and come live with you in a town where I don't know anyone and have no prospects for a job, but I'll do it because I love you and I want to spend my life with you."

Of course, that's not what happened because it's not what the Lord had planned for me. Not yet anyway, and certainly not with her. Had I known those things then, it would have substantially lessened the pain I was about to go through, but one of the many things I've learned about the Lord's love is this: it's during times of pain and struggling that our faith is tested and, in the end, if we remain true to Him, strengthened as well.

Melanie was seeing another man behind my back. I can't really blame her. I was, after all, the one who had left her alone. When I made the decision to move back to Cedar Rapids, I had done so because I had prayed for it. I believe the Lord gave it to me because it was what He wanted for me as well. It had been a hard decision and a long journey. The same thing was happening now, but I was having a hard time seeing it that way, what with my pride and all. I found out about what was going on quite innocently enough when a good friend of mine, Gabe, a client who lived in Davenport and still did business with me, told me he had been to a bar called the Rusty Nail with his wife. It happened to be the same night that Melanie had told me she was going to the Rusty Nail with a bunch of her friends for a party. When Gabe told me where he had been, I asked him about Melanie. He hadn't seen her. In fact, he and his wife had been there from seven until nine, eating and shooting pool, and they had been the only two people there.

I asked Melanie about it the next day and she said simply that she had been there with all of her friends and that was that. Someone was lying to me. I reasoned that Gabe had absolutely nothing to gain by lying; I knew it was Melanie. I eventually caught her in her lies one night when I foolishly drove to Davenport unannounced, mostly, I think, to convince myself that she wasn't lying. When I got there, I parked down the street from her house and watched as she and "the other man" walked arm in arm into the front door. I thought about knocking on the door but I was too upset, so I drove back home and called her the next day and listened to her tell me that there was nothing going on. There wasn't anyone else. There was only me. Always me. Yadda, yadda, yadda.

I would be lying to say I wasn't hurt by it all. I would also be lying to say that I stood up to her and tossed her out of my life. It took me a while to come to grips with what was going on, especially when she finally confessed a couple of weeks later that there was, in fact, someone else, and she needed some time to sort everything out.

At first, I tried to win her back, as if it were a game I needed to win even if I knew in my heart that I had no desire to keep the trophy. What finally brought me around was the fact that God had answered my prayer. I had prayed for resolution; He had revealed to me that He had something better for me even if I had no idea at the time what it was. I got to the point where every time I would think that I needed to do something to get her back, I would think instead of how, by doing so, I was going against God's will for me in my life. If I would call her, it would be followed by a prayer asking for forgiveness because I felt I had sinned; I was in direct opposition to what God had given me: His answer to my prayer. He was offering me freedom, a chance to grow in faith and to step out from what had been the safe and comfortable existence I had at one time known with her but that had long since vanished. He had other plans for me; He also wanted me to see something about myself that I had never had the chance . . . or the desire . . . to see.

I have never been able to imagine the pain I caused Mary with my infidelity. The pain I felt because of what happened with Melanie couldn't begin to come close to what Mary had gone through, but it was enough to bring clarity to the damage I had done to her. While I couldn't relate to the depth of her despair, I could, in some small way, begin to empathize with her feelings of rejection and abandonment. I realized that the pain I was feeling through everything with Melanie was in fact due in large part to the pain I was feeling about what I had done to Mary and, in no small part, to my daughters. One day, I went to Mary's office and did something I had never done before. I told her how deeply sorry I was for all I had done to her. She had forgiven me by then. She hadn't forgotten what had happened and I'm certain she never will, but she had found forgiveness. But that day, for the first time, I asked for her forgiveness. My pain could not match hers; it did, however, bring to light for the first time a small part of what she had experienced. I knew that I never wanted to be the cause of that kind of pain ever again.

I eventually walked away from Melanie. I learned some valuable lessons from this time, hard lessons that I think everyone might learn at one point or another in his life. I learned that God does know what He wants for us and if we sincerely and unceasingly ask for it, and He wants us to have it, we will get it. It won't always be given to us the way we would like to receive it, but He will give it to us nonetheless. It's what we do with it once He gives it to us that matters.

I learned that faith will get anyone through a difficult time. It got Mary and our daughters through the pain of my alcohol abuse. It got me through my recovery and it got me through the heartbreak of being less important to someone than I mistakenly thought I needed to be.

I learned that pride is a terrible thing. It's okay to be proud of your children and your country and even your ability, through God, to overcome a terrible addiction. But pride itself, that deadliest of the deadly sins, is a terrible thing to walk hand in hand with through life, trying to convince yourself that you know what's best for you. Pride kept me from getting help when I needed to get help and when I didn't think there was a problem, and when I realized I might be wrong, I figured I could take care of things myself. Pride stood in my way when I should have walked away from Melanie at the first lie or the second or third but didn't because I was convinced that she really must love me; why else would she lie to me? It's hard to break pride's grip on us, but we can't embrace God's will or strengthen our faith unless we do it.

I learned so much from all that happened. I learned so much about God's love and His desires for us and His willingness to not just hear but answer our prayers when they are in line with His will. I learned . . . again . . . that an answered prayer is a call to faith. It's a chance to grow in the faith we profess to have and trust Him that His plan for us is, in fact, more wonderful than we can imagine given what we might find ourselves going through. I learned all of that as I left Melanie behind and trusted that God must have something incredible in store for me.

CHAPTER 30

"Sedlacek's Greatest Success Story"

I FINALLY FINISHED MY MANUSCRIPT in April of 2003. *The Unopened Box* was two hundred and eighty pages of my heart and soul that I at times thought I would never finish. When it was finished, I had no idea what to do with it. It was a story of my recovery, loosely fictionalized, that dealt with the harsh reality of how alcohol abuse can derail a man and, ultimately, how faith can begin to put him back on track.

The central character, Jack Andrews, was a lot like me or, more specifically, how I had envisioned my life becoming. He had overcome his disease and was a successful writer and speaker, doing what he felt he had been called by the Lord to do. I guess I could think of myself as a successful writer; I had, after all, written the manuscript that I had failed to write earlier in my life. I just didn't know what to do with it. I left some things out; I didn't talk about my relationship with Laurie; I didn't go into depth about what had happened in Bethel; I didn't talk at all about that desperate night in the motel when the deep sleep called me to take all the pain away. I'm not sure why I still felt that I couldn't share these things, especially the parts about what had without question been the Lord's salvation. I think I didn't know yet how people would accept it or if anyone would believe it. I somehow felt, though, that I was now surrounded by people at work who might if I ever decided to break my silence.

In addition to Steve, I had made a good friend at work, Joan Brown, our office manager. Joan was a follower of the Lord, a woman who had never married, and a self-proclaimed caretaker of her family, a role at which she excelled. She was the one who revealed to me an interesting part of my first meeting with Steve at United. After I left that meeting, he immediately went to Joan and said to her,

"I can't explain it, but God told me that I need to have Steve come work for us."

He had been right all along; there are no coincidences. God had wanted us to meet.

Joan and I became friends and she immediately took an interest in my manuscript and my dream of being a writer, a desire that I continued to believe was being encouraged by the Lord. I had shared my story with her, except, of course, the significant parts which I had yet to share with anyone. She became a supporter of what I wanted to believe my life would be one day; it was the same kind of life my main character, Jack Andrews, had lived. Like me, he had overcome his addiction and was sharing his story through his writing and also spoke to recovering alcoholics to encourage them in their own recoveries. This belief was bolstered in May of 2003 when I got a call from Bill Sackett, still a counselor at Sedlacek, asking me if I would be interested in becoming a speaker at the treatment center. I had been sober for seven years, time enough, he felt, that my story was worth sharing to others who were struggling. He asked me to meet with him and I gladly accepted.

This time, unlike when I had gone to see Bill Martin, I got off the elevator on the fourth floor with much more confidence. As I walked down the hall toward Bill's office, I passed Dave Robertson's and Andy Peterson's offices, stopping to say hello to both of them and relish the looks on their faces when they saw me. Andy called me "a miracle," and Dave said I was "Sedlacek's greatest success story," sentiments with which I could hardly argue. It was good to see them both although it was a little strange as I thought back to the time spent in both offices, especially Dave's, when I had been drowning so deep in denial that I could hardly breathe. It was hard to believe that part of my life had existed.

I still think about that often. That time in which I had found myself was like a nightmare from which I had almost never wakened. There are still moments in my life when I'll see something . . . an old oak tree standing in the middle of an empty field . . . and a vision is triggered of slogging through a late December afternoon with a bag of money in my hand, quietly hoping for a gunshot to ring out and put me out of my misery. I'll hear something . . . the sound of the rain on my windshield when I drive . . . and I'll hear the water that was rushing through my head the day of my breakdown; the day when the voices and the visions and the call of death were all in my house, inviting me to "open the door and everything will be all right." As I walked the hall that afternoon, my footsteps echoing on the tile floor in the empty hallway, I was consciously aware of how many single steps I had taken to move my life away from that time. I was more aware of the fact that I had never taken one of those steps alone. He had always been with me; I'm certain there had been more times than I'll ever know that He had picked me up and carried me. I only knew that I would have never done it without Him; no one can ever do anything without Him.

I met with Bill, he, too, excited and happy about my recovery. We talked briefly about my journey and the difficulties those in recovery face daily, and then the conversation turned to the speech he had asked me about. He wanted me to speak on Monday, May nineteenth, less than two weeks away.

"It's a little different from when you were in," he said. "We stopped meeting on Sunday mornings a year or so ago when we knew we were getting ready to do away with the inpatient program."

I didn't have to ask.

"Funding," he said. "We still detox on the fifth floor, but if someone needs to be hospitalized for treatment, we don't do that up here anymore. Because of that, we obviously had to do away with the Sunday morning talks."

I thought back to the Sunday morning talks I had endured when I was in the hospital. They were given by old men, men who had endured hard lives with hard drinking, but they hadn't been very inspirational. I'm certain that a lot of that had to do with the fact that the audience hadn't been very receptive from the start. It was Sunday morning; it was the only morning we thought we would get to sleep in a little but instead had been hauled out of bed at seven to go listen to some old man tell us how much he drank and how it had affected him. I remember thinking at the time that I really didn't need to know about his drinking; I had obviously mastered that part of the journey. I remember thinking that what I wanted to know was what it was like when you finally decided to stop. The thing about treatment is, while you're in, you deal a lot with why you drank, what it did to you and to your family. You talk a lot about consequences and regret but never really hear a lot about what it's like once you get out. Maybe that's why so many people ended up coming back. They had no idea how hard it was going to be and there was no blueprint, no map to lead from simply being sober to being in true recovery.

Bill told me that on every other Monday night, speakers who had successfully completed the program and who had at least five years of sobriety could come and speak to the current batch of people in the intensive outpatient program. He said that the talks were one hour long and should be broken down into three twenty-minute segments: what our lives had been like and what it was that brought us to treatment, what treatment had been like for us, and what life was like now, five or ten or twenty years into recovery. My first thought was that one hour was not going to be enough time. He said there would be anywhere from ten to twenty-five people, maybe more at times, and they would range in age from teenagers on up. That fact hadn't changed much from when I had been in as I thought back to Chris, my first roommate, the nineteen-year-old kid who I had prayed had lived to see twenty, and to Loren, my smoking buddy in his early sixties who was still probably drinking wine. There will always be some things that will never change; alcohol addiction has no age limits or restrictions. It can—and does—affect everyone.

On Monday, the nineteenth of May, I walked down the hall to the large double doors, behind which was the group room, the room I had gone into with Sarah the day she sent me home when I came to treatment drunk. I sat in one of the two chairs across the hall from the small nurses' station where I had blown over the limit and found myself again surrounded with memories of a time in my life that didn't seem as if it could have possibly existed. I was armed with a loose collection of notes that I had jotted down on the outline that Bill had given me, things I wanted to try to touch on, and the story I wanted to use to begin the talk. It was the story about the guy walking down the street and falling into a hole. He keeps calling out for help until his best friend comes along and jumps into the hole with him, telling him, "It's okay, I've been in this hole before and I'm here to help you out."

There's more to it than that, but my point was that I felt I could enlighten them somehow into what recovery really is. I had never feared speaking in front of a group of people, especially a group such as the one behind the double doors. I had been in their shoes; I knew exactly what they were going through. I had prayed all the way to Sedlacek, asking God to give me the words to speak and the peace to speak them. I was ready. Ready, that is, until the doors opened and Andy pushed his way through.

"Hey, Steve, good to see you!"

I stood and took his hand. "Andy, I can't tell you how excited I am to be here."

He looked quickly over his shoulder and then back at me. "Tough crowd in there tonight," he said, smiling.

I smiled back, thinking to the times I was in the crowd and knew that we weren't that tough. "I'll be okay," I told him.

"The prisoners from Oakdale are up here tonight," he said. And then he said it again, still smiling. "Tough crowd."

Oakdale State Prison, originally built as the Iowa Security and Medical Facility, was constructed in 1967 as a psychiatric hospital for the evaluation of men and women prisoners. In 1984 it expanded and became the Iowa Medical Classification Center, the starting point for convicts entering Iowa's penal system. It holds prisoners with special health problems, and on this night some of those prisoners, mostly men, had been sent up to Sedlacek to take part in the outpatient program and hear the speaker, two prospects that I'm certain excited them to no end. I knew right away that I would have to scrap my story about the guy in the hole; most in the crowd were in a hole I had never seen before. Still, I figured recovery is recovery whether you're in prison or not and since I had a captive audience, so to speak, I didn't plan to change what I was going to say.

I started by telling them about my history as an alcoholic. I talked about my first time drinking with Ronnie Olson when I threw up in the back of his car. I talked about college life and then life

in Ruthven when Craig and I would get drunk on my boat and
how my dad got drunk on my boat and broke down and told me
he was a failure. I told them about the move to Cedar Rapids and
how I lived with Allen and how he and I would drink Absolut from
the freezer and how I had started keeping a bottle under my bed. I
shared about my time at Millhiser, how my dad died, and how that
time in my life triggered my complete dependence on alcohol. I
talked about my breakdown, the voices, and the fear, the relapse, and
my escape to Minneapolis; I told them about Bethel but I didn't
tell them the specifics. I just told them that someone came and sat
at my table and made me realize that I needed to stop. I think that
even seven years into my journey, there was still something that was
keeping me from sharing that with anyone. I was hopeful that the
Lord would let me know when I was ready.

The whole time I was talking, I was moving. When I had taught,
I never stood behind my desk when talking to my students. I was
always on the move. I guess I wanted to see who was paying attention, whose eyes would actually follow me. That night, I was
doing it primarily because there was one guy in the group, one of
the Oakdale prisoners, who was one of the scariest men I had ever
seen. He was dressed in camouflage pants and a black T-shirt and
had more tattoos on his arms than most people have idle thoughts
in their heads. His long hair was pulled back in a ponytail; he had
a goatee and there was a pair of dark sunglasses covering his eyes.
He was leaning back in his chair with his legs straight out, his arms
folded defiantly across his chest. When I started moving around, my
initial hope was that his head wouldn't follow me; I was hoping
that maybe he had no desire at all to hear what I had to say. No
such luck. No matter where I went, he turned his head to follow
me, and his eyes, even though I couldn't see them, were open. He
looked like the angriest person in the world and he looked to be
directing it all at me.

I spent the next fifteen minutes talking about my two stays in Sedlacek and how they differed. I talked about the denial and the games I played with Dave and then Mary. I told them about how the first time all I was doing was plotting how to be a more efficient and effective drinker, and how the second time I was beginning to plan on how to never drink again. I told them about Robbie and Loren and Janet and how the odds are stacked against us all when we leave and told them that part of that problem is that we have no idea how to prepare for what recovery is all about. I talked about the dry drunk and David Jeremiah and then went into the crux of my talk, and all of my talks since: how to deal with life "above the line."

What I do when I talk is go to the dry-erase whiteboard in the room and take a marker and draw the line. I have someone tell me his addiction. Most of the people in there are in for alcohol abuse but I've used whatever someone tells me to put. After that, I ask everyone to tell me one thing that was impacted by the abuse, much like I did that first day in my office in Davenport after I had encountered my very own "turning point." It usually takes a couple of minutes for someone to say something. I'm never surprised by that, given how long it took any of us to say anything when I was in treatment. Usually though, once someone says something, and it's usually either "family" or "job," others become less reluctant to say something. There's usually something that has really hit each person hard, and most of the time I get quite a bit up there. It's surprised me through the years as I've spoken that no one, not one single person, has ever said "spirituality" or "God" or "religion" or anything like that at all. It's now the first thing I put on the list, right in the middle and all in capital letters. Through the years, I've grown comfortable sharing my story when I speak. I have reached the point where I make sure that when I leave, people know that the only real way to overcome any addiction is through the salvation of the Lord.

"*. . .We all need to be saved.*"

That first night, there were a lot of people that seemed to get into the idea that to recover, you had to do more than not drink. I think most people believe that if you're not drinking, you're in recovery. It's become the focus of my talks, whether it's at Sedlacek or in a high school, a health forum, or an addiction class in a college.

The only person who didn't seem to be getting into it at all was the one guy who I had figured by now had to have been a serial killer or something. This guy just sat there, arms across his chest, and if it weren't for the fact that his head did follow me around the room when I moved, I would have thought he was asleep. The fact that he was listening to me, still looking angrier than I must have looked to my sister the night she sent me off to my salvation, wasn't settling all that well with me.

I finished up a few minutes before eight thirty so I could allow for questions. I didn't figure anyone would have any; I don't recall that anyone ever asked any when we had speakers on Sunday mornings. We just wanted to get out; I'm sure everyone in the room was now feeling the same way. I was surprised, and more than just a little uncomfortable, when the first hand that went up was that of Charles Manson himself.

I could hear him now.

"Hey, scum bag, why don't you come down and see me at my place sometime? Me and my friends would love to have you for dinner."

"Hey, momma's boy, you ever killed anyone before? I mean other than the fact that we're all sittin' here dyin' listenin' to you."

There was no way I couldn't acknowledge him; his was the only hand up. I looked at Andy, who was busy passing out the evaluation forms that would be completed by those who wanted to comment on how the talk had impacted them. I didn't have any choice. I looked at Charlie and nodded.

He stood up and looked at me. No one said anything.

"I been to a lot of these meetings; hated every one of 'em. I just want to say that this is the best talk I ever heard. I ain't fillin' nothin' out. You just need to keep talkin' to people."

He sat back down and I looked at him and smiled. He just held up his fist and nodded at me. I'm sure in the underworld that must be some sign of acceptance or something but I don't know. All I know is that every time I've spoken since then, I've come to accept that all I want to do when I speak, whether it's to ten people or fifty people, is to have one person walk out of the room, or shuffle out with shackled ankles, and believe that what he's heard from me might run through his head when he thinks he can't go on and realizes that hey, if that guy that spoke to me that night can make it, after all he went through, then maybe I can make it too. One person. That's all I've ever asked for.

I've thought about that a lot through the years and I think about the Lord and how He spoke to people. I think that maybe He had the same hope, that if He could just reach one person—one person who was tired of living his life the way he was living it and had just about run out of hope that there was any other way to live it—if He could just make one person realize that there is a better life, then He'd had a pretty good day. If that one person could share that thought with one other person, and then he would share it with another, and another, and then another, pretty soon, there are a lot of people living a spirit-filled life centered in Christ.

It hit me that night as I walked out of the group room and down the hall to the elevator that I wasn't afraid anymore, that God had not only been with me that night, but He had shown me what He wanted me to do. He wanted me to help others turn from the life they were leading, the very same life I led, and turn to Him as their last and only hope. I felt that He was telling me that this was part of His plan for me; this was what He knew I needed to do, not just for them, but for me as well.

CHAPTER 31

Just One Person

BY THE MIDDLE OF 2003, I was feeling pretty good about my recovery. As I looked at the paper I had drawn in my office in Davenport back that very first day I had heard David Jeremiah, I realized that I was slowly confronting those issues that I had identified as having been impacted by my disease. My walk with the Lord had become paramount in my life. It was the one thing from which everything else grew; without it, there would be no recovery. My relationship with my daughters was good and getting better all the time. The time I spent with Laura on weekends was some of the best time I'd ever had and I was seeing Katie whenever our schedules would allow. I was finally being the father I hadn't been; I knew that I was fulfilling my godly duty. I loved my job, but more importantly I loved the people with whom I was working. I was working in an environment unlike any other in which I had ever worked. Steve was a man of God and whether he knew it or not, he had become my mentor. I now counted two men as close friends, Steve and Jim, and both were the kind of men that I needed in my life. Both were holding me accountable in my walk even if neither knew he was doing it. I felt that I was now more a man of integrity and honesty even though I knew I needed to be more forthcoming about what had happened in Bethel.

While I knew I was making progress, there were still things that needed a lot of work. Socially, I was uncomfortable in public. I found it ironic that the most comfortable public place I'd been since my journey began was when I spoke at Sedlacek. I felt at home there and even though I didn't know any of the people I spoke to, I knew that I was where the Lord wanted me to be. Other than that, it was still hard to be out. Joan and I would hang out together, grabbing a bite to eat somewhere or going to a coffee shop, but other than that, I stayed in a lot. I was moving toward being more comfortable at church, trying not to feel that everyone was pointing at me and whispering about what I was convinced they must have known about me, but even that was hard at times. Eventually it got easier to go there, mostly because I finally came to realize that most people there were there for the same reason I was: they had been in pain and were looking for the love of the Lord to help them heal.

The biggest issue, still, was finances. I was slowly making progress at United but the past continued to close in fast behind me. As Scott had told me, it took a while for everyone to learn I was off the program, but once they knew, the collection calls started rolling in and most of the callers weren't nice about their intentions. One day, out of fear mostly, I dug out the business card Scott had given me and called Linda Merritt, the attorney he had told me about.

I knew that it was time to do something, but this was the last thing I wanted to do. I had thought about how to get out of the mess I was in, but there really wasn't any way to do it. All told, I was about $26,000 in debt and barely making ends meet. No bank being run by anyone other than circus people would loan me money to pay off that kind of debt with the income I had. I had prayed on it and spent some time talking to Jim about it. He knew my financial situation better than anyone else, having done my taxes for the past four or five years. He knew there was nothing else to do; I think I wanted him to tell me that he'd give me $26,000 and call it even given the remarkable spiritual journey I was on. Kind of like God wringing a sobriety washcloth over me one night and making me sober. The thing I've learned about this journey and the thing I stress to others just starting out is that there are no easy steps. There might be fewer of them the further we go but none of them is easy.

My first meeting with Linda served to put my mind at ease even if I still carried a tremendous amount of guilt over what I was doing. Like Scott, she listened to my story and agreed, given all I had been through, that I was doing the right thing. Even so, I still struggled to convince myself that it was the right thing to do but I knew that the financial matter had become too big for me to overcome on my own.

I thought back to the time when I came to realize that my drinking had become too big for me and how I had finally turned to the Lord and asked for help. I wanted to believe it was the same kind of thing here, but I think the thing that was holding me back was the idea that it wasn't an honorable thing to do, walking away from this kind of responsibility. I found myself in an odd position emotionally. In the past, I would have walked away from whatever I could simply so I wouldn't have to take responsibility. Plus, I had been far from honorable in my life; I was struggling now with the idea that this far into my recovery, I was looking at the distinct possibility of turning my back on the very same honor that I was trying to make fit into my life.

It was confusing, and by the time my meeting with Linda was over, I didn't know what I was going to do. She told me the next step was going to be for me to come back when she had all the paperwork done and sign off on everything and let the process begin. In the meantime, she told me to stop paying any of my creditors, empty my bank accounts, and tell any creditor who called to call her instead. That was the only part of the scenario that sounded like a positive to me.

:::::::

My manuscript was officially a manuscript by the fall of 2003. Amid all the phone calls I was getting from my creditors and the emotional struggle I was going through trying to figure out if I was doing the right thing, I focused most of my attention on the work that I had felt God was giving me with what I had written.

One day I went to the Budget Copy around the corner from my office and handed over my two hundred and eighty pages to the woman behind the counter and asked if she could make five other copies and bind them for me. I had printed it off at work from one of about ten disks I'd saved it on so nothing would happen to it. She asked me if I was an author; I'd never had anyone ask me anything like that before.

I wanted to say yes, because it had a much better ring to it than, *"No, I'm just a bankrupt, alcoholic insurance man who likes to write,"* but that sounded like I was feeling a bit sorry for myself so instead I told her, "Not yet, but if the Lord keeps encouraging me to do more things like this, then you never know."

She smiled. "Well, I hope when you become a famous author, you'll let everyone know that we made the first copy of your book."

It made me feel good, hearing that. I think it made me realize that someone else out there, even if she was working in Budget Copy, might just believe in my dream as well. I couldn't help but feel, especially after my talk with Bill Martin and my speech at Sedlacek, that the Lord was hacking the underbrush off the path He had laid out for me, the one I had chosen not to take years ago when the addict had grabbed hold of me and pulled me down the dark road of abuse.

I sent a copy of my manuscript to my sister, gave one to Joan, and mailed one to a friend of mine in Davenport, Beth, who I had gone to high school with and who had reconnected with me when I lived there. When we had discovered that we lived in the same town again, we had met for coffee one morning and she had asked me if I was still writing. I had written in high school, bad poems and darkly humorous short stories, but she had remembered and assumed I must still be writing. When I told her that I hadn't quite finished anything yet, she had laughed and said to be sure I sent her my first novel. When I got my manuscript from Budget Copy, I couldn't resist sending her a copy; I had no idea how the Lord was behind all of this as well. The other person I sent a copy to was a woman by the name of Elaine Hilliard. She was the admissions director at Sedlacek, the first person I had met there when I went in, and someone, ironically, who had become a very dear friend. I stopped in to see her from time to time to visit and share our faith and when I had told her I had written my manuscript, she insisted on reading it.

The thing about writing is that you want feedback, good preferably, but feedback if for no other reason than you know that someone has read what you've written. It takes people a long time to read two hundred and eighty pages of anything, but eventually Joan told me how much she enjoyed it, and even my sister emailed me and told me how proud she was, a statement that I did my best to make sound like she really loved what I wrote. Elaine was the first to tell me how meaningful it was from a recovery standpoint and how she thought others could benefit by it. She even asked if she could share it with Bill Sackett, who also read it and thought it would be good for people in recovery to read.

I was encouraged by what they told me, but the best message I was to get was going to come from someone I didn't know. I got a call from my friend Beth but wasn't available to take it, so after listening to her message, I called her back. I was in my car and had been praying for the Lord to continue to hack away at all that brush on my path so I could see more clearly where He wanted me to go. When I called Beth's office, another female answered the phone.

"Hi," I said, "is Beth there?"

"Who's calling, please?"

"This is Steve Sellers."

There was a slight pause.

"You're the author. The one who wrote the book."

She wasn't asking; she was telling me: *"You're the author."*

Wow, first the woman at Budget Copy and now this woman who I didn't even know. I didn't know how to respond.

"Well, it's not really a book," I said, "and I'm mostly just someone who likes to write."

She didn't hesitate. "You need to get this published."

"Excuse me?"

"I said you need to get this published. People need to read this."

She was sounding more serious, like she really believed what she was saying to me.

"I don't—" I started to say.

"My mom died of alcohol abuse," she said, and then she paused. She had started to cry. She wasn't sobbing but I could tell that she was crying. "I was so angry at her," she said after a moment. "I carried so much anger for so many years because I thought she had chosen not to stop. I thought she had chosen alcohol over me. Over my daughter . . . her own granddaughter."

She was crying more freely now. I had even pulled over into the parking lot of a carwash. I needed to listen to her.

"I didn't know she couldn't stop. Until I read your book, I didn't know that she couldn't stop." She was silent for a moment because she couldn't talk.

I was silent because I didn't know what to say.

She finally spoke again. "You need to get this published." She took a deep breath and said it again. "You need to get this published so that when my little girl is old enough to read it, she'll be able to understand what happened to her grandma."

I thanked her and we talked a little more before we hung up and I realized that I hadn't even asked her name or spoken to Beth. It also hit me, as I thought back to Bill Martin and my speech at Sedlacek and how I had been praying that the brush be cleared a bit from my path, that He had done just that. I felt as I sat in the parking lot of the carwash that He had again spoken to me, this time through an unnamed woman who had suffered a loss that still burdened her and who, even though she had never met me before, was reaching out to me, telling me that I could help her and her daughter and maybe even others who had been burdened by the same kind of loss. He was telling me to have faith in Him, to continue believing in His plan, and to continue to work on the things that I needed to do, no matter how hard they were. As I pulled out of the parking lot, I thought back to "Charlie Manson" and my talk at Sedlacek and how it had hit me that night like it was hitting me again: one person. Just let me get to one person.

: : : : : :

I began to turn my focus on my manuscript, trying to figure out how to get it published. There was never a time when I didn't think of the financial crisis that continued to loom over me but, in time, as Linda had said would happen, the phone calls stopped. Of course, I had yet to go see her to sign the final papers even though she had called and told me that she had completed everything. The papers were ready; I wasn't. I still wasn't quite ready to swallow the pride I was hanging on to and take what was very obviously the easy way out. None of my recovery had been easy; I didn't see why this should be any different.

I read once somewhere that there are three thousand books published every day so I was assuming that it was going to be pretty easy for me. I'd seen some of the books in Barnes and Noble; while I hadn't written a masterpiece by any stretch of the imagination, I believed my book had to be better than *The History of Reusable Coffins, The Mating Habits of Imaginary Rabbits,* or *How to Read a Book Without Really Knowing How to Read.*

I learned how to query both agents and publishers and then compiled a list of both that I thought seemed eager to take on a new author. I targeted publishers that specialized in substance abuse and agents that marketed to the publishers that did the same. I looked at Christian publishers, spiritual publishers, religious publishers, small companies, large companies, and companies that had any Iowa connections I could find. I went to bookstores and looked at books about recovery and found out who published them and added them to my list. I even emailed authors and asked them who represented them and if it was okay for me to use their names and contact their agents. When I was all done, I typed letters to everyone on my list and then waited for the responses to come in, all the while trying to figure out how I would decide who I would let publish my book. I even started to convince myself that this was why I was waiting to go to Linda's office to sign the bankruptcy papers; I would make enough money to pay my debts. I would redeem myself and do it walking brush-free along the Lord's path for me.

Rejection is a hard thing. I was rejected once in high school by Peggy Stanton, a girl on whom I had a huge crush. I had walked by French class and saw her in the room as she turned and smiled and winked at me. She winked at me! I summoned all my courage and called her that night because I was convinced she had been harboring a secret crush on me as well.

"Oh, no," she had laughed into the phone. "I wink at everyone. Really, it's no big deal." She had to hang up then because she was laughing so hard.

You'd think after that, rejection would be easy for me. I wasn't prepared for the letters that came back as undeliverable, merited no response, or came back with the same canned response:

Dear Stan:

Thank you for your interest in our agency/publishing company/ furniture mart.

We're sorry but we're not able/willing/desperate enough to take on your work.

While you no doubt have talent as a writer/dancer/glass blower, we are not in

a position to represent you/publish you/take you seriously.

Best regards/Good luck/Stick with your day job,

(Fill in the blank)

I soon found myself frustrated, wondering how the guy who wrote *An Intellectual Study of Paste* ever made it to print. It was dawning on me that maybe what I had written simply wasn't that good. I kept plugging away, praying, and continuing to believe that even if I never saw print, I had done what I had failed to do earlier in my life: I had written something that, if someone were to decide to publish it, would be a book.

The year 2004 rolled around and I still hadn't gone back to see Linda. She had sent me letters reminding me that the $800 I had originally paid was going to retain her for only a short time and if I had decided not to sign the papers so she could file them, she was going to have to send the money back, less about $200 for her time. My thinking was that I was getting an almost $600 gift and if nothing else, I had bought some time. I was struggling with what to do, but my biggest fear was that I was doing nothing, a strategy that hadn't worked well at all when I was against the wall with my drinking.

It was disheartening that, this far into my journey, I was slipping back into denial. I wasn't denying that there was a problem but rather denying that I needed anyone's help to do something about it. I tried to take comfort in the fact that since I recognized the situation as being a bit dangerous, I must be okay, because if I weren't, I would pretend the problem didn't exist at all. My delusion was disheartening, especially given that I continued to speak at Sedlacek, encouraging people to let go of the things they knew were holding them back; I wasn't even doing it in my own life. I continued to pray; there was never a time when I didn't pray and listen for Him to tell me what to do.

I continued to either not hear from people to whom I had submitted my manuscript or hear that they weren't interested. As the rejection list mounted, I was slowly coming to realize that maybe all the Lord had wanted me to do was finish the manuscript. I had prayed to be able to touch someone with my words and I often thought back to the conversation I'd had with the woman who had worked with my friend Beth and realized that maybe I had already reached her.

I had talked to someone once, I don't remember who it was, who told me he had a friend who had written four manuscripts and never once looked to publish any of them. He would simply write one, bind it, put it on a shelf, and then start the next, hoping that it was better than the one he had just finished. He was much like the weekend golfer who may dream of the PGA tour but in reality wants only to shoot a better score on Sunday than he did on Saturday. Maybe all I was supposed to do was work at becoming a better writer and wait until the Lord told me what to do next.

It was this thought that I shared with Him one day while I was in my car, driving out to the middle of nowhere to take a picture of a client's house. Normally when I'm in the car, I have Christian music on or am listening to whatever pastor I can happen to find, but this particular day I left the radio off and talked with the Lord. I asked Him what I was supposed to do. I felt that I had looked everywhere and done everything I could and that I felt I had run out of options. I asked Him if all I was supposed to do was write and then write something else, and if that was okay; I had no problem with that if that's what He wanted me to do. I enjoyed writing; I always had. It was nice to have finally finished something, and if that's what He wanted me to do, write and get better at it, okay. He had given me a gift; I was finally using it. I think I needed to know if there was anything else He wanted me to do. As always, I thanked Him for all He had done and then I rode the rest of the way in silence, waiting to hear His voice. I had heard it many times since my journey began; it was always a wonderful sound.

The next day, March twenty-fourth, He spoke to me again. I was in my office when I got an email from a company I had queried but not yet gotten a response from. The email was from a woman named Katherine Michaels, an assistant acquisitions editor, and she wanted to know if I would be willing to send them my manuscript. Within the hour, Joan had helped me email the entire thing to Katherine, who thanked us when she received it and said she would be in touch. Nearly two weeks later, I received another email from another woman named Melinda Cook, the acquisitions editor and Katherine's boss, who had a couple of questions to ask me, mostly about who else was looking at the manuscript, had I ever been published before, and what expectations I had about publication. I was trying to keep all my expectations low but could feel the Lord at work, and when He's at work in your life, it's hard not to get excited.

On April 8, 2004, I found out that my book was going to be published. I was in my office when the email came, which was followed by a phone call from Melinda confirming that, yes, it was true. I stood there while she talked to me telling me about the email that would follow in a couple of days with all the details. I don't remember much of the conversation; Melinda was talking into one ear but all I heard was the Lord's voice whispering in the other:

"I know the plans I have for you. . . ."

CHAPTER 32

The Rest Finally Told

THE YEAR OF 2004 WAS significant in my journey. In late April, shortly after I learned about my book, I felt that it was time to further cement my commitment to the Lord, and on May second, I was baptized at First Assembly, the church where Mary and the girls had been going and the church I had been frequenting for some time.

I had been baptized twice before, once when I was little and my parents were members of the United Presbyterian Church in Newton. I think I was four or so but still seem to have a vague memory of the event. I was baptized again in 1990 in the Catholic Church after Laura was born and I had made what in reality was my half-hearted attempt to convert to Catholicism. Neither had the emotional and spiritual impact on me that I felt that May night. It was the first time that I stood in front of a crowd, other than the alcoholics and addicts to whom I had spoken, and publicly confessed that I was an alcoholic. I stood in the baptismal tank with Jason McCoy, then the youth pastor at the church, and looked out at the congregation and told everyone that I was an alcoholic. It seemed to be the perfect place to make such an admission, and as I stood there I saw Mary, Katie, and Laura and, farther back, Steve and his wife, Debbie. It was an incredible experience for me, and when it was over, I stood in the back of the church and wept. Laura then Katie and then Steve all came back and embraced me and I felt closer to the Lord than I had since He came to save me at Bethel. It was symbolic of what was happening in my life: a cleansing.

Through the rest of spring and into the summer, there was much time spent quietly working with my publisher preparing my manuscript for publication and trying to avoid the phone calls that had started to trickle in from my creditors when they realized that I hadn't filed and still owed them money. Melinda had told me that it would probably be early in 2005 before my book was ready, as there was much to do. There was editing, cover design, and at least two complete read-throughs from my end before they would set it to print. I had read the thing probably six or seven times already but had no problem with reading it again. The editing went smoothly and the cover design, created by Cory Edelstone, was better than I would have imagined.

Joan was a tremendous help during the entire process. We would work on everything we could in the conference room at United. It was during one of these meetings that we began talking about how the Lord seemed to be leading me to reach out to addicts struggling with alcohol. We thought about how best to organize my life in a more professional manner to help the process along, and, in time, Ship Recovery was born.

The intent was that Ship Recovery would be a ministry that would, among other things, promote me as a willing speaker at other treatment facilities in the area in addition to making copies of my book available, either directly from us or through bookstores. The primary goal, however, was seeking out opportunities to share my story. Speaking at Sedlacek was a passion for me, but as much as I enjoyed it, I had never felt that I was able to do it enough. We were hopeful that Ship Recovery would be the vehicle that would allow me to have more opportunities. We enlisted Katie, by now the finance director at a non-profit company in Cedar Rapids, to oversee the finances, if any, and Joan assumed the responsibility of developing our website. It was great fun; first and foremost, I got to spend a lot of time with Katie. That, combined with the fact that I finally felt that I was doing what the Lord had intended me to do, was an incredible feeling.

Late in the summer, I got a call from Elaine at Sedlacek. She asked me if I would be interested in being interviewed for an article in the magazine that went out four times a year called *The Mercy Touch*. It was Sedlacek's thirtieth anniversary and the hospital wanted to do a feature on the center in the fall issue. Elaine thought it would be good if someone who had been through the program—and succeeded—would be willing to share his story. I told her I would be honored, and after she had given me the details of the interview . . . who would be asking the questions and who would be taking the photograph . . . it hit me that I would again be going very public about my disease, this time though, not in front of any people; the article would go out to close to one thousand homes in the Cedar Rapids area.

I was interviewed by a woman named Ilene Malone who did the interviewing over the phone. She told me that they would like to have a picture to accompany the article and she sent a great guy, Don Benson, who owned his own photography business, over to my apartment to take a picture for the article. Like Ilene, Don did a great job, and together they produced a wonderful article that went out to more homes than I could have ever imagined. I would run into people in the mall or at the store, people who I knew and even some I didn't, and many would comment on the article and congratulate me for my courage and commitment. I would like to think that the article touched a life or two and had some small impact on people who were struggling against the same beast I had battled.

I could feel the Lord working in me, encouraging me to continue to take the small steps I needed to take—that He wanted me to take—to keep growing in my spiritual walk. He was opening doors for me; I needed to have faith and walk through them, knowing that He was always by my side.

In September, Joan convinced me that I should join her in taking "In Christ's Image," a six-month class that was the first of three classes that made up the course that would ultimately certify us to teach the course ourselves. I was initially reluctant to participate but, after all the good things that had happened to me that year, I felt that I needed to go. God was calling me and even though I didn't know why, I had learned that when He called, He was doing it for my own good.

The class met at the Eastern Iowa Prayer Center just outside of Cedar Rapids and was run by Mike and Susie Daniels, a strong Christian couple who had moved from Lincoln, Nebraska, two years earlier. There were only four others in the class: Todd and Marie Carter, a husband and wife who had very obviously struggled with some aspect of their marriage at one time but who now seemed strong in their walk together; Lisa Talbot, an early thirty-something single woman who came about every other week; and Vicki Abrams, a married grandmother in her fifties whose husband was a strong Christian but hadn't felt the Lord's pull to commit to every Thursday night for the next six months. We met for two hours and mostly we studied examples from the Word on how we should strive to live in a way that would exemplify Christ. I enjoyed the class for the most part. It helped me understand that I had made tremendous strides in how I was now trying to live a more "Christlike life" and hadn't even been fully aware of how far I had come.

The real reason for my being in the class was revealed to me one very cold late October Thursday. Lisa and Vicki were both gone and we were meeting in a small classroom in the Prayer Center. As was often the case, we had gotten off the subject and were talking that night about how God has worked in our lives. Susie, also a recovering alcoholic, was telling us about the night that she was struggling not to drink, how there was a bottle of alcohol hidden in a kitchen cupboard and how she knew if she drank it and crossed the line that Mike had drawn in the sand, there would be dire consequences. She said that as she started to take a step toward the cupboard, she felt the Lord's arms clamp around her and she was unable to move. He held her and told her that He loved her too much to let her do what she knew in her heart she shouldn't do but couldn't stop doing.

As she told the story, I thought back to December thirtieth, nearly eight years earlier, when I was in the guest room in the lower level of our house. The voice was calling me from behind the door that led to under the steps and I was terrified to move but knew . . . believed . . . that Laura was under there and I had to get her out. I remembered trying to take a step toward the door when I, too, felt the power of the Holy Spirit wrap His arms around me and stop me from going any further.

I hadn't shared that with anyone before, but, hearing Susie share her experience, I knew then why the Lord had led me to the class. It was time to step out and share my salvation with others. I told them the story. I told them how He had stopped me and then how I had snapped and gone upstairs and called the police. I told them how I had stood at the door and had felt the rush of cold air and turned to see white mist blow by me and disappear around the corner and into the laundry room. They all confirmed as easily as telling someone the sky is blue that it was the spirit of the

Lord that blew by me and that there was spiritual warfare going on in my home that night. Satan had come for me and if I had opened the door, if I had listened to the voice and believed the thoughts he had placed in me, I would have been gone. I believe to this day that I would have lost my soul to Satan that night, but God would not let that happen to me. The amazing thing to me was that those people in that room with me on that cold October night believed me as well.

With that, I told them what had happened in Bethel. As I was telling the story and got to the part where I had closed my eyes and bowed my head for just a couple of seconds, right after I had heard the words I still hear to this day, ". . . *We all need to be saved. . . ,"* Mike knew what was going to happen next before I even told him.

"He was gone," I heard him whisper, a slight smile on his face as he nodded his head. He knew and believed that the Spirit of God had come to me that night and offered me forgiveness. They all believed it because His Spirit had come to all of them. Maybe not the way He came to me, sitting across the table from me and telling me I needed to be saved. But He had come to them, and because He had come to them, they believed that He had come to me. For nearly eight years I had been too afraid to tell that story for fear that no one would believe me. God put me in that class, not to finish the course, because I didn't. He put me there at that point in my life because He had allowed Mike and Susie and Todd and Marie and Joan to be there with me so they could hear my story and never bat an eye because there was no question that they knew it was true.

I thought back to what Steve had told me when I had first met him, about how there are no coincidences. God had brought us all together for a reason. Mine was so that I could finally be free to share my story about how I had been saved and to share it knowing that the people who needed to hear it most would come to believe that the same thing could happen to them. I realized that night that if you're going to be a disciple, if you're going to reach out to others through your own experiences and share with them the salvation that is offered only through Jesus, you couldn't hide behind the fear of someone not believing that what you're telling him is true. It was an incredible experience and it changed me; I came to understand that the only way I could share my story with others who needed to hear it was to make sure they heard the whole story. I was out of hope when He had come to me; most of the people I talked to were just about out of hope as well. They needed to hear what He would do for them.

: : : : : :

I had stayed in touch with Melinda through the entire publication process and enjoyed working with her. Everything went smoothly and I was excited to get an email from her stating that the official release date was set for January 7, 2005. Cory emailed me the proof of the cover he had designed and I forwarded it to Joan, Katie, and Steve. The next day, Steve came into my office with a color print of the cover that, to this day, hangs with great pride in my office.

We worked at organizing Ship Recovery as best we could, mostly working on the website, securing a new phone, designing business cards, and setting up our own email account. We were having a blast and looking with great anticipation to the release of my book. Joan and Katie decided that we should have a local book launch, sponsored by Ship Recovery, to make copies of the book available but also to let people know what we were hoping to accomplish.

The book was released sooner than we had been told. I had gotten a call from Melinda in early November telling me that she was going to ship out a couple of copies via FedEx for me before they were officially released anywhere else. I was like a kid waiting for Christmas, and the day FedEx came to my apartment to deliver them, I was, of course, at work. They left me a sticky note telling me that they would be back the next day, but I was taking no chances. That night, November fifteenth, I drove to the FedEx station in Marion and waited for the trucks to come in, telling each driver where I lived and asking if I was on his route. I finally found the driver I was looking for and he found the package I was looking for. As I carried it to my car, the enormity of the moment overwhelmed me.

A million thoughts ran through my head: the nightmare of December thirtieth, almost nine years earlier, when my soul was very nearly taken from me; the week I spent in the hospital, trying to come to grips with what was going on yet still planning to continue living the same kind of life that had brought me there in the first place; the trip to Minneapolis, the great intervention at Laurisa's, and the visit that had changed my life.

I thought of the journey since then and all the prayers that had been heard and answered: the desire to come back to Cedar Rapids and the eight months of commuting ninety-three miles one way to show Him how much I wanted it; the resolution He gave me to a relationship that was not the one He knew I needed, even if it was painful to get out; the man He had put in my life who had become, whether he knew it or not, my mentor. All of these things ran through my mind as I held that package in my hands and realized that no matter what happened with my book from this point on, with His help, I had finally done something I could be proud of. I owed it all to Him. I owe everything to Him. In some small way, I believed that I had taken another step in letting Him know how much I appreciated the new life He had given me.

We planned the book launch for Tuesday, January twenty-fifth, the day after a scheduled talk at Sedlacek. I was eager for the book launch, and Joan, Katie, and I had spent a lot of time planning it, down to the food and music and what I would read. It was exciting for all of us but I knew I also needed to stay focused on the talk on Monday night.

It was an interesting time that evening. When I speak, I try to zero in on the people in the room and read into them as much as I can. My goal has always been, and remains to this day, to find one person during the speech that I know has had a nerve hit. That night, January twenty-fourth, it was a woman who looked to be in her early thirties. When I talked about Katie and Laura and how hard it was to realize that my addiction had taken me away from them, she had started to cry. She was sitting in the back row and was sobbing quietly so very few other people knew what was going on except for the young girl beside her who had put her arm around her and pulled her close. She didn't say anything when I would ask people to identify the things in their lives that had been impacted by the addition. However, when someone said "family," she nodded sadly and put her head on the young girl's shoulder.

After I was done, and everyone had asked anything that needed to be asked, she came up to me and introduced herself. Her name was Jessica, a single mom, and she had in fact lost her children; they were taken from her because of her alcohol addiction and subsequent legal problems. She thanked me for sharing my story and took great hope in the fact that I now had such a wonderful relationship with my daughters and could see them anytime I wanted. She asked if I spoke anywhere else and I told her about the book launch and how I was going to talk, both directly and indirectly, about my experiences. She asked if she could come and

I told her yes and told her where it was. I left Sedlacek, never in a million years believing that I would see her again.

Tuesday night was one of the most wonderful nights of my life. Good friends and people I worked with were there. Ken, my old neighbor who had come over on the thirtieth and searched my house for the voices and footsteps, and Kelly, his wife, who had given me the hug I so desperately needed when Mark brought me back from Bethel, were there as well. Steve and Debbie were there, as was Jim Iverson, who introduced me. Mary was even there and had accepted our invitation to greet everyone as they came in. Bill Sackett came carrying with him the best wishes of Bill Martin, who had left Sedlacek and become the director at the recovery facility in Tama. There were people I barely knew and some people I didn't know at all. A lot of Katie's friends were there and it was wonderful to see the smile on Katie's face that told me she was proud of me. Laura was proud too and during the evening became the unofficial hugger for anyone in need.

It was indeed a wonderful evening, but the best part for me, and the most surprising as well, was when I saw Jessica walk in with an older woman. I was talking to my ex-neighbor Ken about the night he had come to my house when I saw her and excused myself. I went to her and gave her a hug.

"I'm so happy you came," I said as I released her. "I didn't think I'd see you here."

She smiled at me but I could tell she was uncomfortable.

"Let's move over here a little," I said, nodding to an empty corner away from the crowd of people milling around. "We'll have a little more privacy."

Jessica looked relieved at the chance to be away from people and I realized that she hadn't been in a sober world very long. I'd been in it for almost nine years and I *still* wasn't all that comfortable around people.

When we got to the corner, she smiled at me again, more relaxed this time, and turned to the older woman.

"Mom," she said, "This is the man I told you about last night. This is Steve."

She looked at me. "I'm sorry; I don't think I know your last name."

"Sellers," I said as I turned toward the other woman. "I'm Steve Sellers."

"I'm Louise Henderson," she said. "I'm Jessica's mother."

We shook hands and before I had a chance to say anything, Louise spoke again.

"I just had to come and thank you for last night. Jessica told me about your speech when she came home. She's staying with me at my house right now until, well, until things settle down a bit." She looked at her daughter and smiled, then looked back to me. "Last night was the first night in, well, I don't even know how long it's been, but it was the first time in a very long time that she finally felt hopeful about her life. She said it was because of what you talked about last night about your faith. She said you've been through a lot but that you've never lost your faith. I just wanted you to know how much I appreciate what you said to her last night."

I looked at Jessica and smiled. She had tears in her eyes.

"I finally believe that I can do this," she said as she fought to compose herself. "I just wanted my mom to come and meet you so she would believe me when I told her last night that I had finally met someone who had given me hope. I think she finally believes it now too."

I didn't know what to say and before I could say anything, she reached out and gave me a hug, and before I knew it, Louise was hugging us as well. The three of us stood there for a minute before Jessica stepped back.

"I'm sorry, I can't stay. I have the chance to see my kids for a short time tonight and Mom is going to take me. I really want to stay but I think you know how important this is to me."

"Of course," I said. "But do you have two minutes? There's something I'd like you to have."

"Sure," she said. "Of course."

I left and quickly made my way to the long table where Katie was sitting with a couple of her friends, copies of my book on display. Smiling at Katie, I grabbed one and made my way back to where Jessica and her mom were standing.

"Here," I said as I handed it to her. "I would be honored if you would accept this as a gift from me. I am so happy you came tonight and I want you to take it so if you ever find yourself struggling, you can read it and be reminded of that hope."

She looked at the book and then at me and she started to cry again. She gave me one last hug, as did Louise, and then they turned and walked out into the darkness. I never saw her again but I believe very strongly that Jessica has remained on her path. I believe that the Lord brought her to me that night for her benefit as well as my own. As wonderful as the night was, full of laughter and tears and hugs, it was also full of the knowledge that the Lord was there as well, reminding me with Jessica that His plan for me, as it had been shown with "Charlie Manson" during my first speech at Sedlacek, is always finding one person. He had again reminded me of the same thing.

One person. Just bring me one person. . . .

CHAPTER 33

Hitting the Wall and Burning the Past

IN TAKING MY INVENTORY IN 2005, I was happy with my recovery for the most part. I felt that I was grounded spiritually, walking with the Lord on the path He had laid out for me. I felt better since I had shared the story of my salvation with my class at the Prayer Center and no longer kept it out of my talks at Sedlacek even though I didn't feel that I had the freedom there to share it all. I had come to learn, and was doing my best to tell others, that the only way to recover from the addiction was to give it over to the Lord.

My relationship with my daughters was unbelievable. I was spending time with Katie working on finding ways to grow Ship Recovery. My time with Laura, especially the weekends when it would be just the two of us, was creating some of the best times in my life. I felt like a father again and knew the Lord was smiling at me as I was fulfilling my godly duty as a father. Professionally, I liked where I was, especially because I was right across the hall from a man who walked with the Lord the way I wanted to. He was an example of how I wanted to live my life and it was a true blessing to have him so close every day. I felt good about what I had finally accomplished with the gifts God had given me and took great pleasure in the opportunities I had to speak to other addicts. The feedback on my book was positive and the website continued to attract visitors; people were beginning to know that Ship Recovery was available for anyone who needed help.

In March, I began working on my next manuscript. I wanted to become a better writer and try to utilize some of the things I had learned in college about literary technique in hopes of challenging myself to improve. *Through the Deep Darkness* was a story set in the resort in Minnesota I used to go to as a kid. It was where Laura and I had gone in the summer of 2002 to meet Katie and my mom and the place I loved more than any other. It was also somewhere I felt I might never see again so I wanted to go there vicariously through the characters that I was able, with God's help, to create.

On the surface it was a story about a young boy vacationing with his mother and learning how to fish from a writer who lived on an island near the resort. The boy had lost his father, the writer had lost his son, and the two of them came together to learn how to be father and son for each other. On a symbolic level I had tried to create a book about salvation and overcoming the sin . . . the deep darkness . . . that holds us all back from being what the Lord wants us to be. It was full of symbols that would challenge readers to see the story for what I had made it, and even if they didn't see it all, I still wanted it to be a quiet, easy read that would remind them of a relaxing vacation by the lake.

The other thing it gave me the chance to do was create my vision of a perfect woman, and a man who felt blessed that he had the good fortune to find her and marry her. The woman's name was Gabrielle and she was the perfect complement to the writer, and they enjoyed a wonderful marriage grounded in faith and hope.

When I write, I ask the Lord to give me the words and the story and then He leaves it up to me to discipline myself to get it done. When I finished the manuscript in September, I felt that He had shown another part of His plan for me even if it didn't all make sense to me at the time. I was happy with the manuscript and believed that God had me write it for reasons I did not yet understand but was eager to see unfold.

The negative in my life continued to be my financial recovery. It became evident early that I was not going to make the money necessary to pay off my creditors, and they had started calling again with a vengeance. I sought relief in wonderful opportunities the Lord gave me to promote Ship Recovery. In April, Steve and Debbie hosted a private reception and reading in their home, inviting some significant and influential people in town to come celebrate with us. I read from my book, seated by the fireplace in a beautiful light green director's chair that they had purchased for me for my readings. It was an awesome experience, but the best part of the night was having Katie and Joan come up and talk about Ship Recovery—our ministry—and letting everyone know that our true desire was to reach out to people addicted to alcohol. I felt the Lord wanted us to take the disease from out of the shadows of shame and make people aware of the fact that, like any disease, it can be overcome. It wasn't a choice; it was an addiction, and I had come to learn quickly that people did not know that there was a difference.

Also, later in the spring, I was invited to my hometown, Newton, to take part in National Library Week and do a reading. The director of the library, Randy Landers, was actually a friend of mine with whom I had graduated from high school. Randy was also a recovering alcoholic and, in a press release in the Newton paper, he praised my book as "an important read for anyone directly or indirectly affected by the disease." It was a great opportunity for me, along with Katie and Joan, to go back home and see some old friends. The best part was to have my mom come and listen to me speak. It was a joy to see the smile on her face, proud not only of the book but also of the fact that her son had been reborn.

No matter what relief I sought, or got, it was becoming apparent that ignoring the financial crisis in my life wasn't going to make it go away. As happy as I was with my recovery, I was growing more dissatisfied with myself at my unwillingness to address this issue. I would find myself speaking with alcoholics and addicts and emphasizing that they could not hide from the problem, pretending· it didn't exist, hoping to wake up the next morning and find that everything was okay. I knew all too well that I was being hypocritical by doing the very thing myself that I was telling them not to do. I feared I would allow to happen with my finances exactly what had happened with my alcoholism: I would wait until I hit a wall and had nowhere else to turn. Procrastination had always been an issue in my life; I had even put it on the list above my line, but it was becoming obvious to me that I hadn't done a very good job of addressing it.

Things changed in May when I was at work and Heather, our receptionist, called me and told me there was someone up front to see me. It was a deputy sheriff; I hadn't seen one up close and personal like this since the day Mark had driven me back from Bethel and two of them came into the emergency room to serve my commitment papers. As I walked into the waiting area of our office, my stomach sank; I had hit the wall. It would have been an unnecessary collision if I had done something about it sooner, but sometimes we all have to continue to learn things the hard way.

I was getting sued, just as Linda said might happen. I don't know who it was; I don't even think I looked at the papers. The deputy was a very nice guy and, after hearing the condensed version of my recovery, told me that I should call my attorney again and take care of this. He told me I had twenty days to do something and that I shouldn't wait. He wished me luck when he left and I left as well and went home, gathered all the paperwork Linda had given me, and called her office, telling her secretary that I was on my way down.

I am not, nor will I ever be, proud of filing bankruptcy. I have learned through the years that carrying guilt is not a healthy thing to do and it's a point I emphasize more than most others when I speak. This, however, is something that I still have a hard time leaving behind me. Linda was remarkable through the entire process and emphasized with me more than once that there was nothing else I could do. My situation was born out of need, not greed. I never once bought anything for myself, instead using the only available means I had at the time to survive. Looking back, I was ill-equipped to do anything professionally that would have been of benefit to me.

My confidence took a long time to recover and to this day still hasn't come back all the way, so I especially struggled early on when I made my way back into the working world as a sober man. There is no excuse for what happened and there is no justification. Both Scott, my credit counselor, and Linda, my attorney, had seen more than their fair share of people go through things like this and had encouraged me from the very beginning to give up and start over again. It still hurt to do it; I share this with people when I talk but I never encourage them to do what I did unless, like me, there is absolutely no other way out. It is a stigma . . . a burden . . . that I will carry with me for years to come but one with which I will have to learn to live. It is still my belief—my promise, really—that if and when I ever reach a point in my life that I can repay this debt, even though it has been excused, I will pay it. That is one of the focal points of every prayer I offer up to Him. Even though I know He is proud of all I've done with the new life He has given me, I cannot help but feel that I disappointed Him a bit, and that is not a good feeling to have. It's funny given all the things I used to do that brought tears to His eyes and I never felt anything. But this still hurts, knowing that I hurt Him.

In October, Linda and I went to court; Joan came along for the moral support she had become so good at giving, and in five minutes it was all over. I would like to say that having that burden lifted from me was one of the happiest moments in my life, but instead, when I got home and went to bed that night, I wept harder than I had in a long time. It's a hard thing, walking away from responsibility like that. I had done it before and it hadn't seemed to bother me a bit. I took no comfort in the fact that it bothered me so much now. I did not view it as growth in any way. I still don't.

: : : : : :

February 23, 2006 marked the ten-year anniversary of my sobriety and I wanted to do something special to celebrate. Joan's birthday is also on the twenty-third, the day I celebrate as my "re-birthday," so she and I, along with Katie and Connie, a good friend of ours, got together for dinner. Joan gave me a 10-Year Medallion from Hazelden, a recovery facility in Minnesota, and it's one medallion I will carry with me forever. We had decided that after we ate we were going to go out to the country to the home of some people Connie knew so we could have a fire and burn part of our past. We were all going to get rid of something we had hung on to for far too long. We weren't going to share what it was but we were all going to throw in something we were ashamed of or angry about, something from the past that needed to be put away once and for all. When we got out there, we went to the big fire barrel they have and filled it with whatever we could find that would burn and then, using the Serenity Prayer lighter that Matt had given me when I was in treatment the second time, we started the fire.

Katie, Connie, and Joan each dropped in paper, notes perhaps or letters that were too painful to keep, more painful to read. There may have even been a picture or two. It didn't take long for these things to burn, and in the light of the fire, I could see the tiny smiles that were trying to convince them that it was a good thing to be rid of whatever they had thrown away.

My past was going to be a more exciting burn. God knows there were enough things in my past that I could have thrown into the fire, but by then, I had gotten rid of just about everything that had anything to do with the man that died that night in Bethel ten years earlier. The one thing I still had was my leather briefcase, the one that had been used solely to transport the plastic Gilbey's bottles in and out of the office and my house. I had gone everywhere with that briefcase because it carried two bottles of my lifeline wherever I went. I don't recall that I had ever used it for anything other than my own bootlegging. I had kept it through the years, using it mostly to store papers I had nowhere else to keep because I never seemed to have enough space for everything. The problem was that every time I would open that stupid briefcase, I could see the bottles in there and could almost smell the poison that had at one time been the best thing I had ever smelled.

That night, it went into the fire. I had no idea how long it would take a leather briefcase to burn and I doubt that all the brass on the hinges and snaps and lock ever disappeared into nothing, but we all stood there a long time while it burned. Occasionally we would hear a big *whoosh!!* followed by a popping sound, and I imagined it was the ghosts of the alcohol that had been locked up in there for so long finally meeting their end. Whatever it was, I was happy to see it gone from my life. There's no sense hanging on to the past when it's done nothing but bring you pain.

CHAPTER 34

Just One Thing Missing

I HEARD A WONDERFUL PASTOR at First Assembly, Don Mc-
Garvey, speak recently about a "discontentment" in his life. He said
that he was happy with where he was and thrilled that he wasn't
where he used to be but that there was discontentment because
he didn't feel that he was where the Lord wanted him yet. That's
the way I found myself feeling in the spring of 2006. It had been
ten years since the Lord came and shared with me His desire that
I give myself over to Him so He could recreate me as the man He
had intended me to be. For the most part, that had happened.

As I thought back to that piece of paper I had drawn in my office the day of my own "turning point," I realized how far I had
come. Virtually everything I had written above that line, those
things that had been so negatively impacted by my alcoholism,
had been addressed. Even though they were all things that I would
continue to work on every day of my life, I felt good about how
far I had come. Even the intangibles, the core issues that make us
who we are, had become integral parts of my daily life. Cursing,
taking the name of the Lord in vain, had vanished and, like the
ex-smoker who can no longer stand the smell of smoke, I would
find myself cringing when I heard it come out of someone else's
mouth. I strived to be honest with myself as well as everyone else.

It was probably harder being honest with myself than with others. I think we've all spent so much time trying to convince ourselves that everything was okay when we were drinking that it was a hard habit to break.

I strived to be a man of integrity in all I did, professionally and personally, because, other than the simple fact that it was the right thing to do, I knew that I couldn't stand in front of the alcoholics at Sedlacek and *not* exude integrity in what I was telling them. I even worked at being a better parental partner with Mary. Through the years, our relationship has been rebuilt into one that I believe is based on what it should have been based on when we were married: communication. I am open and honest with everyone, and it has made for wonderful new relationships and made those from the past, with my sister for example, even better than I could have imagined.

My relationship with Laurisa was strong even if we were separated by more miles than ever before. The time we were able to spend together was genuine and we were both enjoying learning about each other for the first time. And without question, I was a better father. I had missed a lot of time with both my daughters, but wounds had healed, especially since I had made the decision to move back to Cedar Rapids. I think Katie especially had come to understand how difficult that process had been for me and she knew that I had done it because I missed them both and wanted to be a viable part of their lives.

Professionally, I was thrilled to be at United, but that had more to do with Steve than anything else. He had become my mentor, the man I looked up to and felt I could turn to for anything. Perhaps without knowing he was doing it, he was setting the bar for me on how to be a true man of faith. God had led me to Steve and, like my sobriety and the chance to come back home from Davenport, his guidance and leadership were gifts to me. He gave me a chance to get my feet back under me professionally while walking alongside me spiritually in the process. As a result, I learned to like myself again and in time finally let go of the guilt I had been carrying with me for so many years. He became a friend and a brother and I love him more than he knows.

My physical, mental, and emotional health were all in excellent shape. Physically, I felt better than I had felt in a long time. I was eating well, sleeping more at night than I had in years, and continued to go diligently to the gym. I felt smart again, mostly because I was making smart decisions, and when a person feels good and is doing the right things, he enjoys his life. Emotionally, I was off the roller coaster that the addict had ridden with me. I still had bad days but I knew that when the day was over, tomorrow was right around the corner and it would be better.

I was not happy with how my financial issues were resolved but have come to accept that there was no other way out for me. I've been blessed to have run into Scott Bradley, my credit counselor, two or three times since I filed and, after he asks how I'm doing, he always tries to reassure me that I did the right thing. My attorney, Linda, even contacted me on my tenth anniversary after Joan and Katie sent out a mass e-mail to everyone to let them know of the significance of the date, and she told me how proud she was of what I had done and also reassured me that I'd had no other choice. It was hard to do and I'll probably never fully agree that it was the right thing to do, but it was, at the time, the only thing I could do and I have to live with that. It is the biggest wound I still carry, the one that, if it ever heals, will leave the biggest scar. The consequences of the disease are relentless in their pursuit. Even when you've got as much distance between where you are and where you've been as I had in February of 2006, you will never be totally free from what the addiction has done. All we can do is have faith that we did all we could and that, with the Lord's help, we will continue to get better.

Without question, the biggest issue that has been addressed, and continues to be addressed every single day, is that of my relationship with God. He saved me; of that, there is no doubt. The Spirit of the Lord came to me in my darkest hour and sat with me and saved me. He did not change me; I am not a changed man. I am a new man in Christ. The old man died that early morning in Bethel and a new man has been created. I don't even know if it's accurate to think that I've had a second chance because that implies that I'm the same man and I have another opportunity to do it right. I believe that I am a new man.

The night I got home from our little burning of the past, I thought about the past ten years, the hardships, trials, and difficulties that I had endured, and realized that I had gotten *through* them because of God. In the past I would have tried to get *around* them with alcohol, to avoid them as if they didn't exist. The thing I've learned about recovery is that it's not easy; there is no getting around anything anymore if a person is sincere about true recovery. It requires faith and the knowledge that you're not alone.

After the Lord came to me at Bethel, I had a feeling that He was pretty sincere about being with me on the journey. I stay connected to Him every day in prayer, walking in the Word and living my life the way I know He would like me to live it. As I sat at home that night, February 23, 2006, and looked at my recovery map, I was grateful for all He had done for me. There wasn't anything that I had not identified and was working on to continue on my journey.

Well, there was one thing.

I hadn't dated anyone very seriously since I had split up with Melanie. Part of the reason was that I didn't ever want to go through that kind of pain again. If a cat burns his paw on the stovetop, he's not going to get back up on the stove. I felt at times that I didn't even want to go into the kitchen. I went out a couple of times with women, but they seemed needy and clingy, with lives full of more drama than the soaps I used to watch when I was home trying not to drink before I would go to my self-esteem class.

I enjoyed being at home writing and trying to find a home for my manuscript. I relished speaking opportunities when they would present themselves and hanging out with Joan or Katie or picking up Laura and taking her to the mall or out for ice cream. It dawned on me that I liked my independence; I liked coming and going as I pleased and not having to be anywhere. Once, a year or so earlier, Steve had everyone in the office over for a cookout in his back yard. I was sitting around the fire after dinner watching the flames and enjoying the late summer evening. I was talking to Chad, who by then was working at United. His family was there, now larger by one more child, and he was constantly checking in the darkness of the yard for his kids and seemingly not able to relax and enjoy the evening. I was so relaxed I was having a hard time staying awake.

"I think I'm going to get going," I said as I stretched. "I need to get home."

He laughed, looking at me like I was kidding. "What do you mean you need to get home? You don't have to go anywhere," he said, stretching his arms out toward his kids while his wife chased them through the darkness. "Believe me, man, I would love not having to go anywhere."

I laughed but remember realizing that he was right. I didn't have to be anywhere.

Eventually, however, I also came to realize that there were times when I missed companionship. I got tired of eating alone and soon found myself in a habit of not eating the greatest food in the world.

374   The Sobering Truth

It's not that I was a bad cook; it just isn't much fun cooking for one. As a result, I would buy a lot of meals that required only that I turn on the oven or the skillet and heat them up.

By now, I had moved to a different apartment and was no longer allowing myself the luxury of the Internet, as I didn't want it to interfere with my writing. However, on nights I wouldn't write, I found myself watching a lot of television and going to bed early. I was beginning to realize that I missed conversation and someone to ask me how my day was. I was lonely and started talking to the Lord about it, not so much to ask Him to help me find someone but mostly, if I was going to be alone, if He was sure that this was what He wanted for me. I knew from reading His Word that man wasn't created to be alone, so if I was going to stay alone, I wanted to make sure it was okay with Him.

Summer came and I immersed myself in writing something I had never written before. Comedy. I wrote three short stories that I enjoyed working on, I think mostly because I was growing unhappier about being alone. I had dated a couple of women but wasn't feeling the connection I had hoped for and was coming to the conclusion that I didn't want to look anymore. I decided that I wanted to get a buzz haircut, buy a motorcycle, and take a week and ride to Boston to see my sister. I have no idea where those notions came from but I started looking at motorcycle ads and trying to work up the courage to go get a haircut. It has to frustrate the Lord to know that even though He gave man common sense, it doesn't necessarily mean we're committed to using it all the time. All I know is by this time, I had given up the search for someone with whom to share my Skillet Sensations.

On Wednesday, May thirty-first, I was sitting in my office, daydreaming about how if I had a buzz cut I probably would have no use for a do-rag when I went east on my motorcycle. I went online to my Yahoo account to check my email and found a spam from a website called Relationships.com which touted itself as a "Christian Singles Site." This wasn't the first singles site I had come across and I knew that they all offered the same thing: a three-day free trial, which basically meant that they would take my money . . . in this case $24.95 . . . for three days. I couldn't imagine it would be hard to get my money back. After all, this was a Christian singles site. How bad could it be?

I closed my door and went through the enrollment process, paying for the first month and then proceeding to create a profile. It's odd doing that. It's hard to walk that fine line between sounding pathetic and pompous, but by the time I was done, I felt that I had made myself sound pretty much as I was. I also used the photo that had been taken for the article in *The Mercy Touch*, as it was about the only picture I had of myself. I didn't want to overdo it so I kept everything pretty simple; after all, I was going to get a haircut pretty soon and World of Bikes had their summer sale going on.

Once the enrollment process was finished and I had paid for the first month so I could have my three-day "free trial," I proceeded to create my screen name, choosing "Restored One." Katie and I had gone to a Jeremy Camp concert at our church once and I bought a T-shirt that said "Restored" on it, as it was the name of an album he was getting ready to release. I wore it to an AA meeting once when I accompanied a friend who needed the encouragement and, afterwards when we were having a cup of coffee, there was a young guy standing with us, looking at my shirt. He leaned in and squinted at it and then started to laugh.

"What's so funny?" I asked.

"I'm sorry, man," he said. "When I first saw this, I couldn't understand why you were wearing it to an AA meeting, but now that I see it, it makes sense."

"What do you mean?" I asked. "I got it at a Jeremy Camp concert. It says 'Restored.'"

"Yeah," he said, chuckling again. "When I first saw it, I thought it said 'Restoned.'"

I didn't figure "Restoned One" would make it very far on a Christian singles site so I went with my original idea. I had Joan read my profile and she thought it was good so I posted it. After it was approved by Relationships.com, I began looking for the woman who would, at the bare minimum, keep me from getting my hair cut.

Less than ten minutes later, I realized that there were no women within a hundred miles of Cedar Rapids who were members of the site. None. Nada. Zip. There was one in far western Iowa and one from a small town in the southwest corner of the state. The rest, maybe five or six, were congregated in the Des Moines area and none of them appeared to be capable of taking the scissors out of the barber's hand. My three-day free trial hadn't even lasted ten minutes and I knew that I had just done one of the most foolish things I had ever done in my life.

I immediately went to the home page and looked for a button that would allow me to cancel my subscription, as I saw no reason to continue as a member. I decided it was foolish of me to think that I was actually going to find someone on the Internet. There had been a hint of desperation to the whole thing and I knew that I had been wrong to think that something would come of it. These thoughts kept running through my mind when I realized there was no escape button; I was going to have to call. I wanted my money back.

They can't do this to me!

I dialed the number for customer service, and while I waited for someone to answer, I realized that I was done looking for a relationship. I felt I had put forth the effort, albeit a weak one, to find someone. I had dated; I had joined a singles site; I had looked up and down every aisle at the grocery store because I had read somewhere that a grocery store is the best place to find someone. Solitude, even though a lonely venture, seemed to have settled comfortably around me, and I had pretty much resolved to spend my life alone. All I needed now was for someone to answer the phone.

"Hi! Welcome to Relationships.com. This is Amy. How may I help you?"

She sounded cheerful, which, in the customer service business, does not always equate with helpful.

"Hi, Amy. My name is Steve Sellers and I want to cancel my three-day free trial and get my money back."

I didn't see any point in getting into the details about why I wanted out, even though the uncomfortable silence from the other end of the phone certainly would have given me the time to do that.

"Uh, I'm sorry, sir. Relationships.com doesn't have a free trial."

Now I was the one who didn't know what to say. The silence lasted until Amy spoke again.

"Sir?"

"I . . . I thought that if you paid for a month you could cancel after three days and get your money back. I thought all singles sites were like that."

"Oh, no, sir," she said cheerfully because she knew that they were going to keep my $24.95. "We don't have a free trial, but you're certainly able to cancel after the first month. When did you join?"

"About fifteen minutes ago."

She laughed, then caught herself. "I'm sorry. If you don't mind me asking, why did you want to cancel after only fifteen minutes?"

"It only took me fifteen minutes to see that there isn't anyone within a hundred miles of me. I'm not really into long-distance relationships. I tried one once; it didn't work out so well."

She paused for a minute and I prepared myself for an argument. She wasn't ready to argue. She was ready to speak what the Lord, in His infinite wisdom, had given her to say to me even if she didn't know He had done it.

"Steve, you need to have faith; you need to expand your horizons and believe that if there is someone out there for you, miles shouldn't keep you from finding her."

I didn't know what to say, so she continued.

"I can go ahead and make a note to cancel your account in thirty days if you'd like, but in the meantime, look around. Don't think about the distance; love doesn't have boundaries."

I couldn't argue with her because she was right. I had faith; maybe I should just do as she said and see what happened. If nothing else, maybe I would make new friends and have interesting conversations with people who knew more about motorcycles than I did.

CHAPTER 35

Always the Faith

SINCE I DIDN'T HAVE THE Internet at home, I would usually come back to my office at night after grabbing something to
eat and see who else was out there, hopefully with the same kind
of faith that I had. Relationships.com allowed a person to "wink"
at someone if he or she finds a profile that looks as if there might
be some compatibility.

The first woman I winked at, "Earth Angel" from Lincoln, Nebraska, winked back at me on Thursday and I decided to email her,
but our correspondence only got as far as me directing her to my
website. I decided that since I only had a month, I might as well get
it all out there for anyone to see and I discovered, thanks to "Earth
Angel," that a lot of women searching for love on the Internet are
often fleeing from the very kind of man that I am: an alcoholic.

I continued to look, now somewhat half-heartedly, until Friday
night, the second of June. I had grabbed some food and brought
it back to my office and was sitting at my desk, eating a three-
strip dinner from KFC, my version of "the other white meat,"
and looking at the world of Christian lonely hearts when I saw
her. T Wilson. It was her smile that grabbed me first, a smile that
melts a man's heart when he sees it. A smile that makes you wonder what someone like that is doing on a singles site in the first

place. A smile that lingers in your mind long after the computer is shut off for the night. A smile from, of all places, "Somewhere in Indiana." As in, on the other side of Illinois. As in, two states and another time zone away. As I looked at her and read about her, I kept hearing the Lord, Who sounded an awful lot like Amy from Relationships.com, saying,

"... *Miles shouldn't keep you from finding her.*"

Her name was Trisha and, without hesitation, I winked at her. And then, like a seventh grader, I sat at my desk and waited for her to wink back, or to pass Amy a note to give to me in study hall. I kept looking that night, finding women like "Holy Holly" from Denver, "Angel Eyes" from St Paul, Canton, Ohio, and Palm Beach ("Angel Eyes" was a very popular name on Relationships. com), and "Judith Priest" from Little Rock. I read their profiles, but between them all, I kept going back to my own page, hoping to see that TWilson had winked back at me. She hadn't.

I then decided to stay home the whole weekend writing and try-ing not to go to the office until I broke down at seven on Saturday morning and went anyway. I was anxious and hopeful and all sorts of things that I hadn't been in a long time, but when I got online and checked, I hadn't heard a thing from her. I was disappointed but not surprised. She was a beautiful woman and that smile could no doubt win over someone who was at least in her own zip code. There was nothing from her for the entire week and I had pretty much given up on her and, as a result, I found I had pretty much given up on anyone else that might be available. There wasn't any connection with anyone else as there had been when I had first seen that smile that was, to the best of my calculations, over three hundred seventy miles away.

On Sunday, the eleventh, I had taken Laura back to Mary's and stopped at the office on my way back home. By then, I had pretty much given up on hearing anything from T Wilson but decided to check anyway and very nearly fell out of my chair when I found I had an email from her. She was very nice, telling me she decided to "bite the bullet" and drop me a line. She told me a little about herself, and I read and re-read everything she had to say. I wrote back to her right away and again found myself waiting to hear from her but, as quickly as I had heard from her, she disappeared again and this time, I didn't think she was going to come back. I thought about calling Amy at Relationships.com to see if she would send a note for me or tell her in the hall between classes that I really liked her.

I didn't hear from her again until the twenty-sixth of June, and from then on, it was as if there wasn't anyone else in the world. Over the next five days, we generated sixty-seven pages of email. I would sit in my office and send her something and then wait, staring at my screen, frozen into inactivity until I heard that sweet *ding!* that told me I had another message.

It went on like that all week: writing, sending, waiting, receiving, reading, and then the cycle would start again. I sent her to my website and she admired me for my courage and did not run. We talked about families, faith, past pains, and future hopes. We shared everything; we held nothing back. We calculated the distance and knew that only three hundred eighty-eight miles stood between us; it suddenly seemed like nothing. We learned everything we could about each other, protected I suppose by what little anonymity the computer was still giving us, but in time, even that couldn't keep us from opening our hearts to one another. We both thought for a moment that it was all going too fast and, had we been those seventh graders passing notes back and forth, it would have been. We knew, however, that there was something special happening; we hadn't simply happened upon one another.

There are no coincidences . . .

On Friday the thirtieth, we decided that we needed to talk to one another. We needed to hear each other's voice even though we both knew it wouldn't matter. I had Laura that weekend, and after she went to bed, I called T Wilson. I was back to being that seventh grader dialing the phone, the high-school kid calling Peggy Stanton because she winked at me. Nervous. Excited. Listening to the phone ring and hearing His voice, *For I know the plans I have for you. . . .*

When she answered, surrounded in her own house by candles and soft music, the same anticipation making her heart dance as mine was, I knew it was the voice of an angel. We talked for three hours and could have talked for hours more. We talked all weekend; the phones were never out of our hands. We talked about everything we had already written about. We talked about nothing. We talked about our children, our parents, our sisters, our disdain for pets, our love of coffee, work, play, dreams, heartaches, and joys. We talked much about our faith and how the Lord had taken us through the dark times in our lives and had told us never to give up hope because He had something good waiting for us if we would just continue to believe in Him. Always believe; always have faith. Never doubt His mercy and His love, and He will shower upon you blessings that you had never before imagined in your life. As I listened to that sweet voice on the phone, the picture from her profile in front of me, the smile and the eyes making it seem as if she were right there in front of me, I knew that I had to see her. We knew how we felt even if it seemed impossible—we knew because He had brought us together. How else could it be?

There are no coincidences. . . .

By the end of the weekend, we had made our plans to meet. I would leave on Wednesday, the day after the Fourth of July, and drive to Indianapolis to meet her. I was going to have to miss three days of work but that didn't matter to me. I didn't even think about it. On Monday, I went into Steve's office and closed the door.

"I have to be gone for a few days. I'll be out Wednesday, Thursday, and Friday. I hope that's okay."

He looked at me. "Is everything all right?"

I smiled at him. "The Lord is speaking to me. I need to go somewhere and find out His plan for me."

He didn't even hesitate.

"Bless you, brother," he said, smiling and giving me a hug. "You'll be in our prayers."

I got up on Wednesday morning and left, knowing that it was a six-hour drive, knowing also that it might seem a lot longer than that. Anticipation will do that to a person. We talked a lot on the way and it wasn't until I was about halfway there when I had pulled into a small town to get gas that I got nervous for the first time. I prayed, sitting there in the parking lot of the Busy Corner Café, and the nervousness went away and I knew it was just the enemy putting fear into my mind. He'd had me in his hands over ten years ago and the Lord had plucked me from his grasp. He wasn't going to let me go without a fight, but he also knew that he didn't stand a chance anymore. I had been faithful; I had never lost hope in what God was doing for me and in me. Now, He was taking me exactly where He wanted me to be. As always, when we have faith, the enemy doesn't have a prayer.

Trisha directed me into Indianapolis. I had never been there before, had never imagined a reason why I would ever go there. She had planned to meet me at an Italian restaurant called Maggiano's where she had been dropped off by a friend.

The last time I called her before I got to the restaurant, I knew our lives were never going to be the same. I even told her so.

"I was just thinking about something," I said to her.

"What's that?" she asked.

"I'm about to have my last first kiss," I said. I knew. He had brought me here and I knew.

When I got there around four, I parked in the lot and walked through the door, peering into the darkened room, waiting for my eyes to adjust. I walked up to the hostess stand where a tall blonde was smiling, waiting.

"May I help you, sir?" she asked.

I peered past her into the dining room, looking for that smile.

"I'm here to meet someone," I said.

"Are you Steven?" she asked, smiling.

"Yes," I nodded, smiling as well. "Yes, I am."

She stepped out from behind the stand and walked past me, away from the dining room, and opened the door to the outdoor patio. She held the door for me as I stepped through. There was a fountain in the middle of the room, the clink of glass and silver, and quiet conversation all around. I looked first to my left and saw an older couple sitting at a small table; they were holding hands and laughing.

As my eyes moved to the right, past the fountain, they stopped at the sight of the most beautiful woman I had ever seen in my life. She was dressed in white, as all angels are dressed, her tanned skin shimmering in the light. She was smiling, that same smile I had seen that Friday night when I had first laid eyes on her. I remember bringing my arms up to my heart and taking a step toward her and then everything went silent. There was no running water, no laughter, no sounds of the glass and silver. I saw her stand but I have no recollection of her coming to me. I only know that the next thing I remember is that she was in my arms, the intoxicating aroma still with me to this day. I held her close, a thousand things running through my mind. The darkness, the voices, the anger, the tears, the rage, the salvation, the struggles, the pain . . . and then, the faith. Always the faith.

She was in my arms, finally, but we had yet to say a word. I knew exactly what I was going to say. I had thought about it the whole way over, but as I held her, everything I had thought I would say was taken away by what I knew He wanted me to say. It's the way it had always been on this journey. Let go and let God. He knew what He wanted for me ... for us. So I said what He wanted me to say.

"Will you marry me?" I whispered in her ear.

"Yes," she whispered back.

I stepped away from her and looked, for the first time, into those eyes that are still the most beautiful eyes I have ever seen.

"I'm serious." And I said it again. "Will you marry me?"

The sound of the fountain returned and the tears ran down her cheeks.

"Yes," she said, and then she said it again. "Yes."

Epilogue

TRISHA AND I WERE MARRIED in Indianapolis on November 25, 2006, four-and-a-half months after we met. Our kids stood up with us. Katie was my "best woman," Trisha's daughter Brooke and sons Bryan and Ben stood with her, and her youngest son Brandon walked down the aisle with Laura, who scattered flower petals on the way. Steve and Debbie drove us to Indianapolis and then drove Katie and Laura back home to Cedar Rapids. It was a wonderful wedding, the culmination to what most would call a whirlwind romance. We called it the fulfillment of God's will in our lives.

Everyone who met Trisha in Cedar Rapids, the important people in my life, fell in love with her, as did I, the first time they met her. Katie and Laura both love her and they now spend more time with me than ever before. They love the home Trisha has made for us and love being a part of it when they can. I took her to meet Steve and Debbie, and then Jim and his wife, and these two men, my spiritual mentors and men for whom I have the utmost respect, never batted an eye when we told them of our plans. They, too, had been blessed by being led to their life mates; they understood perfectly what the Lord had done for us.

Her friends and family embraced me as well, except perhaps for her mother initially, but that was only because she felt that I was taking her daughter away from her. Dottie has come around in time and has come to accept the fact that I can make Trisha as happy as

Dottie's late husband, Vic, had made her. Trisha's dad, Sam, and his wife, Joyce, are incredible people and couldn't be happier for us.

I had called my sister on my way back from meeting Trisha for the first time and she wept on the phone when I told her that the Lord had led me to such a wonderful woman. She loves my wife dearly, as does Arnie, and my relationship with both of them, much like my relationship with my daughters, has changed in ways I would have never imagined.

There was no doubt that Trisha was going to move to Cedar Rapids. Even though I told her up front that I could not move, not after what the Lord had done for me to bring me home, I knew it wasn't necessary to say anything. She told me she was ready to move. She said that the Lord had put it on her heart months before we met to prepare to get "untangled" from her life, and even though she didn't know why, she knew it was what she was supposed to do. It was almost as if He had told her to say to me,

"Well, I've thought about it and I've decided to sell my house and give up my life here. I'm going to move away from my friends and family and come live with you in a town where I don't know anyone and have no prospects for a job, but I'll do it because I love you and I want to spend my life with you."

It's funny how the same words you thought you *wanted* to hear from one person are the exact same words you *needed* to hear from *the* one person the Lord knew He was going to bring into your life before you even had life.

We have a wonderful life together. Trisha helps me address recovery issues and at times doesn't even know she's doing it. She makes me want to go out socially with people, mostly because I love being seen with her and everyone enjoys having her around. I'm learning to be comfortable with people and not to feel that I'm less of a man because of what I've gone through but rather that I'm a better man for exactly the same reason.

I have been given a new life, and with it come responsibilities—godly duties, as Steve calls them. I am a husband again, and a father, and to my mother, stricken with Alzheimer's, the son she never had and needed more than ever in her final days. These are the blessings God has given me with my freedom from my addiction . . . the things He has asked me to do as a new creation in Him. It is no longer about me; it is about Him and being everything that I wasn't able to be for Him when alcohol had me in its grip. These are things that most men take for granted. I count them as blessings and as a chance to be the man God intended me to be.

This was a hard thing for me to write. It's hard to visit the dark places in our lives, to be reminded of the wreckage we left behind, the damage done, the shame, and the suffering. It's hard to put it all out there for everyone to see but necessary so if someone like me comes across this, he too can see that there is hope for salvation through Jesus. He often becomes the last hope, but my prayer is that people will come to see that He is the only hope. He saved me. I would be dead by now if it were not for Him and the fervent prayers of the people who brought Him to me.

I have been blessed beyond imagination and have finally come to accept the fact that I am exactly where I'm supposed to be in my life. I have been steeled through the fires of adversity, my patience and faith now the very foundation of my existence. I am loved by a woman who will never quit believing in me and whose patience and faith will serve to continue to strengthen the mold of my own. I have true friends—the kind of friends I can call any time of the day or night just to tell them how much I love them and they will always be happy to hear that from me and happier still to tell me the same. My daughters, I'm certain, have finally reached a point in their lives where they can look at people and tell them in the honesty that comes in everything they say that, "Yes, that's our dad and we are proud of him."

I was sitting in my office one day, helping a client of Steve's when he was out of town. We had never met one another before. As she sat in the chair in front of my desk, she picked up a copy of my book, turned it over, and read the back cover. I heard the quiet whisper: "Praise God."

I looked up at her and smiled, the smile giving away the question.

"I was walking down the hall at church one Wednesday evening," she began. "It was quite a few years ago. I walked past a room and it was full of people and they were all standing in a circle holding hands. They were praying; I went in and joined them. I had no idea who they were praying for but I prayed with them." She looked back at the book and then at me again. "Everyone was praying for you." She smiled again. "It's so good to know that the Lord answers our prayers."

A room full of people that probably had no idea who I was, and yet they were all praying for my salvation. It's no wonder that He came to me when He did. People had prayed earnestly and He had heard them and He had come to me. The power of prayer is an amazing thing.

There's a plaque in my office that Joan gave to me some time ago that I cherish, the words of which have become my mantra. It says simply, *God not only knows where He is taking you but He also knows how to get you there.*

That is my life. That is the one thing I try to impart to everyone, *every one*, with whom I come into contact. It's what I convinced myself to do right before I met Trisha, before the first day I saw her, when we melted into one another and flew headlong into the odyssey that has become our life together when nothing could have been further from the imagination less than one month earlier. It is the simple concept that people have a hard time grasping, but it's all there is and all there ever needs to be:

"Trust in the Lord with all your heart and lean not on your own understanding."

May you all be richly blessed.

Recovery "Above the Line"

1. When was the first time in your sober life that you thought it would be easier to give up being sober and simply go back to the life you had tried to leave behind?

2. If you had to list the reasons for your decision to stay sober, how would you rank the following with 1 being the primary reason?

   ___Family   ___Financial Repercussions

   ___Faith   ___Job/Career Considerations

   ___Legal Concerns   ___Treatment Program Considerations

   ___Friends   ___Spiritual Considerations

   ___Health Concerns ___Other: _____

   ___Character Issues ___Other: _____

3. If you weren't able to resist the old temptation, are you able to identify why? How did you feel afterward?

4. What are some of the consequences that you have had to face because of your behaviors?

5. What was the difficulty in making your way through them?

6. Discuss some of the significant health issues that you have had to face as a result of your addiction.

7. Since moving beyond your addiction/addictive behavior, what steps have you taken to restore your mental, emotional, and physical health?

Spiritual

"On hearing this, Jesus said to them, 'It is not the healthy who need a doctor, but the sick. I have not come to call the righteous, but sinners.'" Mark 2:17 (NIV)

1. Do you ever remember being fully aware of pushing God aside to satisfy your addiction/addictive behavior?

2. Knowing what you had to lose, why do you think you kept on doing it?

"'For a brief moment I abandoned you, but with deep compassion I will bring you back.'" Isaiah 54:7 (NIV)

3. Did you ever feel that the Lord had abandoned you? When and/or why? What have you done to bring Him back into being the focal point of your "recovered" life?

"'You have rejected me,' declares the Lord. 'You keep on backsliding. So I will reach out and destroy you; I am tired of holding back.'" Jeremiah 15:6 (NIV)

4. When do you think you first "rejected" the Lord because of your belief that He was not helping you?

"'Who knows? God may yet relent and with compassion turn from his fierce anger so that we will not perish.'" Jonah 3:9 (NIV)

5. Have you ever felt God's fierce anger?

". . . He reached out his hand and touched the man. 'I am willing,' he said. 'Be clean!'" Mark 1:41 (NIV)

6. When was the first time you felt cleansed by the Lord's compassion?

"'So he got up and went to his father. But while he was still a long way off, his father saw him and was filled with compassion for him; he ran to his son, threw his arms around him and kissed him.'" Luke 15:20 (NIV)

7. When did you first feel like the prodigal son upon his return to his father?

"Be kind and compassionate to one another, forgiving each other, just as in Christ God forgave you." Ephesians 4:32 (NIV)

8. When was the first time you forgave someone in your recovery? Who was it and how was your forgiveness received?

"Therefore, as God's chosen people, holy and dearly loved, clothe yourselves with compassion, kindness, humility, gentleness and patience." Colossians 3:12 (NIV)

9. During your recovery how have you struggled with the following?

Compassion:

Kindness:

Humility:

Gentleness:

Patience:

Relationships

Family

"'For how can I bear to see disaster fall on my people? How can I bear to see the destruction of my family?'" Esther 8:6 (NIV)

1. What specifically about your addiction/addictive behavior caused the most significant damage to your relationships with members of your family?

2. What steps have you taken in your recovery to repair this damage? What has been the most difficult part of this work?

3. In what ways are you striving to become a better partner, spouse, parent, son, or daughter to those family members most impacted by your addiction/addictive behavior? How do you feel these efforts are being received?

Friends

"My friends and companions avoid me because of my wounds; my neighbors stay far away." Psalm 38:11 (NIV)

1. If you had to write a letter to one of your "old friends," who would it be and what would you say?

2. Can you identify at least one person (other than a family member) who has remained a close friend through your "greatest mistakes"? Why do you think he/she has remained your friend?

"'. . . I have called you friends, for everything that I learned from my Father I have made known to you.'" John 15:15 (NIV)

3. What are some of the qualities you look for in friends now that weren't important to you "then"?

Character

Honesty

"So justice is driven back, and righteousness stands at a distance; truth has stumbled in the streets, honesty cannot enter." Isaiah 59:14 (NIV)

1. Looking back, at what point did you realize that it was easier for you to lie than to tell the truth in regard to your addiction or addictive behavior?

2. What has been the hardest part about becoming more honest in your recovery?

Patience

"The end of a matter is better than its beginning, and patience is better than pride." Ecclesiastes 7:8 (NIV)

3. How has God helped you learn patience?

4. At what times in your struggles were you most negatively impacted by your anxiousness and impatience?

Integrity

"Whoever walks in integrity walks securely, but whoever takes crooked paths will be found out." Proverbs 10:9 (NIV)

5. When were you first "found out"? How did you deal with it?

6. Did you accept blame or try to justify your actions?

Self-Esteem

"As Scripture says, 'Anyone who believes in him will never be put to shame.'" Romans 10:11 (NIV)

7. How did you feel about yourself when you first quit drinking?

8. What things did you do to change any negative feelings you may have had about yourself?

9. How would you identify the difference between guilt and shame?

10. Did you ever feel guilty about what your alcoholism had done to you? Your family? Do you feel that you still carry that guilt and if so, how has it affected you in trying to repair these relationships?

11. Are you ashamed of what you've done? How do you believe that you can begin to overcome these feelings of shame?

Professional/Career

"A sluggard's appetite is never filled, but the desires of the diligent are fully satisfied. The righteous hate what is false, but the wicked make themselves a stench and bring shame on themselves." Proverbs 13:4–5 (NIV)

1. How has your addiction/addictive behavior affected your job or career?

2. Have you ever missed work because of your addiction/addictive behavior?

3. Have you ever been confronted at work about your addiction/addictive behavior? What did you do during that confrontation?

4. Have you ever lost a job because of your addiction/addictive behavior? How did it make you feel or how did you react? Did you accept responsibility for what happened?

5. Have you ever put people in the workplace at risk because of your addiction/addictive behavior?

I'm sober.
Now what?

fotojenn/inc

Ship Recovery
Anchored in Faith

If you or a loved one
desires to discover a life
of *true* recovery...
we can help.

For more information

www.ShipRecovery.com
(319) 427-SHIP
(319) 427-7447

All calls are private and
confidential.

Ship Recovery provides
Christ-centered education
and support for individuals
and families who are
struggling with addiction or
addictive behaviors through

- Small group study
- Accountability
- Mentoring
- Workshops/Seminars
- Event speaker

The MISSION of Ship Recovery is to help others
Navigate the difficult waters of addiction
Embrace life beyond sobriety
Seek a God-directed life of recovery

Proceeds from the sales of *The Sobering Truth* provide financial
support for the ministry and outreach of Ship Recovery.